# KARACHI

## THE LAND ISSUE

# KARACHI
## THE LAND ISSUE

• Arif Hasan • Noman Ahmed • Mansoor Raza
• Asiya Sadiq-Polack • Saeed Uddin Ahmed
• Moizza B. Sarwar

OXFORD
UNIVERSITY PRESS

# OXFORD

UNIVERSITY PRESS

Oxford University Press is a department of the University of Oxford.
It furthers the University's objective of excellence in research, scholarship,
and education by publishing worldwide. Oxford is a registered trade mark of
Oxford University Press in the UK and in certain other countries

Published in Pakistan by
Oxford University Press
No. 38, Sector 15, Korangi Industrial Area,
PO Box 8214, Karachi-74900, Pakistan

ISBN 978-0-19-070868-9

Typeset in Minion Pro
Printed on 68gsm Offset Paper

Printed by Kodwavi Printing Services, Karachi

# Contents

# List of Appendices

# List of Figures and Tables

# List of Maps

*Between pp. 112–113*

# Acknowledgements

This book is a much-expanded version of a working paper: Arif Hasan et al., 'Land ownership, control and contestation in Karachi and implications for low-income housing' (London and New York: IIED and UNFPA, March 2003). The research for the paper was initiated by Arif Hasan and was funded by the International Institute for Environment and Development (IIED), through a research grant from UK Aid. The research was a partnership between Arif Hasan (architect), Mansoor Raza (engineer), Dr Noman Ahmed, Asiya Sadiq-Polack (architect), and Saeed Uddin Ahmad (architect) of the Urban Research and Development Cell of the NED University, Karachi. The research was supervised and put together by Arif Hasan, Noman Ahmed, and Mansoor Raza and Moizza B. Sarwar substantially added to the research from primary and secondary sources and edited the final document.

A number of persons have supported the authors of the report in their work. The inputs from the Urban Research and Development Cell of the NED University have been supported by Rahat Arsalan (architect); research assistants Madiha Salam and Samia Shahid; and surveyors Muhammad Younis Khan, Mirza Kamran Baig, Azeem Ahmad Khan, and Faheem Rafique.

Arif Hasan and Mansoor Raza's work was supported by Nurjehan Mawaz Khan (architect); Fatima Zaidi; Fawwad Hasan; and Humayoon Waqas. Israr Ahmad Rana (secretary to Arif Hasan) and Nurjehan Mawaz Khan helped in putting the pre-edited study together.

# Introduction

This book discusses the formal and informal mechanisms governing the ownership and management of the land market in Karachi. The information is based on primary and secondary research, and presented in a format that is accessible to all the stakeholders and practitioners concerned.

Karachi is a megacity with a population of about 18 million. Although the effects of urbanization on the development of land in Karachi are similar to those in other megacities in the south, three important aspects of this city combine to set Karachi apart from other megacities. First, its strategic location in the regional conflict associated with the Afghan War. Second, its immense economic importance within the general context of Pakistan and IN the particular setting of Sindh province, of which it is the capital. Third, the migrant population of Karachi far outnumbers its native Sindhi and Baloch people. An understanding of these features is necessary to understand the persistent land management and governance problems in Karachi.

## WHO OWNS THE LAND IN KARACHI?

Karachi division currently covers 3424 square kilometres and is governed by thirteen different land management authorities. A review of the roles and amount of land managed by these agencies shows that, although state land is easily available, Karachi has been unable to foster commercial growth or provide low-income housing, amenities, and utilities. There are two reasons for this:

– First, the presence of numerous landowning agencies with no shared plan or coordinating mechanism results in a serious clash of interests, frequent disputes over land transactions, and conflicts between various parties. The increasing incidence of litigation in courts of law, armed conflicts between powerful interest groups, speculative hoarding by landowning agencies and the use of land to grant favours to friends and political allies or win over political opponents has created an inefficient and opaque land market.

– Secondly, a clash between the province and the city and Karachi's importance in the Afghan War, have left it with a weak and contradictory land governance system. This means that powerful political, ethnic, and commercial interests are able to dictate land use policies and exploit conversions to their own advantage rather than act in the interests of the city and its poorer inhabitants.

## HOW IS LAND REGULATED AND MANAGED?

There are numerous laws, statutes, and regulations relating to land in Karachi. These include procedures for land disposal, laws on cantonments, railways, informal settlements (*katchi abadis*),[1] land acquisitions and land revenues, the Societies Acts, and building control and town planning regulations. The Sindh Katchi Abadi Authority (SKAA) Act of 1987 (dealing with *katchi abadis*) has sufficient provisions to protect the tenure of low-income groups, and environmental laws, if properly observed, can ensure that development is socially and environment friendly. The building by-laws and zoning regulations could also contribute to a healthy physical and social environment, despite the fact that they are anti-street, anti-pedestrian, and anti-dissolved space. These laws are routinely violated as they are too rigid and take no account of the incremental manner in which poor communities often build their homes. The cantonment laws are anti-poor and do not facilitate the transition from informal to formal settlements. Meanwhile, the Land Acquisition Act has been used to provide land for questionable development projects sponsored by the government and powerful interest groups, which have displaced a large number of poor settlements.

An evaluation of these laws shows that the method of governance in Karachi makes their implementation problematic. Governance is compromised by an ongoing conflict between the city and the province, bureaucrats, and government ministers who violate the objectives of these laws by using discretionary powers for patronage, and powerful 'mafias' who invest their money in lucrative formal and informal real estate businesses. Interestingly, one product of the informal real estate business is housing for the poor; if the mafias did not exist, the poor would not have homes. Another element in the mix is the constant interference in land related matters by the armed forces and other federal landowning agencies.

A number of development plans have been formulated for Karachi since independence, most notably the master plan made in collaboration with the Swedish company Merz Randal Vetten, the MRV Plan of 1952, the Greater Karachi Resettlement Plan of 1958, the Karachi Master Plan for 1975–85, the Karachi Development Plan 2000, and the recent Karachi Strategic Development Plan 2020 (KSDP-2020). To date there has been no political ownership of these plans (even though the KSDP-2020 was approved by the elected house), which regrettably function as technical documents rather than a framework for implementation. The absence of a legal framework to coordinate planning and development by the different landowning agencies in Karachi is compounded by a lack of government subsidies, appropriate funding allocations, and technical capacity. As a result of financial constraints, the City District Government Karachi (CDGK) promotes the commercialization of the main corridors of movement in Karachi in order to raise revenue from commercialization fees. This is done in an *ad hoc* manner and is the cause of considerable environmental and social degradation.

## WHAT FINANCE MECHANISMS ARE AVAILABLE TO CONSUMERS?

Like many other major cities in low and middle-income countries, the finance systems in Karachi do not reflect the economic conditions of most of its inhabitants. People generally have few savings and survive on a monthly salary, but houses are usually only available for outright purchase rather than through easy financing or mortgage options. A review of the nine formal housing finance institutions in Karachi revealed that they do not offer loans to purchase land. This is partly because the absence of a stable, predictable, and uniform land registration system makes lending for land purchases a highly unreliable and protracted procedure, and also partly because interest rates are far too high to make loans affordable. This is not because the financial institutions charge high rates of interest, but because of the high KIBOR rate, which currently stands at 12 per cent.[2]

## WHO ARE THE MAIN ACTORS IN THE LAND MARKET AND WHAT ARE THEIR RELATIONSHIPS WITH EACH OTHER?

Contributors to the electronic and print media, advocates, activists, and members of research bodies and NGOs have identified a number of key land actors in Karachi. These include the armed forces, the national and international corporate sector, along with local and provincial elected representatives. Rather than developing and implementing master plans, land-use agreements and regulations, and providing easy entry and exit into the land market, they facilitate land grabbing and land conversions, and have turned land in Karachi into a political and ethnic resource. Serving ministers and members of the provincial assembly claim that they cannot rectify the situation because the police are on the side of the encroachers, while politicians have been known to condone or even support violations of law.

The lack of a unified stake in the city and its land means that those who seek to protect it by fighting encroachment on their site or jurisdiction often turn a blind eye to and/or facilitate the violation of rules, regulations, and plans on another site. With no proper documentation, using legal processes to implement the law and resolve disputes is a difficult, lengthy, and expensive—if not impossible—process that rarely ends in justice being served. It also makes it hard for families to access credit to build houses.

The old professional elite that used to control the development of the formal sector has been replaced by traders and traffickers, and legally acquired funds have largely been superseded by funds acquired illegally or through extortion. The availability of large amounts of money has helped 'informalize' formal sector processes. As a result, bribes in money and kind are used to bypass or bend government rules, regulations, and procedures. This allows developers to make profits of over 150 per cent on land transactions alone, while informal payments can add up to 25 per cent to the whole price of the end product. They also make purchasers dependent on middlemen who can help them with the documentation and processes involved in purchasing, building, renting, or acquiring housing loans. Although the 'informalization' of formal processes has given low-income residents access to a large number of affordable plots (something that the formal sector is incapable of doing), these are usually far from their workplace or from the city centre where better social facilities are available.

## WHAT IS THE ROLE OF NON-STATE ACTORS?

Non-governmental organizations (NGOs) serve a small segment of the population in the provision of housing. They are mostly involved in social sector issues such as education, health, and micro-credit for income generation, and are unlikely to make a difference to the existing gap between the supply and demand for housing in Karachi. This means that the state needs to play a more proactive role in housing. While individual NGOs are unlikely to change state policy, a network of NGOs pushing for change could make a difference. Professional education is theoretical in nature and does give students a real understanding of the options and realities available to poor communities. Indeed, it has emerged that architects do not wish to work on low-income settlements, and are unaware of their residents' requirements. Until these changes occur, local contractors and artisans will continue to carry out incremental improvements to housing in poor settlements.

## WHAT ARE THE PREFERENCES OF LOW-INCOME RESIDENTS IN KARACHI?

All housing in low-income settlements is built in the same way (irrespective of its tenure status), with precast concrete block walls and, to begin with, metal or asbestos sheet roofs. Where property is concerned, low-income groups prefer informal deals even when formal processes are available, as they do not trust market operators or government officials, and are not comfortable dealing with them. Information about formal processes is hard to obtain and often difficult to understand. To overcome this, a poor-friendly culture needs to be developed in offices that deal with applicants, and information should be made available in an easily accessible and understandable format and language. The House Building and Finance Company (HBFC) has developed a user-friendly website and materials in order to be more accessible, but few people are aware that these resources exist.

People prefer one unit houses to apartments, as this allows them to enlarge their home incrementally and use it for some kind of economic activity. They also prefer to live in affordable locations close to their workplace and relatives. They spend less time and money travelling if they live near their workplace, and derive greater social, physical, and economic security from being near their relatives. It is interesting to note that the majority of people with informal jobs work near or within their settlements, while those with formal office jobs travel considerable distances to work. People also prefer to rent rather than live in settlements where tenure is insecure. The most vulnerable group surveyed was tenants, who rent because they cannot own a house (formally or informally) in an affordable or appropriate location. Having to pay both rent and transport makes it even harder for them to support themselves and their families. Housing census statistics show that the number of tenants in Karachi is increasing.

## CONCLUSIONS

Simplified rules, regulations and procedures could be used to apply Karachi's land laws and statutes in a more equitable manner, with proper monitoring to identify problems in their implementation and help develop more appropriate rules, regulations and procedures.

The first step would be to establish the Karachi Division Planning Agency to coordinate the different landowning authorities and enact procedures, as proposed by the Karachi Development Plan 2000 in 1989. The aim would be for this body to represent all the landowning agencies, establish consensus between them, and work in the larger interests of the city. Creating this kind of mechanism to coordinate multiple land actors and stakeholders within the law would minimize the room for discretion and political patronage, although care will need to be taken to ensure that the agency is not dominated by the most powerful group. This will require a strong and informed civil society that can exert pressure on the agency and monitor its proceedings and decisions. In order to do so, civil society groups and academics will need to be able to access official information.

One of the major constraints in implementing this proposal is the ethnic conflict in Karachi, which has turned land into an instrument of power. The turf wars between ethnic groups exploit issues such as the discretionary powers of politicians and government officials; unclear land titles and an ineffective system of justice in land and property related issues; manipulation of the market through coercion and the targeted killing of estate agents and property dealers. Moving forward on this agenda will require consensus on the need to resolve these ethnic conflicts, and a willingness among leaders of the ethnic groups to look beyond the politics of 'constituencies' and 'votes' and act in the larger interest of the city and the province.

# 1

# Karachi: The Context

Karachi is a megacity[1] with a population of about 18 million. Preliminary analysis of Pakistan's 2011 census suggests that it is the fastest growing city in the world.[2] Megacities are unique ecosystems whose land-use configurations have a profound influence on the daily living conditions of their residents. Urbanization produces areas of high population density, creates demographic change and concentrates economic and political power in the megacity concerned. All of these processes are currently underway in Karachi.

In some respects the features of urbanization in Karachi mirror those of other megacities. Karachi's population density is 17,325 people per square kilometre, compared with 44,000 in Dhaka, Bangladesh; 12,700 in Lagos, Nigeria; and 9,500 in Mexico City (Cox 2012). Its growth rate stands at about 5.4 per cent per annum,[3] compared with 3.4 per cent in Dhaka,[4] 3 per cent in Lagos,[5] and 1.16 per cent in Mexico City. Socially, Karachi has recorded an increase in literacy in the last few decades and seen the gap between male and female literacy narrow.[6] There has been a sharp rise in the age at which people get married, particularly women.[7] Economically, the processes of structural adjustment, deregulation, and privatization have led to 'the emergence of a First World economy with a Third World wage structure'.[8] This has increased both aspirations and poverty (50.5 per cent of Karachi's residents live below the poverty line),[9] while privatization[10] has led to the removal of subsidies in education, health, and urban services, increasing urban inequality[11] and undermining people's ability to fulfil their aspirations.

The subsequent effects on land use and development in Karachi are similar to those of urbanization in other megacities in the southern hemisphere (see Weinstein 2008, on Mumbai; Sassen 2001, on New York; Gilbert 2003, on Nairobi, and Payne *et al.* 2007, for an overview of literature on urbanization). They include illegal land conversions; the use of funds acquired through coercion and contraband trafficking to develop real estate; turf wars between rival real estate dealers and promoters; large scale evictions; huge gaps between supply and demand for housing and a strong anti-poor bias in planning and policy making.

Despite these similarities, three important aspects of the city combine to set Karachi apart from other megacities. The first is its strategic location in the regional conflict associated with the Afghan War. The second is its immense economic importance within the general context of Pakistan and the particular setting of Sindh province, of which it is the capital. The third is the fact that the migrant population of Karachi far outnumbers its native Sindhi and Baloch people. An understanding of these factors is necessary to understand the chronic land management and governance problems in Karachi.

In the late 18th and early 19th centuries, the Russian Tsarist Empire conquered Central Asia. It aimed to capture the natural harbour of Karachi and access the warm waters of the Arabian Sea so that it could contain the expansion of British Imperial power in India and the Middle East. The British responded by annexing Sindh in 1843, using Karachi as a base to launch the Afghan wars and head off the Russian advance. Karachi became an important British cantonment with strategic links to political and economic events in Afghanistan and Central Asia. In the First World War supplies were sent from Karachi to the White Armies fighting the Red Armies in Central Asia; in the Second World War the Allies channelled supplies through Karachi to the eastern front. Supplies were subsequently channelled through the city's port during the anti-Soviet war in Afghanistan in the 1980s and the ensuing wars of attrition in that country. It still serves as a hub for war supplies, which are now sent overland from Karachi port to NATO troops in Afghanistan fighting the Taliban in the wake of 9/11.[12]

Karachi was destabilized by its involvement in the Afghan war as the city became the headquarters of rival interests in the conflict and some of their local supporters became proxies for different rival international and regional players in the war. The war effort was partly financed by heroin trafficked for both local use and export through Karachi Port (Rashid 2001). Guns were an essential part of the drug trade, with the 1980s marking the beginning of the so-called 'drug and Kalashnikov' culture in the city. It also saw the start of large scale investments in land and real estate businesses through undeclared and 'unknown' sources, further weakening an already deteriorating governance system. In the early 1990s use of arms emerged as a means of settling land disputes and forcibly occupying property. The formal governance system was 'informalized' through a system of bribes and coercion, and violations of land related laws, rules, regulations, and procedures became increasingly common (see Chapters 5 and 6).

As Pakistan's only port city, Karachi was a natural nexus for all forces to meet and trade. The city houses 32 per cent of the country's total industrial base, and generates 15 per cent of national GDP, 25 per cent of federal revenues and 62 per cent of income tax.[13] There are also powerful government institutions with interests in the city, in the form of the Karachi Port Trust (KPT), Port Qasim, Customs and Civil Aviation Authority, and the armed forces which have their own various industrial and real estate activities. These powerful bodies own and administer their own land and manage its development independent of the city government. Their interests often clash with those of the city and provincial governments because the institutional relationship between the different landowning organizations is vague and undefined.

The relationship between Sindh province and the political tier of Karachi is particularly complex. The city contains 62 per cent of Sindh's urban population, 30 per cent of its total population and 22 per cent of all Pakistan's urban population—while the country's second largest city, Lahore, contains only 7 per cent of Punjab's total population.[14] Karachi's large-scale industrial sector employs 71.6 per cent of the total industrial labour force in Sindh; the city produces 74.8 per cent of the province's total industrial output and contains 78 per cent of its formal private sector jobs.[15] Its enormous importance plays into the politics of Sindh, which are increasingly determined by the ethnic composition of Karachi, which is much more heterogeneous than that of other cities in Pakistan.

Its ethnic composition also affects issues related with governance, mainly because the Sindhi speaking population feel that they are becoming a minority in their own province.[16] In 1941, 73 per cent of Karachi's population said that their mother tongue was one of the local provincial languages (Sindhi, Balochi, and Gujrati), 6.2 per cent regarded Urdu or Hindi as their mother tongue, and 2.8 per cent spoke Punjabi. There were no Pashto speakers in the province at that time. By 1998, only 14 per cent of residents spoke local languages as their mother tongue, 48.52 per cent spoke Urdu, 14 per cent spoke Punjabi and 11.42 per cent spoke Pashto.[17] This change was due to several factors: the huge influx of Urdu speaking immigrants known as Muhajirs, or refugees, from India in 1947 and the following years; the continuous migration of Pashto speakers from the North West Frontier Province (now Khyber Pakhtunkhwa) since the 1960s; and the arrival of Punjabi professionals, businessmen, and artisans to service the city's expanding services sector.[18]

These multiple migrations to Karachi have changed the demography of Sindh as a whole, as the Sindhi and local language speaking population of the province declined from 96 per cent in 1941 to 62.64 per cent in 1998.

Karachi's transition into a melting pot has been poorly managed, particularly over the last decade. The Sindh Local Government Ordinance (SLGO) of 2001 devolved power from the province to the city. When elected representatives replaced the old bureaucratic colonial system, the major ethnic party, the Muttahida Qaumi Movement (MQM) representing the Urdu-speaking population, came to power. The local Sindhi-speaking population felt alienated by the MQM's control over the city and its resources, and complained that they no longer had access to the city's assets. Their representatives, who mostly belong to the Pakistan Peoples Party (PPP), pointed out that the SLGO had been enacted by a military government and was unacceptable to them.

When democracy returned to Pakistan in 2008, the PPP had a sweeping victory in the provincial elections, but the MQM emerged as the major winner in Karachi. The PPP could not govern Karachi without MQM support, and the MQM did not have the majority it needed in the Sindh Assembly to govern Sindh. Consequently, a coalition government had to be created. One of the PPP's first acts when it came to power was to suspend the SLGO and replace it with the old bureaucratic system, bringing the city under the control of the province. The MQM resented this because a decentralized system in the province gave the Urdu-speaking population considerable powers in their constituencies. Since 2008, the two main protagonists in Sindh politics have continued to argue over which of the two systems Sindh should adopt: decentralization or pre-decentralization. As they cannot do without each other, particularly in a coalition government, they continue to operate a hybrid system or kind of 'marriage' in Karachi, which creates confusion and further weakens governance systems.[19] Meanwhile, the Pashto speakers who control Karachi's transport system and are major players in its informal economy wish to be represented in proportion to their growing presence, and are demanding a restructuring of the election constituencies. The arms culture and tradition of violent protests and riots dating from the Afghan war means that it takes little for the disagreements between ethnic groups and political parties to turn violent. The current violence in Karachi[20] is exacerbated by weak governing institutions, and has spilled over into the land market[21] as political and economic factions seek to establish corresponding ethnic enclaves in the city.[22] This is happening concurrent to a surge in the development and construction of real estate in

Karachi, driven by increased disposable income and considerable inflows of investment capital from the Gulf States (MPGO 2008).[23] This report needs to be understood in the broader context outlined in this chapter. Insufficient communication amongst policymakers, administrators, and academics leads to misapprehensions about the way that land is linked to issues of governance, economic opportunity, and political stability. Therefore, the aim here is to present information about the ownership, management, and built urban landscape of Karachi in a format that is accessible to all the stakeholders and practitioners concerned.

# 2

## Karachi: The Land

### ISSUES IN CONTROL AND OWNERSHIP

The land market under discussion in this report includes all the institutions that own land and their actions in transferring land ownership. This section begins by mapping the landowning agencies in Karachi, looking at the impetus behind their creation and the amount of land they own in the contemporary city. A review of the laws, statutes, and master plans governing land regulation and management in Karachi in Chapter 3 suggests that the nature of the laws and the manner in which they came about and have been enacted is rife with political interference, which has largely led to anti-poor outcomes. The level of political discretion with regard to land, and the lack of harmony between competing government agencies is highlighted in the final section, which recounts interviews with three functionaries from different landowning government authorities in the province.

In 2001, the SLGO created the city district of Karachi and divided it into eighteen towns. Each had its own elected *nazim* (mayor), and the city also had an indirectly elected *nazim*. Before the SLGO was enforced, Karachi was a division headed by a commissioner. The division was divided into five districts, each headed by a deputy commissioner (DC). The commissioner and deputy commissioners were bureaucrats of the provincial government of Sindh. One of the five districts was rural, consisting of *goths* (villages) and their pasturelands. This subsequently became part of three of the new towns created under the SLGO (Gadap, Keamari, and Bin Qasim), opening up a large, previously rural area to urban development (see Map I). The SLGO was suspended in 2009 and the old five district system was reinstated. However, the once rural district did not revert to its former status, and villages are now being transformed into urban settlements through the Goth Abad Scheme (which is explained in Chapter 3).

Karachi division covers 3424 square kilometres in all, 298 of which come under the cantonments and other landowning agencies. The three towns that absorbed much of the rural district contained 84 per cent of the land in Karachi division, but a very small percentage of the city district's population. The urbanized area of Karachi covers 1300 square kilometres.[1] An urbanized area is land that is developed for various urban land uses, or planned and allotted for such uses (see Map II).

Karachi currently has many authorities that control and manage land.[2] These include Pakistan Railways, the Port Qasim Authority, the Karachi Port Trust (KPT), the Defence Housing Authority (DHA), the Government of Pakistan, the cantonment boards, the Sindh Katchi Abadi Authority (SKAA), new developments such as Education City and Textile City, the Lyari Development Authority (LDA), the Sindh Industrial and Trading Estate (SITE), the Government of Sindh, the Malir Development Authority (MDA), and the Karachi Metropolitan Corporation (KMC).

These authorities have various levels of powers to plan, develop, and maintain land under their jurisdiction, and varying standards and sets of by-laws. This results in conflicts of interest and issues with the overall planning and functioning of the city. According to the law, the origin of landownership rests with the provincial government of Sindh, which exercises this right through its board of revenue (BoR). The BoR is authorized to manage land records and keep details of transactions with public and private agencies and the status of land until transactions are completed. It also manages the records of land and properties held by private owners and public agencies as a result of transactions made before Pakistan came into being in 1947 (Farani 2011). BoR leases land parcels to authorities, organizations, and societies for approved land uses, which should ideally be in line with the Master Plan for the town or settlement. The status and duration of leasehold ownership is normally governed by the purpose for which the leased land will be used. Leases for agricultural use are short-term (lasting 1–5 years), medium-term for agro-based industry such as poultry or dairy farms (10–33 years), and long-term for residential, commercial, industrial, and amenity uses (usually 99 years).

During the British colonial period, the provincial land administration allocated sizeable land parcels to different agencies for different purposes. After independence, the administration preserved these allocations and accorded them legal cover. Military-related activities dominated the city at the time, and the British enclaves were designated as cantonments. The present cantonment areas of Karachi are a heritage from this period. The allocation of 2.1 per cent of all the land in Karachi for military use was justified by the fact that it was the base for the British army's excursions against the Russian empire and subsequent campaigns in both the world wars. The Military Lands and Cantonments Group (ML&C) is currently responsible for administrating Military Lands & Cantonments boards that do not fall under the jurisdiction of the city's civil administration (Mahmood 2010). Under Cantonment Ordinance 2002, these boards are supposed to consult the civil administration on development and planning decisions, but are not bound to follow its advice (ibid.).

In addition to their military developments the British also established a trading infrastructure, mainly to enable them to ship Sindhi and Punjabi cotton to British textile mills via Karachi. This led to the emergence of two more stakeholders in land, the railways, and the Karachi port. The first railway line was opened for use on 13 May 1861.[3] As the railways developed as an organization, appropriate land rights were transferred to facilitate the functioning and future expansion of the organization. Land was allocated for rights of way, workshops, stations, marshalling yards and related activities. Some 4 per cent of all the land in Karachi is allocated to the railways, although much of it has been encroached upon by formal and informal developments.[4]

Parallel with this development, the legislative council of Bombay passed Act IV of 1886, which established the Karachi Port Trust (KPT) and led to the designation of land and sea rights to the KPT for the purpose of trade and commerce.[5] KPT has since become an important stakeholder due to its strategic location and the nature of its activities. It owns 2.8 per cent of all the land in Karachi.

A municipal commission was set up in 1852 to oversee residential zones outside the specified military and commercial lands, and determine their corresponding land uses. Under the Bombay District Act of 1837, this was extended to Sindh in 1878 and subsequently included the urban areas of Karachi. In 1934, the city of Karachi Municipal Act was promulgated, leading to the formation of the Karachi Municipal Corporation (KMC), which was responsible for developing and maintaining the city. The KMC's mandate as a development and management agency changed after independence, when the Karachi Improvement Trust (KIT) was created to tackle the unprecedented rise in the city's population following the partition of India. KIT was responsible for developing the first post-Independence master plan for the city, in conjunction with the Swedish firm Merz Randal Vetten (MRV). In 1957, KIT was transformed into the Karachi Development Authority (KDA). In a clear separation of development and management tasks, KDA became responsible for land developments while KMC was put in charge of maintaining developed land in urban areas of the city.

Land was subsequently transferred from the BoR to KDA for development purposes. KDA now had the lion's share of land in the city and a mandate to develop any land that was transferred to it, but not land possessed by federal agencies such as the cantonments, railways, and KPT, or provincial land already owned or utilized by the government and its agencies. Following devolution and the ordinance of 2001, KDA was merged into the CDGK,[6] which became the development and maintenance authority for Karachi, acting simultaneously with other landowning stakeholders. This went on until 2009, when the KMC was revived with a mandate to develop and manage the land under its jurisdiction. Although KMC is considered to be the representative of the city, it only controls one-third of the total urbanized area of Karachi, and its decisions, including the provisions of the KSDP, are binding only on the land under its jurisdiction.

The Pakistan (Federal) Estate Office controls 0.5 per cent of the land in Karachi, due to the fact that it was the capital of Pakistan until 1958. Now that Karachi is the provincial capital of Sindh, the Government of Sindh controls 17.7 per cent of its land in the form of virgin land, provincial government offices, and housing for government employees (Sehgal 1990).

Cooperative societies developed under the 1860 Societies Registration Act are also important stakeholders in land. Many societies emerged in the city before and after partition, taking responsibility for the development and maintenance of their respective land parcels. These include the Pakistan Employees Cooperative Housing Society (PECHS), the Sindhi Muslim Cooperative Housing Society (SMCHS), and the Pakistan Defence Officers' Cooperative Housing Society (PDOCHS), now the Defence Housing Authority (DHA). Excluding DHA, these cooperative societies control 6.8 per cent of all the land in various parts of the city (see Map III). Of all the above mentioned cooperative societies, DHA is the largest, having about 7,000 acres of land or 5.0 per cent of the city area.

The PDOCHS started as a normal cooperative housing society that was registered under the 1860 Societies Act, and was part of the welfare received by retired army officers. At the end of 1970s development was proceeding at a snail's pace and the society's financial situation was deteriorating. In order to avert a crisis, the then military dictator of Pakistan, General Zia ul-Haq, dissolved PDOCHS through an order and formed the DHA as an autonomous new authority with extensive development rights.[7] Clifton Cantonment was also established as part of this process, with the express purpose and mandate of looking after and maintaining the DHA. The city's newest cantonment was established with very different objectives from those set up by the British, and has evolved from a civilian controlled organization to an army controlled authority whose administration is headed by a serving Brigadier.[8] The DHA now has its own development plans, strategies, and by-laws, and is not bound to follow development decisions made by the city administration. Like other cantonments, it can share, consult with and receive advice from the city government regarding development decisions, but is not bound to follow its advice. DHA is one of the largest land stakeholders in Karachi, not only because it holds five per cent of all the land in the city, but because this land is located in prime sites (see Map IV). It recently acquired an additional 5080 hectares of land to develop DHA city. Through the power of the army, the DHA and its affiliated cantonments have become major players in land politics, leading to land and property speculation for and by the elite.

As the financial and industrial capital of the country, Karachi houses thousands of industrial units that cover 3.3 per cent of the city's land (see Map V). These are developed and administered by different authorities, which are also stakeholders involved in land related decisions. After partition, most industries developed near the port. The KPT Industrial Area was developed in 1947. This expanded rapidly, and in 1948 the Sindh Industrial and Trading Estate (SITE) was established adjacent to what was then the northern limit of the city. In 1958, the industrial areas of Korangi and Landhi were chalked out under the Greater Karachi Resettlement Plan (Master Plan), and in the 1960s and 1970s small industrial areas of Federal 'B' Area and North Karachi were developed. The government then established three new industrial areas in the 1980s: the Export Processing Zone, Bin Qasim Industrial Area, and the Super Highway Industrial Estate. The newest industrial area is being planned with an educational city.[9]

Port Qasim and the Steel Mills are important stakeholders in industrial land, with a 1.5 per cent share of the city's land. Both were established in the 1970s as part of the government's self-sustenance policy. Port Qasim was established in 1973, when 12,000 acres of land from the Sindh board of revenue was allocated for the port and related industrial areas under the PQA Act XLIII of 1973.[10]

The newest land stakeholders are the Malir Development Authority (MDA) and the Lyari Development Authority (LDA). The MDA was created through an act in 1994.[11] It holds 3.9 per cent of the city's land, most of which is rural land within the city limits that used to be managed by the District Council (DC). The DC was responsible for managing rural lands through its six union councils until the devolution ordinance of 2001.[12] Some of the MDA's land was transferred from the KDA in the form of existing schemes, such as Shah Latif Town. The LDA was established in 1993. It acquired its land from the BoR, different district councils, and the KDA, and currently holds 5.6 per cent of the land in Karachi. Like the MDA, the LDA became the owner of schemes already developed by the KDA, such as the Hawksbay Scheme-42.[13] The MDA and LDA were both dissolved and merged into the CDGK after the devolution ordinance of 2001, but have since been reinstated by the Pakistan Peoples Party(PPP) (see Map VI).

There are two reasons for their reinstatement. Firstly, both authorities mainly operate in the former rural district of Karachi where large parcels of land are available for development. Secondly, given the ethnic conflict between the local Sindhi-speaking population and the Muhajirs or migrant Urdu-speaking peoples who settled in Karachi during and after 1947, the LDA and MDA can be used to patronize Sindhi, Balochi, and Brahvi speaking groups (Mujtaba 2012; Wichaar 30 April 2012). Both authorities have jurisdiction over areas that come under the Goth Abad scheme. Converting land from rural to urban use involves formal procedures to officially change land use from 'agriculture' to 'urban'. This change in status increases the value of the land, making the process fraught with opportunities for corruption, money-making and political influence.

In addition to the major stakeholders mentioned above, there are many others who also have an impact on land related issues in the city. For example, land held by the Karachi Water and Sewerage Board (KWSB), universities, and other utilities and amenities falls under the jurisdiction of the provincial government. A tract of land around the link road connecting the National Highway to the Super Highway near Malir Housing Scheme-01 has just been allocated for educational and industrial purposes.[14] The government of Sindh has still not identified institutional arrangements to develop and manage these land parcels, even though they amount to 1.07 per cent of the all the land in the city. A graphic summary of the statistics is shown in Figure I.

### Figure I

#### Profile of Land Ownership and Control in Karachi

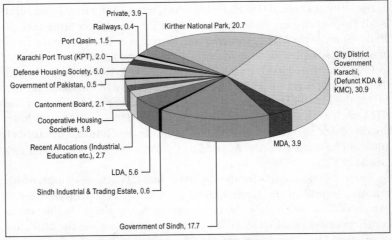

Source: Karachi Strategic Development Plan 2020: CDGK–2007.

Figure I shows the range of formal landowners in Karachi. They have many, often conflicting claims on land, and their reluctance to work together is compounded by the absence of a coordinating authority among these landowning agencies. Interviews with former and current employees of CDGK (now KMC), KDA (merged with the KMC), and the Karachi Building Control Authority (KBCA) now Sindh Building Control Authority (SBCA) revealed that while the Master Plan Group of Offices (MPGO) is technically the centre of control, officials were unclear about how they were supposed to seek its input and approval. They seemed to view contact with the office as voluntary rather than compulsory.

The emergence of the informal land and housing market in Karachi is often blamed on the failure of formal sector to service the demands of the city's population. However, it appears that the problem is not land scarcity, but distribution policies and procedures that do not favour the poor (see the figures on land distribution in Table I). Land in Karachi is a precious resource because of its value in a commercially vibrant port city.

Control of land ownership comes hand in hand with a degree of power and control over the city, its population and its investors.

Land transaction procedures are confusing and lacking in transparency. Land is bought and sold between public agencies and private sector stakeholders in a clandestine manner, and property values are often distorted by shady deals. Public agencies like the KMC suffer due to loss of revenue, and the city's citizens are denied access to open enterprise.

The public agencies' reluctance to sell land is due to its dual role as both an investment and a commodity. Land speculation plays a large part in determining their decisions about supply, reducing the amount of land available on the market and setting it aside for the highest bidder and most profitable use (as a tool for patronage or more direct financial gain).

It is no surprise that Karachi consequently has a very strong and dominant informal sector in which housing is developed without official planning permission. A study for the Karachi Strategic Development Plan 2020 found that informal residential developments account for 8.1 per cent of the total urbanized area. Despite its small share of the total occupied land, this sector meets over 50 per cent of the city's housing needs. These informal settlements are known locally as *katchi abadis* (even when they have been regularized). Few are officially documented, although a sizeable number of them acquire legal status by obtaining leases through the SKAA. This was set up under the Sindh Katchi Abadis Act of 1987, with the mandate to legalize informal settlements by notifying (officially registering) them if they conform to certain prescribed standards. These settlements are usually created by informal developers on land belonging to a government agency, and built on a rectilinear or grid-based plan that makes it possible to regularize them at a later stage. The majority of such settlements have been notified for regularization.[15] Once they have been notified and leased, settlements come under the jurisdiction of the SKAA, which is then the landowning authority. Most informal settlements are developed on BoR land, in railway rights of way, along natural drainage systems and on KWSB land (see Map VII).

It is difficult to distinguish between developed and vacant areas of the city due to the lack of reliable data and the government authorities' reluctance to determine the extent of undeveloped land, which is often allotted to their constituents, friends, and potential political allies for agricultural, mining, or development purposes.

The study undertaken in 2007 for the KSDP-2020 can be used for to identify the urbanized area of the city, although it only shows 7.3 per cent of the urbanized area as vacant. The actual amount of vacant land in Karachi is much greater if the total city limit is taken into account, as it contains a good deal of rural land, especially the vacant land available in Gadap Town. Vacant land refers to an area that has been allotted for different planned uses, but has been not used for this purpose for various reasons. According to the KSDP study (Master Plan Group of Offices 2007), 27 per cent of the total urbanized area is residential and 2.2 per cent is commercial. It is important to note that the entire city district of Karachi was administratively considered as an urban area under the repealed SLGO 2001. This generated confusion as the reality was very different.

We have seen that land ownership and management functions are divided amongst many public agencies, which lack a common coordinating mechanism or shared purpose. There is no system of accountability for land transactions or land related decisions in current governance procedures, and the socio-political culture of the city is such that informal access to and use of peripheral land is seen as a workable alternative—it is not deemed necessary to obtain the documentation or follow the procedures to acquire proper legal status.

Efforts have been made in the past to develop an authority to guide all the landowning authorities in physical planning. The Karachi Development Plan 2000 floated the idea of a powerful physical planning agency for the city with a steering committee composed of members of all the landowning agencies in Karachi, and administrative and technical staff to facilitate policy and coordination. Its functions would include reviewing the status of land ownership by various public agencies; developing a strategic framework for land allocation, utilization, and further transactions; coordinating the planning and development of physical and social infrastructures; facilitating land related decision making and developing and managing land related databases. In the end this agency was never created because successive governments were reluctant to give the plan legal cover. The desire to retain political discretion regarding land allocation and development overcame the need for an overarching planning agency.

**Table I**

Distribution of different types of land use in Urbanized Areas of
Karachi and the KSDP-2020 Study Area

| Land Use | Percentage of Total Urbanized Area |
|---|---|
| Formal residential | 27.0 |
| Informal residential | 8.1 |
| Goths (villages, i.e. residential) | 1.6 |
| Commercial | 2.2 |
| Health | 0.5 |
| Educational | 2.6 |
| Government | 2.3 |
| Other institutional | 0.9 |
| Industry | 7.1 |
| Cottage industries | 0.0 |
| Transport | 0.6 |
| Warehouses | 0.4 |
| Mining | 0.1 |
| Vacant land | 7.3 |
| Open space | 10.6 |
| Agriculture | 5.6 |
| Water | 1.8 |
| Road space | 17.7 |
| Other land uses | 3.6 |
| Total | 100% |

Source: Karachi Strategic Development Plan 2020: CDGK—2007.

## CONCLUSIONS

Despite the advantages of easily available state land, Karachi has
not been able to meet the need for low-income housing, commercial
growth, amenities, and utilities. There are two reasons for this. Firstly,
the presence of numerous landowning agencies with no shared plan or
coordinating mechanism results in a serious clash of interests, frequent

disputes over land transactions and conflicts between different parties. The increasing incidence of litigation in courts of law, armed conflicts between powerful interest groups, speculative hoarding by landowning agencies and the use of land to grant favours to friends and political allies or win over political opponents has created an inefficient and opaque land market. Secondly a clash between the province and the city along with Karachi's importance in the Afghan war has left it with a weak and contradictory land governance system. This means that powerful political, ethnic, and commercial interests are able to dictate land utilization policies and use land conversions to their own advantage rather than in the interests of the city and its poorer inhabitants.[16]

# 3

# Land Management in Karachi: Review of the Laws, Statutes, and Regulations

## THE IMPORTANCE OF LAND

Land ownership, management, and government functions in Karachi are fragmented and spread across multiple agencies. The situation is further complicated by a lack of coordination and collective decision-making, a wide array of laws and statutes, and the institutional framework in the city. Because land is an important asset, control over its distribution and development becomes a primary political and administrative objective, with continuous adjustments to accommodate the demands of political parties, military institutions, religious pressure groups, transport operators, builders, developers, and international stakeholders. It is useful to bear this in mind when reviewing the various sets of laws, regulations, and statutes relating to land.

This chapter discusses the procedures for the disposal and acquisition of land, the framework for recording land sales and purchases, processes for leasing and switching from public to private land use and the building regulations that are supposed to be enforced in the city. All these laws are drafted and published in English, with some (but not all) translated into the national language Urdu. Given that the literacy rate in Pakistan stood at less than 43.92 per cent in 1998 (UNESCO 2012), many people are unlikely to have a good grasp of a second language. In this context, formulating and publishing laws and regulations in English can be seen as a mechanism for excluding a large proportion of the population from land matters.

The numerous offices involved in each stage of changing land use or status make the land market inflexible, create huge opportunities for political and bureaucratic officials to control the way it operates (through balloting, for example) and ultimately inflate land prices. It would be cheaper and simpler for applicants to deal with a single centralized office that coordinates the different agencies, rather than having to navigate complicated procedures involving multiple organizations.

Another point worth noting is the lack of any specific provisions for housing in the land laws. Housing seems to be seen and treated as a separate issue from the land and building industry. This may be partly explained by the fact that many of the laws discussed below originated from unilateral presidential decrees (on land disposal, for example), or non-accountable bodies (such as the military and cantonment laws), and those that were drafted on broader principles have not been legally or practically enforced (as with KSDP-2020).

## DISPOSAL OF URBAN LAND

After Pakistan came into being in 1947, land was officially set aside for planned 'displaced peoples' townships' to accommodate the large influx of refugees from India (some 600,000 arrived in three months). Other neighbourhoods and colonies were also developed under the overall supervision of the national Ministry of Rehabilitation and Resettlement. The Karachi Improvement Trust (KIT) was formed in 1951 to provide basic services and infrastructures in these settlements. Although it was created under the auspices of the central ministry, it was assigned the status of a local government organ and upgraded to the Karachi Development Authority (KDA) in 1957, with a mandate to plan, develop and dispose of various types and sizes of plots in the city. It is worth noting that KDA acquired land from BoR in limited sections, and that the four initial schemes accounted for less than 100 hectares of land. Land allocations increased in the 1960s as the demand for land grew.

The Disposal of Land and Estate Regulations passed by the government of West Pakistan in 1965 were probably a conscious effort to streamline the disposal of urban lands under the jurisdiction and control of the KDA. Defining a clear institutional structure and procedure for land disposal was an important element of this statute. The regulations for transferring ownership included balloting[1] and discretionary allotments by the Director General of KDA. The KDA used a uniform price list for land parcels, applying the same rates regardless of whether the land was allotted through a discretionary process or balloting. It was assumed that the smaller plots of 60, 80, and 120 square yards would be purchased by people on low and lower middle-incomes, but this did not happen (Hasan 2000). The statute also laid down procedures to curb malpractices such as speculation, lack of occupancy, multiple land allotments and informal disposals (Government of West Pakistan 1965).

A few years later, the government promulgated the KDA Disposal of Land Rules of 1971, which streamlined the disposal of lands according to category (as shown in Table II). These rules did not change the discretionary powers vested in the chief executives of KDA, Sindh province and other respective bodies (Government of Sindh 1971).

**Table II**

Land disposal procedures adopted by the KDA since 1971

| No. | Plot Type | Proportion of Disposal | Remarks |
|---|---|---|---|
| 1. | 120 sq. yards or less (Category A) | General public (disposed both by way of discretionary allotments and balloting) | To be allotted to *Jhuggi* (shack) dwellers |
| 2. | 121–400 sq. yards (Category B) | 15% to employees of provincial government 5% to employees of central government 10% to defence personnel 35% to construction companies/trusts 35% for general public | To be allotted after inviting applications, scrutiny and disposal (through direct allotment or balloting in case numbers of applications exceed plot numbers) |
| 3. | 401–1500 sq. yards (Category C) | 15% to employees of provincial government 5% to employees of central government 10% to defence personnel 70% to general public (though auction) | The disposal was to be carried out through public auction except for categories specified for direct allotment |

Source: Dr Noman Ahmed's interpretation of KDA Disposal of Land Rules 1971. These allotments are held under 99-year leases.

The rising demand for land for housing and other uses from the 1970s onwards (due to the Green Revolution, industrialization, and the war in East Pakistan) was reflected in the subsequent Sindh Disposal of Plots Ordinance 1980, which laid down some revised considerations. The maximum size for residential plots was kept at 1000 square yards. Most categories of plot were allocated by ballot, although smaller plots that were previously obtained through public auction started to be reserved for civil servants and government employees. Each landowning department was also allowed to use its own procedures to allocate land left over from balloting, with no stipulation for a coordinated public procedure. The new formula for land disposal is shown in Table III.

**Table III**

Land disposal procedures adopted by the KDA since 1980

| No. | Plot Type | Proportion of Disposal | Remarks |
|-----|-----------|------------------------|---------|
| 1. | 80 sq. yards or less | 60% by ballot<br>8% to civil servants and low grade government employees<br>2% to retired civil servants and government employees<br>5% to defence personnel<br>5% to poverty related hardship cases<br>20% to displaced or relocated persons | Open applications for balloting announced in the press. Remaining categories processed by departments of relevant government agencies |
| 2. | 81–120 sq. yards | 75% to general public by ballot<br>12.5% to government employees<br>2.5% to retired civil servants<br>5% to defence personnel<br>5% to federal government employees | Balloting for general public. Other categories allocated through departmental applications and procedures. |
| 3. | 121–400 sq. yards | 65% to general public by ballot<br>8% to government employees<br>3% to retired government employees<br>5% to defence personnel<br>4% to federal government employees | Balloting for general public. Other categories allocated through departmental applications and procedures. |

Source: Dr Noman Ahmed's interpretation of Sindh Disposal of Plot Ordinance, 1980.

The promulgation of the Sindh Disposal of Urban Land Ordinance (SDULO) in 2002 marked a departure from the usual approach to land disposal, inasmuch that it uses incremental housing development as the procedure for allocating residential plots of less than 120 square yards. In this context, incremental housing refers to housing schemes sponsored by the government of Sindh or another authority that provides plots of up to 80 square yards exclusively for housing. This initiative was the result of learning and lobbying by public spirited citizens and experts who wished to ensure that certain groups—especially the urban poor—could access land for shelter. However, the SDULO stripped the provincial chief minister of discretionary powers to distribute land to house the poor—although pressure from powerful interest groups forced the provincial legislature to repeal it in 2006 and restore the pre-existing status quo. All land disposal laws left the regulation of day-to-day functioning of various landowning authorities in the city to the discretion of the public agencies, provided they did not contradict the provisions of the main land disposal laws or ordinance. However, none of the documents mentioned a specific regulating authority, to ensure that the ensuing functioning of these authorities met the criteria set out in the land disposal laws or ordinance.

The rising demand for housing from the end of the 1970s prompted the authorities to institutionalize land delivery and allocation in periphery urban areas of Karachi and other pressure points in the province. Goth Abad or village development schemes first emerged in 1987 to deal with suburban and rural housing needs for communities in Karachi involved in farming, livestock rearing, poultry, and other agricultural occupations (Government of Sindh 1987). No independent survey has yet been undertaken to ascertain the actual number of villages and their status that were affected by these schemes, although sporadic estimates have been made over the years. There is consequently some confusion about the amount of state land used for housing and other land use schemes, and rural land expropriated from local landowners.

According to records maintained by the Provincial Assembly of Sindh, a survey of villages in and around Karachi conducted in 1989–1990 recorded 808 villages. Some 458 of these villages were regularized, with ownership titles issued by various government agencies to 51,421 individual households or clans. This occurred on an *ad hoc* basis before 1987, and 350 villages still await regularization (Government of Sindh 2008). This will depend on whether they meet the criteria set out in the Province of Sindh Goth Abad (Housing Scheme) Act of 1987, whose objective was to give settled villagers land ownership rights free of charge.

The process used to dispose of rural land, grant villagers legal ownership and pave the way for village infrastructure and planning soon became accessible to formal and informal developers, who had developed settlements on former rural land in Karachi. Although these developers are often referred to as 'encroachers' or 'mafias', many are supported by local political interest groups as they offer poor families reasonably priced land on the periphery of the city. Indeed, the Orangi Pilot Project—Research and Training Institute (OPP-RTI) regards them as land suppliers for the poor. Their arrival on the scene reflects the growing importance of rural land for urban housing and development, crowding out the claims of rural inhabitants of the village, but making land available to urban residents. In short, the Goth Abad scheme was used by land developers to encroach on the land and sell it to new residents against the payment of hundreds of thousands of rupees.

The enforcement of SLGO 2001 integrated the rural district of Karachi into the towns of the newly created Karachi city district, making all urban and rural areas of Karachi available for urbanization (apart from a few sensitive locations). Under KBCA regulations, the LDA and MDA were responsible for their planning and development. This policy move accelerated the transformation of Goth Abad Schemes into peri-urban housing areas like Malir, Gadap and Bin Qasim.

Estimates of the number of *goths* in Karachi after the year 2000 vary. Press reports claim that there are 588 (*The Express Tribune*, 16 February 2012), while the OPP-RTI, which supports the regularization and upgrading of these villages, puts the figure at 2,173. It is not clear how many are genuine rural areas used for agricultural purposes, and how many have been informally created and promoted in order to benefit from the current regularization scheme. The latter is highly likely, as most land records in Pakistan are manually maintained by record-keepers and clerks (*patwaris* and *tehsildars*) who make their own judgments about the nature of the land in question. Efforts to centralize available land records have been very limited, and media reports claim that most are a part of a well organized land scam supported by political parties (for details on this see sections on 'Data Gathered from Visual Media on Karachi' and 'Data on Land in Karachi from Five Case Studies' in Chapter 5). As mentioned earlier, there is dire need for an independent verification of the state of land affairs.

## CANTONMENT LAWS

Cantonments in Karachi are defined as estates with mixed land use that are under the planning and administrative control of the military authorities. Most were originally used for military purposes, but their military functions were phased out over time and the land turned over to residential and commercial use as the city expanded. There are now six cantonments in the city: Manora, Faisal, Clifton, Korangi Creek, Malir, and Karachi cantonment (see Map VIII), which exist as separate entities and are still developed for and by the military authorities. However, since the cantonment authorities decided to develop housing schemes in these areas and float them on the market, most residents are now civilians rather than military personnel.

The Cantonment Ordinance of 2002 promulgated by the President of Pakistan has a strict mechanism for dealing with encroachment, despite the lack of a clear and consistent definition of encroachment across different regulations. The management of the cantonment boards act very swiftly in this respect, and have almost absolute powers to remove what they consider to be 'encroachments' once notice has been served. They take a very different approach to civic agencies, and while there are provisions to appeal against their actions, the nature of the statute allows for very little redress from the process. Those responsible for alleged encroachments are liable to have their property confiscated and auctioned to cover the cost of removal operations. The law is anti-poor because it does not define any procedures to safeguard movable or immovable articles on the location concerned. Even pushcart vendors peddling their wares stand to lose their merchandise if they happen to get caught in eviction operations. There are very few residential encroachments on cantonment lands because swift action is taken against alleged offenders.

People from poor and less privileged communities may also routinely suffer the consequences of these brusque evictions in these areas where they come and work as domestics, painters, and plumbers or repairing tyres or providing other small-scale services. Vendors and workers in the informal sector provide essential services for a wide range of people, but operate in precarious conditions where they are as likely to be evicted as they are to find customers. Most of the tyre repair stalls that routinely serve cars and other vehicles operate through temporary erected structures. Each eviction and displacement erodes the working capital of these small enterprises and creates financial hardship.

The Cantonment Ordinance 2002 also empowers the cantonment boards to undertake their own spatial planning, according to their own development guidelines and standards. They are expected to consult with CDGK while preparing these plans, but are not bound to do so. This separate approach creates significant management and coordination issues with other landowning agencies, especially in terms of inaccurate assessments of infrastructure requirements.

When asked about his experience of planning with the cantonment authorities, one former employee observed that the agency's priorities reflect commercial rather than public interests, like most other landowning agencies. Board members with a military background may occasionally consider the planning rationale on a city-wide basis, but most think in the short-term and only take into consideration their area of jurisdiction. This former employee reflected that half of the meetings with the CDGK to check on planning are merely cosmetic exercises; the recommendations are not taken on board and members who persistently oppose the plan under consideration run a real risk of being transferred.

The resulting intensive expansion of higher income residential developments in cantonments is contributing to an exponential increase in vehicles, electricity loads, and water and sewage networks. Trunk and bulk services such as electricity, sewage treatment plants, and landfill sites for cantonments are located outside the cantonments themselves, and are often shared by other areas. This leads to distortions in estimated need and distribution in other parts of the city.

The Cantonments (Requisitioning of Immovable Property) Ordinance of 1948 empowered the central (now federal) government to requisition any property for cantonment related activities, with no redress or possible contestation from the court. Although this ordinance is rarely invoked, and then usually only under extreme circumstances, its very existence undermines other planning authorities.

The Cantonment Rent Restriction Act 1963 is similar to the Sindh Rent Control Ordinance 1979. It is a cumbersome process devised to resolve conflicts and disputes between landlords and tenants regarding their premises. Tenancy agreements normally last for eleven months, and are extendable. Landlords are entitled to serve notice of a month or more to repossess their property, while tenants can prolong their stay and may use delaying tactics such as legal action. As legal processes are time consuming, informal arbitration under the auspices of local political activists is often used to resolve conflicts.

Urban development and management functions are conducted separately on military lands and cantonments in Karachi: the DHA is responsible for executing development works, while the cantonment boards perform urban management functions. Many *katchi abadis* have developed on military lands, in much the same way as in other municipal areas of Karachi. The Clifton cantonment board has thirteen notified *katchi abadis* in its remit. They start as informal settlements that provide services for adjoining neighbourhoods, shelter for labourers and service providers and sites for low and medium rise, mixed use developments, and then they go through a process of regularization similar to other municipal areas. As noted above, their relatively advantageous location gives the residents of informal settlements in cantonments better employment and livelihood opportunities, although they may be threatened with eviction if their settlement is on land earmarked for infrastructure or land development schemes. People living in settlements along riverbanks and natural drainage channels, road shoulders, and similar locations are routinely evicted. There is no extraordinary provision in the cantonment laws to protect these settlements or extend any compensation to their residents, unlike those in areas covered by the CDGK.

## RAILWAY LAWS

According to the Pakistan Railways Commercial Manual (1935), railway lands cannot be used by railway companies or any other agency to erect buildings of a permanent or semi-permanent nature for non-railway related facilities. However, railway land can be leased to other government departments and used for government purposes once the necessary entry has been made in the railway land register. This should be maintained by the Railway Divisional Superintendent of Karachi for all the uses, licenses and other forms of land transactions made under his jurisdiction. The authorities may also initiate surveys to ensure the status of land and verify entries in the register.

The leasing of railway land to other government departments for various purposes is subject to considerable political discretion. For example, in 2007, the then chief minister of Sindh used his 'discretionary powers' in direct opposition to professional counsel to allow commercial construction exceeding the recommended floor area ratio (FAR) on an amenity railway space that his government had long refused to allow Pakistan Railways to lease (Cowasjee, *Dawn*, 22 July 2007). Yet in 2012, the chief minister made a federal level complaint about Pakistan Railways selling land for commercial purposes (*The Express Tribune*, 8 November 2012). The lack of consistency in policy by the state is reflected in regulations and laws that allow for broad exceptions to the rules (see also the section on Land Disposal Procedures).

Railway lands are scattered across the city in station reserves, operational reserves and special facilities. Poor monitoring has allowed a sizeable chunk of railway owned land to be encroached upon and used for informal settlements and formal residential and commercial functions. Interestingly, since the now defunct Karachi Circular Railways (KCR) stopped operating in 1996, its tracks and rights of way of and many of its branch lines have been used for low-income settlements. Although the laws and procedures allow for the removal of such settlements, the ineffectiveness of the railway department has provided some temporary respite for their residents.

## LAWS ON KATCHI ABADIS

A *katchi abadi* is defined as an informal residential area developed on state land. Originally, these settlements were not organized, but over time they started to follow the same physical planning structure as authorized, normally planned neighbourhoods in order to optimize their chances of future regularization. The Sindh Katchi Abadi Authority (SKAA) Act of 1987 set out the criteria and procedures for regularization. Various studies on Karachi assert that more than half of the city's residents live in *katchi abadis*.

The SKAA Act makes comprehensive provisions for the development and management of these settlements. The core functions of the SKAA, which is constituted by this law, include: (i) implementing government policies on regularization; (ii) developing and improving *katchi abadis*; (iii) preparing guidelines for policy implementation; (iv) identifying and monitoring *katchi abadis*; (v) arranging physical and social surveys; (vi) preparing improvement plans and infrastructure development schemes; (vii) evicting unauthorized persons or groups from *katchi abadis* or areas that are being surveyed to determine their legal status; (viii) developing low cost housing, resettlement schemes and redevelopment schemes; (ix) following up legal and administrative matters relating to *katchi abadis*. The SKAA is authorized to charge residents a prescribed betterment fee, whereby payments for leases are used to fund subsequent works and develop the locality. Over the past few years the focus has shifted to the provision of leases, as 'most settlements have already acquired basic services like water and electricity through their own initiatives, through NGOs, or by directly applying to the service and works departments. The public works agencies then write to the SKAA and ask for a No Objection Certificate (NOC) before services are officially provided to the settlement. Most of the time, the SKAA approves.

The authority is also empowered to notify and regularize *katchi abadis* that fulfil the conditions for regularization. All *katchi abadis* established before 30 June 1997 are eligible to apply. The criteria for regularization include a minimum size of forty households and a location clear of hazards such as embankments, high voltage overhead electricity conduits, waterways, sensitive installations, and coastal wetlands protected by compulsory conservation orders. The relevant landowning public agency or department on whose land the *katchi abadi* is located also needs to be willing to allow it to be regularized and to cooperate in the process. The settlements then become eligible for various kinds of development scheme, which usually require individual occupants of plots or properties to acquire leases before the work starts. The time period for processing lease applications varies between six months to two years. Detailed schedules of payment for the leases are prepared, with instalments normally set according to local socio-economic conditions. None of the regulations stipulate that residents should improve their homes before or after getting a lease.

The *katchi abadi* laws are reasonably pro-poor if they are applied effectively and the prescribed actions undertaken on a regular basis. It is essential to conduct continuous surveys of squatter settlements, adjust jurisdictions, articulate physical boundaries, register new *katchi abadis* once the procedural work has been completed, promote and collect lease and development charges, and prepare and execute infrastructure development schemes in identified areas. However, very little progress has been observed since 2003–2004, mainly due to the limited political interest in upgrading these settlements. By 2010, just 376 of the 702 settlements surveyed had been notified for regularization. As a result, the poor are unable to access formal housing credit and are increasingly dependent on informal transactions, the relevant public institutions have lost revenue and political patronage has increased.

## THE SOCIETIES ACT

The Societies Registration Act of 1860 is a law inherited from British colonial times. It lays down the provisions for the creation and management of a society for a wide variety of purposes, including housing, and applies to the land owned and controlled by the CDGK and the province of Sindh.

Key steps in creating a cooperative society include preparing a formal constitution, enlisting members, completing registration formalities and opening a proper bank account controlled by the society's office bearers. Once they have fulfilled all the procedural requirements, registered societies are eligible to apply to acquire land from the government to develop housing. All residential units must be constructed and developed in accordance with the local zoning and building by-laws promulgated by the local or provincial government concerned. The society's trustees and executive staff are responsible for managing and maintaining the area. A 2006 amendment to the act sets out the framework for acquiring land and property for religious seminaries (*deeni madrasahs*), and regulating them.

The Societies Act provided a formal option for all social groups to acquire land, including the urban poor, who were meant to be major beneficiaries of residential schemes like Gulzar-e-Hijri (KDA Scheme-33). Most of these schemes targeted low-income and the lower grade employees of large public or autonomous organizations, giving them an opportunity to acquire land. The enormous KDA Scheme 33 managed to develop 26,000 acres of land, but was ultimately of little benefit to the urban poor due to the extremely slow pace of development, encroachments onto the site (often by armed gangs), opportunities for speculation and the fraudulent reallocation of land parcels. Informal operators usually seek protection from political parties or their clandestine armed outfits, which often leads to the emergence of competing informal conglomerates that clash over land grabbing ventures (see Map IX).

## LAWS ON LAND REVENUE

According to these laws, land is owned by the provincial government, which transfers or delegates it to other government or private agencies as requested. All land and revenue records for the province are kept by the relevant provincial board of revenue department. In the case of Karachi, this is the government of Sindh.

Land revenue laws apply to non-urban lands, determining the rental status and land tax schedule applicable to various categories of land. Rural areas of Karachi were clearly demarcated in the district and union council jurisdictions until 2001, when the promulgation of SLGO 2001 amalgamated all of Karachi Division into the newly constituted Karachi district. The SLGO was repealed in November 2011, creating a temporary void. Sindh Assembly is now contemplating a new law to determine the future local government structure in the province, and thus also in Karachi.

The amount of revenue generated by land is based upon its categorization. Applicable land categories include *barani* (dependent on rainfall), *sailabi* (flooded or kept permanently moist by river), *aabi* (irrigated by lifting water from tanks), *jheels* (streams or flow from streams), *nahri* (irrigated by canals by flow or lift), *chahi* (watered from wells), *banjer jadid* (land that has remained unsown for eight successive harvests), *banjar qadim* (land that has remained unsown for more than eight successive harvests), and *ghair mumkin* (land that has become uncultivable for any reason, such as land under roads, buildings, streams, canals, tanks and suchlike, or barren sand or ravines). Much of the peri-urban land in Karachi can be classified as *banjar qadim*, *banjar jadid*, and *ghair mumkin*. This land is incrementally incorporated into urban development through formal and informal processes and procedures (Farani 2011).

The Land Administration Manual (2011) lays down the system for managing such land when it is used for agricultural production. Staff is responsible for record keeping, maintaining crop production statistics and filing agricultural returns and mutations. The Land Record Manual sets out the procedure for listing, updating, and revising the land records in a *tehsil*, *taluka*, or town. The statute also includes binding clauses for transferring and altering common village lands (*shamilat*) used for grazing, sand or stone quarries, or containing trees for fuel wood or construction. The key land administration functionary in a rural territory is a *patwari*, or village registrar cum accountant, whose main duties include recording the crops grown at every harvest, noting changes and preparing statistical records of production, and land status. Their functions have survived various changes in the overall administration of the province and city.

The Land Settlement Manual (2011) outlines the various kinds of land rights and privileges enjoyed by village communities. Different types of land tenure include *zamindari* (full proprietary rights), *pattidari* (land divided between different owners according to ancestral or customary shares), and *bhaichara* (inferior land held on customary basis). Regular record-keeping and updating are a key aspect of land settlement, undertaken by a land survey unit constituted under the provincial board of revenue. As a standard operating procedure, the provincial government used to appoint a settlement officer to reconcile land records, address and settle conflicts and disputes, and incorporate extraordinary territories that were naturally generated or vacated by humans. Land settlement was a precolonial practice that continued into the 1970s but has since been largely abandoned as an administrative task, causing unresolved disputes and conflicts that often turn into prolonged social clashes between extended clans and other actors. The outskirts of Karachi have been affected by this situation.

It is easy to exploit this facet of land management for political purposes because land records are managed manually and there are no readily available or accessible centralized computer records. Karachi's land records came under judicial scrutiny in 2012, when the Supreme Court took notice of the fact that the revenue department of the government of Sindh had 'deliberately' avoided restoring the land revenue records burned after the assassination of Benazir Bhutto. Government officials had allowed land in different districts of Sindh to be allocated, converted, and changed without verifying its actual ownership. There were instances where land leases granted for thirty years had been 'informally' converted into 99-year leases, causing substantial financial losses to the city and provincial exchequers (Sahoutara, *The Express Tribune*, 5 December 2012).

Land revenue laws are important tools in land governance, but they need to be implemented through the proper, laid down procedures and institutional mechanisms to be effective. Land use needs to be monitored periodically to determine the availability of land for various uses, and land uses requiring amortization need to be identified. The lack of clear land titles and status makes it difficult for indigenous communities and low-income groups to invest in places that they have occupied for several years, and opens the way for corruption when information on land status is routinely traded through informal channels. In normal situations, an undeveloped tract of land can become urban land through the cycle shown in Figure II:

**Figure II**

Transformation of Rural Land to Urban Land

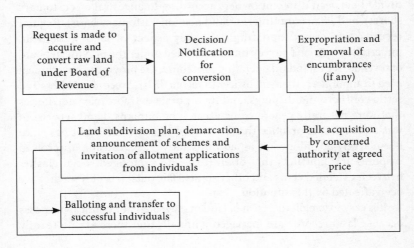

## LAWS ON LAND ACQUISITION

Land acquisition laws are applied for a range of different infrastructure and development functions. The Land Acquisition Act of 1894 allows the electricity and railway authorities to apply to relevant boards of revenue or other authorities to acquire land to generate, distribute, and transmit electricity or operate railway networks. The same provision exists and is normally applied for other forms of development and infrastructure, such as waterways, canals, telecommunications networks, etc.

These laws also cover the acquisition of land for urban development by various development authorities and autonomous bodies. The KDA, MDA and LDA have historically acquired land for general urban development according to the provisions of respective acts. The KDA was created in 1957, and the LDA and MDA were set up in 1993. The KDA was mandated to oversee planning and development in the entire Karachi metropolitan area; while the LDA and MDA respectively focused on facilitating planning and development in peri-urban areas of Lyari and Malir. The new format for urban management under the SLGO 2001 resulted in the repeal of earlier laws and subsequent devolution of these authorities to the CDGK, although many land management functions, regulations, and procedures were protected and carried over into the new dispensation, including land acquisition.

The implementation of SLGO slowed down as the provincial government of Sindh attempted to increase its power and control over local affairs. Local government has numerous advantages for poor urban communities, such as local level representation, participation in the selection of development schemes, basic control of lower level management functions, and the ability to communicate local issues to higher levels of decision making. The SLGO also empowered local institutions at the city level to prepare urban and district master plans. However, the initiation, completion and notification of the much delayed master plan for Karachi reflect the difficulty of reaching a consensus on local government. Although Karachi is the capital of Sindh province, only 11 per cent of its residents speak Sindhi as their mother tongue, while 67 per cent of the province's total population speak Sindhi and local languages as their first language. The province wishes to control Karachi, which wants to be autonomous.

## BUILDING CONTROL AND TOWN PLANNING REGULATIONS

These regulations are framed under the Sindh Building Control Ordinance 1979. Their general provisions set out the procedures for individuals and corporate bodies who wish to develop land, the schedule of areas where such development is possible and the procedure for public notices regarding changes in land use.

The regulations lay down the framework for managing the built environment in designated locations and areas of Karachi, covering key areas such as licensing professionals, procedures for public sales, projects and real estate development, dealing with land development violations, identifying dangerous buildings, managing construction sites, space requirements in and around buildings, safety provisions, heritage conservation, widening existing roads, standards for land development, procedures for land subdivision, amalgamation and change of land use, classification of urban land use and parking, and right of way requirements.

Many of these regulations are difficult to implement and enforce, especially for low-income communities. They may need to be facilitated by consultants and their agents, which entails substantial management costs including fees and levies. In addition to this, provisions are often altered on *ad hoc* basis due to political influence or commercial pressures. For example, in 1995, the NGO Shehri[2] helped the citizens of Karachi campaign against the city government and KBCA; seal about 260 unauthorized structures and initiate disciplinary action against 29 KBCA officers who had colluded with the builders' mafia (Cowasjee 2001). Despite these proceedings, 15 of the 29 KBCA officers remained on the KBCA payroll because of their status as political favourites. (See Chapter 6 for more on the development of the builder's mafia).

Although building control and town planning regulations apply to informal low-income settlements that have been regularized, they are seldom enforced. The densification of informal settlements continues without any recourse to formal approval from the KBCA (now the SBCA).[3] The relevant authorities are only approached for approval or endorsement in rare cases where a formal transaction such as a House Building Finance Company (HBFC) loan is involved. It is difficult to enforce regulations or manage settlements when so few of them are covered by regularization and improvement plans. As a result, they become stagnant, unable to attract investment for formal real estate initiatives, and increasingly subject to the influence of political groups (see Chapter 4 for details).

The Sindh Assembly recently passed the Sindh High Density Development Board Act 2010 to ensure the coordinated and integrated development of high density zones in urban centres across the province, including Karachi. This empowered the board to identify and demarcate high density zones, bearing in mind the general principles of the KSDP-2020. Professional bodies of architects and planners and certain civil society groups were sceptical about the proposed creation of such zones, given the poor regulatory framework for development; fragmentary land management control by various agencies; their adverse impacts on city infrastructure and the composition of the board, most of whose members are ruling party appointees or government agency bureaucrats.[4] It is generally believed that attempts will be made to use this instrument to generate profits for developers, by increasing the population density and activities in the already congested central business districts. Preliminary work to identify and demarcate the first zone in Karachi began in 2010, but has yet to yield any conclusive results.

## ENVIRONMENTAL LAWS

According to the Pakistan Environmental Protection Act 1997, every development project that affects the local ecology and community should be subject to an environment impact assessment (EIA), conducted under the auspices of the provincial environmental protection agencies. The objective is to mitigate the harmful impacts that development schemes, including residential developments, might have on the physical and social environment. In Karachi, this is managed by the Environmental Protection Agency (EPA) of Sindh. Professional consulting firms conduct an assessment on behalf of their clients, which is then deliberated in public hearings that are advertised and open to all citizens. These hearings provide a platform where objections and observations are recorded and considered for further deliberation. So far this procedure has done little to safeguard the urban environment due to the influence of powerful interest groups that promote *laissez faire* construction practices. Nevertheless, growing public interest has seen a number of schemes modified and two cancelled as a result of public hearings.[5]

## BUILDING CONTROL LAWS

The SBCA regulates the built environment under the framework of Sindh Building Control Ordinance, 1979 (see previous section). The authority was originally set up as the Karachi Building Control Authority (KBCA), but the present regime extended its jurisdiction to cover the entire province. In 2002 the government issued a set of regulations known as the Karachi Building and Town Planning Regulations. Builders and developers are supposed to follow these regulations, but often flout them in connivance with KBCA functionaries. Building practices and procedures are widely perceived as riddled with malpractice, procedural irregularities and approvals of inappropriate proposals. One reason why these laws are not followed is because they are not enforced. During an interview, an SBCA official[6] observed that all the SBCA district representatives are based in the head office some distance from the areas under their jurisdiction and that the corridors are full of applicants waiting to negotiate and get approval on commercial FARs (floor area ratios). The SBCA seems to function as a demand-led agency that responds to applications in its offices, but has neither the manpower nor the political will to go and inspect buildings to ensure that they conform to building control laws.

## CONCLUSIONS REGARDING LAWS AND REGULATIONS

There are numerous laws, statutes and regulations relating to land in Karachi. The SKAA Act of 1987 has sufficient provisions to protect the tenure of low-income groups, and the environmental laws and EIA process could help ensure socially and environment friendly development. The building by-laws and zoning regulations could also contribute to a healthy physical and social environment, despite the fact that they are anti-street, anti-pedestrian and anti-dissolved space. These laws are routinely violated as they are too rigid and take no account of the incremental manner in which poor communities often build their homes. The cantonment laws are anti-poor and do not facilitate the transition from informal to formal settlements. Meanwhile, the Land Acquisition Act has been used to provide land for questionable development projects sponsored by the government and also of powerful interest groups, which have displaced a large number of poor settlements. Some 40,900 houses have been demolished since 1992, displacing 286,300 persons.[7]

The problem is not the laws, but governance. It is difficult to implement and enforce laws when the city and the province are locked in conflict; when bureaucrats and government ministers use their discretionary powers for patronage rather than to serve the objectives of these laws; when powerful mafias invest their money in the lucrative formal and informal real estate sector and openly flout plans and laws with the help of a willing establishment and when the armed forces and other federal landowning agencies constantly interfere in land related matters. In the case of the Land Acquisition Act, the term 'public good' needs to be revisited and redefined and proposed development projects judged accordingly, to make it more difficult to bulldoze homes.

## REVIEW OF LAND AND URBAN MASTER PLANS

A number of development plans have been prepared for Karachi since Independence, most notably the MRV Plan 1952; the Greater Karachi Resettlement Plan 1958; the Karachi Master Plan 1975–85; the Karachi Development Plan 2000; and the recent KSDP-2020. A review of these plans is as follows.

The macro form of urban Karachi was shaped by the Greater Karachi Plan and the Greater Karachi Resettlement Plan 1958. The former laid down the key corridors of movement and growth, while the latter opened up satellite towns in the relatively remote locations of Korangi and North Karachi. Land and housing for low-income residents was located far from the key manufacturing areas and city centres where employment opportunities are found, establishing an inbuilt social injustice that forces the urban poor to survive on the peripheries of the city.

The Karachi Development Plan (1975–1985) was a pioneering initiative in terms of urban and regional planning. Various possibilities for growth and development were considered, along with short and long term proposals for land use and development. This plan laid down the principles for distributing plots to low-income communities and individuals through the Metrovilles Programme scheme. This aimed to supply sites and services for the growing low-income population, using massive public sector initiatives and state subsidies to develop four 10,000 plot schemes per annum. These schemes did not achieve the desired targets due to administrative shortcomings; handicaps to occupancy; the parallel development of *katchi abadis* in more desirable locations and speculative land acquisition by middle-income groups wanting to profit from future sales. Nevertheless, the plan provided a useful framework for land management and development, through strategic interventions such as proposals to safeguard and conserve agricultural lands; adjust cantonments and defence lands and consolidate coastal recreation areas.

At the end of the planning period for the Karachi Development Plan (1973–1985), the KDA's Master Plan and Environmental Control Department (MPECD) started preparing the Karachi Development Plan (1986–2000). The field work and design surveys undertaken for the final report and detailed sector-wise studies for this plan generated useful land data and the final document included valuable information about the large reservoir of vacant land on the outskirts of the city; bulk infrastructure provisions; the overwhelming proportion of public land ownership; the growing number of 'squatters' who accounted for 40 per cent of the population; increasing land prices; rising unemployment and increasing affordability. Several strategies were proposed to streamline land distribution and management in different areas, by prioritizing the completion of existing housing and land development schemes; providing new development areas (with a special focus on low-income communities); planning new KDA schemes towards the end of the planning period; consolidating existing land development schemes by prioritizing the provision and consolidation of infrastructure and mechanisms to reduce the population concentration in core areas of the city and establish partnerships between key real estate groups. Few of these provisions have been implemented because the government did not fulfil the institutional commitments to provide legal cover for the plan.

The most recent planning exercise was the Karachi Strategic Development Plan (KSDP) 2020. This was undertaken by a relatively powerful local government that came into being after the KDA, KMC and many other local authorities were devolved under the umbrella of the CDGK. Since the objective of the plan was to transform the city into a world class metropolis, the provision, distribution and development of land and infrastructure were linked with investment, business, and trade. The importance of mixed use development was recognized and promoted through liberal provisions for the densification of existing core locations; the promotion of high density developments in and around the city centre; exclusive land development schemes for higher education, textiles, bus terminals, truck terminals and the media; a new site for an airport and provisions for coastal development. The plan was passed and officially notified by the CDGK in its council deliberations, and work has begun on several developments, with land distributed in the educational, textile, and other industrial zones. However, the CDGK has since been dissolved, and implementation of the plan has been heavily compromised by political uncertainties.

## CONCLUSIONS REGARDING LAND AND URBAN MASTER PLANS

The municipal authorities have identified multiple ownerships and the control of land management as major issues. These might not have emerged as a hindrance to effective planning and development if a competent, overarching platform for decision making and implementation had been in place above all the authorities. Various plans prepared for the city consistently identified the need for this and a decision making and implementation framework was even identified in the plans prepared in 1973–1985 and 1986–2000 (the Karachi Division Physical Planning Agency), but the different authorities and their controlling federal or provincial ministries never actually agreed to this proposition. The government of Sindh, which is the largest public landowner through the Board of Revenue Department (BoR), preferred the short term, scheme based approach of releasing raw land to the defunct KDA, the port authorities, SITE, the DHA, and other agencies.

The supply and allocation of urban land has been and continues to be regarded as a key political tool in negotiations between stakeholders. Land management institutions have lost much of their bargaining power due to rising market pressures, and land supply has become *ad hoc* and haphazard. The urban and regional planning principles and axioms of social justice enshrined in various statutes have proved ineffective against prevailing *laissez faire* attitudes. Thus, balloting is still used as a procedure to supply residential land, even though it is known to accelerate speculation and limit the chances of genuine target groups to access land (see Chapter 5 for details on how balloting is used).

Most of the provisions of KSDP-2020, the current plan, are technically valid and socially relevant. The failure to implement proposals to develop and redesignate certain core areas as mixed land use zones; regularize informal low-income settlements: complete older housing schemes; limit spot land use conversions and develop closer coordination between the local and provincial government, can be ascribed to the uncertain status of local government and lack of consensus (backed by appropriate laws and institutions) between major political stakeholders.

# VIEWS OF THE PROVINCIAL GOVERNMENT AND THE CDGK ON THE KARACHI STRATEGIC DEVELOPMENT PLAN-2020:

## THE VIEWS OF THE PROVINCIAL GOVERNMENT[8]

In principle, the government of Sindh owns all land in the province of Sindh. It can allocate, lease and dispose of land through its Board of Revenue (BoR) and, as the ultimate landowner, revoke leases. Although the government of Sindh has a special housing office in its local government department, it does not act on the issue of housing provision, but relies on local governments in the cities of Sindh to provide housing for their urban poor. The BoR in the government of Sindh transfers underdeveloped land parcels to the city's development agencies and different departments of its own in Sindh for development and disposal. Planned developments in Karachi include the Education City, the IT City, the Super Highway—National Highway Link Road, and many other similar projects.

Under the Sindh Urban Land Disposal Act, which is administered by the government of Sindh Land Utilization Department, the BoR can convert parcels from their original agricultural land use to commercial, housing, or industrial use (see earlier section for details). The disposal, conversion, and development of land does not always follow the guidelines laid down by the CDGK in the KSDP-2020. Although the KSDP-2020 is a legal document, the government of Sindh is not bound by it because it is not a provincial act or law applicable to all projects. All the private developers, cooperatives, and individuals who provide formal planned housing for low-income groups take advantage of this provision by approaching the BoR directly in order to obtain land for their developments. This creates a conflict of development priorities and real estate allocations in the city, and leads to disorganized densification, urban sprawl and *ad hoc* land use patterns that bear no relation to the city's infrastructure, transport networks, or land use plans. All this places considerable strain on the city's resources and the agencies responsible for its operation and maintenance.

The development and planning agencies of the federal government in Karachi and the cantonment boards of Clifton, Keamari, and Manora do not follow BoR laws when executing their respective area plans and projects. The autonomous LDA and MDA do follow CDGK and SBCA rules because they cannot make independent decisions on development. The aforementioned agencies, cantonment boards, and federal development authorities can also buy land directly from the BoR and develop projects on it, in further violation of the KSDP-2020.

This leaves the CDGK as a spectator to the situation, trying to accommodate the Government of Sindh (GoS), BoR and federal government agencies as development partners and adjust the master plan to fit in with their projects. If their proposed projects impinge on CDGK jurisdiction, they use the 1984 law for public good to forcefully assert themselves.

In 2002, the CDGK proposed the *ad hoc* densification of certain major roads in Karachi to reflect current commercial trends. It was decided to consolidate the existing trend for multi-storey developments and transforming residential spaces into commercial spaces and use land conversion fees to generate income for the CDGK. The legal instrument for this initiative was the Change of Land Use by-laws of CDG Karachi 2003. Modified versions of the same by-laws were promulgated and notified in 2004 and 2006. It may be noted that the erstwhile KDA had allowed the commercialization of plots on Shahrah-e-Pakistan, University Road, Nazimabad 'B' Road, Rashid Minhas Road, Shahrah-e-Faisal, and Tariq Road since 1998, on payment of a conversion fee and other charges (see Government of Sindh Notification dated 20 July 1998). The initial proposal for 6 corridors by 2011 was increased to 27 corridors, including all the major arteries in the city irrespective of their location, existing transport and infrastructure load and social and cultural fabric. The FAR for these corridors was increased from 1:1 and 1:1.5 to 1:5.5,[9] partly as a result of pressure from the real estate development sector, which wants to maximize the profit on investments. Although this *ad hoc* plan has been heavily criticized amid concerns that it will lead to unplanned densification and land use changes, the CDGK is pressing ahead with preparations for the first cluster of densification plan and regulations, hoping to swell its coffers with this easy money making exercise.

In an attempt to explore real estate potential of the central business district and adjoining areas, the government of Sindh set up a committee to deliberate on this matter through the Sindh Building Control Authority. Committee members included the chief minister of Sindh, GoS functionaries, the controller of KBCA (committee secretary) and selected professionals from four organizations: the Institute of Architects of Pakistan (IAP), the NGO Shehri-CBE, the Department of Architecture and Planning at NED University, and the Pakistan Council for Architects and Town Planners (PCATP).

The committee met several times. After some deliberation, the representatives from the professional organizations suggested that randomly chosen transport arteries should not be allowed to become dense in isolation, as this would create development hazards at the city level. A proper densification scheme requires a city-wide plan, in accordance with KSDP-2020. In the interests of transparency and accountability, it was proposed that neither the chief minister nor any other GoS officer or official be allowed to be sole executor of the plan and that all stakeholders should be taken on board to ensure that the plan is implemented effectively. These recommendations have yet to be acted upon, as the chief of SBCA has not convened a meeting to address the issue. In the meantime, the CDGK and other agencies regularly receive applications for land use conversions and increased FARs, which are dealt with on a case by case basis.

When the GoS, BoR, cantonment boards, and other agencies have many contested cases of jurisdiction over land in Karachi, the CDGK may plan the land use, but can never be sure that it will be implemented. Development directions keep changing due to the involvement of so many stakeholders who are only interested in profitable ventures and not particularly concerned about the provision of affordable housing for low and lower middle-income groups. In this situation, such communities rely on the informal sector and private developers. The absence of government support and subsidies for the provision of land, credit and infrastructure has led to a large housing backlog.[10] There are no hard figures available to gauge the exact situation, but several studies put it at about two-thirds of the total formal supply. This shortfall results in overcrowded formal housing stock and informal expansions in old and new settlements.

## VIEWS OF AN OFFICIAL IN THE CITY DISTRICT GOVERNMENT KARACHI (CDGK)[11]

The City District Government Karachi (CDGK) owns and manages only 31 per cent of the land in Karachi. The rest is controlled by other authorities, such as provincial and federal government agencies, cantonment boards, and the Malir and Lyari Development Authorities. The Karachi Strategic Development Plan 2020 (KSDP-2020) proposed by the CDGK provides guidelines for the development and growth of the city, but it has not been possible to implement it fully due to the multiple landowners involved. Although KSDP-2020 suggests that most of the planning proposals, vacant land allocations and land use suggestions will be formulated solely by the CDGK, and it provides a plan of action (see KSDP-2020, Table 6.1), this has not been the case (see the preceding section, based on an interview with Mr Khalid Siddiqui).

The KSDP-2020 was completed in 2007, but little progress has been made in implementing the master plan since then. According to the MPGO, this is largely due to the fact that jurisdiction over land is divided between independent authorities that do not have to accept any other agency's proposals and sanctions. They have their own development and planning authorities, and do not necessarily need the CDGK to approve their development initiatives. The MPGO has been involved in discussions with the other landowning authorities on behalf of the CDGK, and the following five initiatives are under way to facilitate the effective implementation of KSDP-2020:

- Develop eleven new high-rise, high density mixed land use real estate zones. Most of these lie within the existing inner city, central business district (CBD), and high-income residential and commercial areas bordering the port, the coast, and wholesale markets and businesses. Documents outlining the by-laws and regulations for the development of these zones are being prepared. This development is geared towards middle to upper income groups in the city, offering living, work, and recreational opportunities on the open market.

- Regularize illegal or *de facto* low-income settlements. The MPGO has been working with various authorities on this, including the LDA, the MDA, the SKAA and the CDGK, Karachi Port Trust, and cantonment directorates for *katchi abadis*. Various regularization and improvement projects are under way, which will benefit the poor who already own properties in these settlements. There are no plans to develop new low-income schemes.

- Complete old housing schemes, as the CDGK is not in a financial or administrative position to launch new housing schemes. These schemes were launched years ago but have not been completed due to lack of funds, political will, administrative capacity and corruption. Efforts to complete them will help control urban sprawl, increase the density of existing areas and make use of the physical infrastructure that has been developed. However, it may still take many years before these settlements are fully occupied.

- The CDGK is playing a proactive role in helping the government of Sindh Board of Revenue to regularize its land parcel developments on the outer periphery of the city. These plots are slated for residential, commercial and industrial use and the CDGK is trying to bring them into line with the KSDP-2020 to facilitate coherent future development.
- The MPGO is regularly involved in investigating and approving land use conversions for the CDGK. Many of these cases lie on corridors in the city that have recently been declared commercial areas, leading to the conversion of houses into apartment blocks or commercial plazas. These conversions often spill over into surrounding settlements and the subsequent legal and illegal conversion of houses is causing problems with densification, congestion, infrastructure breakdowns, traffic, and limited privacy.

## VIEWS OF AN OFFICIAL FROM THE SINDH KATCHI ABADI AUTHORITY (SKAA)[12]

The minister for *katchi abadis* plays a big role in deciding which settlements are dealt with by the SKAA. This means that field offices sometimes have to switch focus when a new government comes to power, so that its supporters are rewarded and opponents sidelined. Otherwise there is little demand for leases and tenure as people value informal security more than formal security. Possessing the right paperwork for a lease is not protection enough against evictions, which may well occur at midnight when the media and judicial system are not available to help prevent them. Regularization is largely determined by political discretion, both at the top and at the local level. Although the SKAA does follow the procedures specified in the Act of 1987, its success rate often depends on the director of the field office and head offices,[13] and their degree of support for work in the field.

For instance, bureaucratic procedures were reduced when Tasneem Ahmed Siddiqui was Director of SKAA. The authority set up lease camps in the *katchi abadis* that were due to be regularized so that people who had day jobs did not have to take time off work to go to the office to get a lease. This has continued, but sometimes there is not enough staff to deal with the workload or follow up cases that are stuck in other government departments; contacting all the departments whose approval is needed before the SKAA can start work is a full-time job in itself.

The time taken to issue leases to most of the residents in the area marked out for regularization varies. It can take anything between two months (as in Chakra Goth) and two years (if legal proceedings are involved).

Legal disputes over land ownership occur when other landowning authorities in Karachi refuse to give the SKAA a No Objection Certificate (NOC) because they want to control the land. The KDA and CDGK have been involved in numerous disputes over sites occupied by longstanding *katchi abadis*. It can take years to settle these disputes in court, and in the meantime public agencies cannot develop the land because of its suspended status.

## CONCLUSIONS

The current activities of the MPGO and CDGK (now KMC) suggest that there is little political will to implement the KSDP-2020. The absence of a legal framework to coordinate planning and development by the different landowning agencies in Karachi is compounded by the lack of government subsidies, appropriate funding allocations, and technical capacities. The CDGK is short of money and promotes the commercialization of the main corridors of movement in Karachi in order to raise revenues from commercialization fees. Politicians, bureaucrats, and developers are often more interested in the informal financial benefits offered by development than the advice of the professional committees established to look into the adverse effects of commercialization. This leads to *ad hoc* developments that cause considerable environmental and social degradation. Meanwhile, the MPGO/CDGK accepts the constraints faced by the state and rely on private developers and investors to develop and deliver housing. While the KDA was a major provider of housing in the decades leading up to the 1980s, the CDGK now acts as little more than a regulator. Given this situation and the absence of private and government banks willing to give loans to low-income groups, the poor have little choice but to live in informal settlements awaiting eventual regularization.

# 4

# Land and Housing: Credit for Purchase

## A REVIEW OF HOUSING FINANCE

The information in this section is based on interviews with key staff members in nine formal housing finance institutions, and a review of their records and literature on housing finance. The details, facts and figures for the institutions are shown in Appendix 1.[1]

Like many other major cities in low and middle-income countries, the finance systems in Karachi do not reflect the economic conditions of most of the city's inhabitants. People generally have few savings and survive on a monthly salary, but houses are usually only available for outright purchase rather than through easy financing or mortgage options.

It has been established that the minimum amount required to build a house for a poor family (that can be increased incrementally) is Rs 500,000 ($5,556 at current exchange rates). A family that earns Rs 15,000 ($166) per month should not pay more than Rs 5,000 a month to repay this amount over fifteen years (Hasan 2011). The most important requirement for low-income groups is funding to buy a plot of land in a formal sector housing scheme, especially given that the housing backlog has increased to more than half of total annual supply.[2] It is against these realities that the financial institutions in Karachi have been analysed.

The most important source of funds for housing is the House Building Finance Company (HBFC). Now a private company, this was originally a federal government institution founded in 1952 called the House Building Finance Corporation. It has the largest portfolio of disbursement and active loans relating to housing finance and a strong, dependable relationship with formal sector developers and builders and staff at every level who understand the housing market, operations, and trends. So far it has financed 456,256 houses through disbursing loans worth Rs 47.82 billion ($0.53 billion). Most formal housing projects and initiatives automatically include a loan facility from HBFC. However, the company does face various constraints such as incomplete documentation of its previous dealings; political pressure to approve various loan programmes and credit lines; inordinate delays in the completion of projects; a lengthy litigation cycle to deal with wilful defaulters and a general tendency for customers to delay loan repayments. HBFC staff believes that increasing awareness among ordinary customers could enhance the efficiency of credit disbursement and recovery processes. To develop their awareness, its website explains how to purchase land and property from the open market; lists the documents required to do so; outlines the precautions to be taken against fraud and cheating and sets out the procedures and benefits of HBFC loans.[3]

The stringent and often cumbersome procedures for assessing the credit worthiness of prospective clients were also cited as a core problem that prevents HBFC from utilizing its full potential. A company representative agreed with this, saying that although HBFC claims to work for low-income groups, its rigid rules make it only accessible to middle-income groups.[4] Details of loans conditions can be viewed in Table IV. For example, the 'Ghar Asan Flexi' scheme for home purchases and/or house construction and renovation requires 23 documents *before* an application can be made. This means that applicants have to go to at least nine different agencies to get them validated and attested. Not surprisingly, households below a certain level of income will be deterred by the amount of time and money this entails.[5]

The 60 per cent balance of funding that the HBFC can provide is particularly beneficial for the middle level of the middle-income group, who have been able to purchase land in formal sector schemes and have the wherewithal to pay for up to 40 per cent of the land and construction costs themselves.

The housing credit option offered by Tameer Microfinance Bank is more useful for those in lower-income and lower middle-income groups. It has reduced the minimum disbursement to Rs 50,000, which can be very useful for people seeking small loans to renovate, maintain, extend, or consolidate their house. However, documentary evidence of income and property is required to finalize these loan agreements, thereby excluding the huge number of people who live in settlements and peri-urban localities that have not been regularized, and limiting the chances for those employed in or associated with informal trades, businesses, and enterprises to access a loan package. Although the interest rate is high at 36 per cent, the 3–5 year repayment period makes it relatively feasible for small loans for home improvements and extensions.

The Managing Director of Tameer Bank noted in an interview that for most lending institutions, 'the biggest issue in housing finance is a clean title to guarantee that a default will not be made.'[6] This institutional focus on clean titles automatically sidelines working households in informal settlements that have not been regularized. It also shows how the institutional inefficiencies of the public sector seep into the private sector. Most importantly, widespread corruption in the dispensation of titles by public sector agencies and the lack of a uniform one window operation for dispensing leases to low-income households (under CDGK, BoR and SKAA regulations on *katchi abadis*, for example)[7] compromises their use as collateral by formal institutions. Poorer sections of the population consequently have to rely on informal and sometimes exploitative loans from political patrons, relatives, or employers.

The rise of political Islam has seen a number of banks promoting Islamic banking. Loans under the Islamic system conform to *Shari'ah* law on financing, ownership, and trade. Home loan contracts therefore involve co-ownership of the property because the transaction is not based on lending or borrowing money. The Meezan Bank's Easy Home Programme provides 85 per cent of the cost of the house, but the bank does not fund land purchases or cater to anyone with an income of less than Rs 20,000. For details of the system, see Appendix 1.

Commercial banks (as opposed to housing, micro-credit, and Islamic banks) normally focus on the middle and upper income groups, offering a wide variety of loans and packages for repairs, renovations, purchases, construction, modification, and redevelopment. Loans can be for as much as Rs 10 million, and are negotiable in exceptional cases.

Housing loans and credit lines are not aggressively marketed by bankers. There are several reasons for this. Commercial banks view housing loans as a high risk business to be undertaken only when all the stringent conditions have been met and advise their clients to examine prospective purchases closely to ensure that they are free of any legal or documentary shortcomings. This limits the chances of this business expanding in a market characterized by informal transactions and limited options for clean formal business. Bankers appear to adopt a cautious approach to avoid increasing the number of bad loans in their portfolio.

The housing finance options on offer have changed radically over the last three decades, which have seen a surge in consumer finance. In the fiscal year 2003 alone, the amount of housing finance available jumped by 400 per cent to Rs 3.5 billion ($38.88 million). In January 2004, it was estimated that there was an unmet demand for Rs 70 billion ($777.77 million) of this type of funding (*Dawn*, 25 January 2004). Data from the State Bank of Pakistan show that housing loans increased by 7.6 per cent in the first seven months of 2007, compared with 15.5 per cent over the same period in 2006 (The Asia Foundation 2008). Formal housing credit institutions have also proliferated, and are now willing to offer credit for house construction, repairs and renovations, extension, reconstruction, repurchase, modification and fresh purchases. The ceilings for loans have become fairly flexible although the core conditions for documentation remain unchanged.

HBFC, which has been transformed from a public corporation to a private company, offers the widest range of options and greatest flexibility. As a specialist housing finance institution, it extends numerous packages to a widespread clientele. Tameer Microfinance Bank also provides useful housing loans of between Rs 50,000 and Rs 500,000 for low-income households. Nationalized commercial banks and Islamic and private banks offer a range of loan options with a ceiling of Rs 30 million over a maximum period of twenty years. Yet they still fail to address the huge emerging needs of households that are unable to comply with current banking conditions due to lack of documentary evidence of ownership, informal employment, unverifiable assets and high interest rates. It is important to note that 24 per cent of applications for construction, 11.5 per cent for purchase and 7 per cent for land are rejected due to the lack of proper documentation. This also delays the processing of loans, as does applicants lacking the expertise and knowledge to fill out forms and follow procedures correctly (ibid.).

Table IV shows that the Islamic banking system and the HBFC offer the most attractive 15-year loan schemes available in Pakistan. Yet none of these banks cater for over half of the population of Karachi, who live in informal settlements, have no lease or ownership papers and earn Rs 15,000 or less. They do serve families that earn Rs 20,000 to Rs 25,000, provided they can invest in land; cover some of the construction costs and have a formal job or a formally registered or taxpaying business—which few do.

## CONCLUSIONS

Although there has been a surge in finance for house building, there is still not nearly enough funding to meet the rising housing deficit. This is because housing finance institutions do not cater for the needs of lower-income groups, who account for over 70 per cent of the unmet need for housing finance. The scarcity of institutions offering housing finance to lower-income groups is indicative of a public sector reluctant to facilitate a link between the market and the housing needs of the majority of Karachi's population.

Low and lower middle-income families need to be able to obtain loans to purchase plots of land in formal sector settlements where they can build their houses incrementally. This would give them both security of tenure and an asset, but housing finance institutions currently do not offer loans for land purchases. One reason for this is the absence of a stable, predictable and uniform land registration system, which makes lending money to buy land a highly unreliable, erratic and protracted procedure.

Interest rates are also far too high for loans to be affordable. This is not because the financial institutions charge high rates of interest, but because of the high KIBOR rate, which currently stands at 12 per cent. Various methods of subsidizing interest rates for low-income groups have been suggested, but banking institutions are unwilling to pursue them because it would reduce their profit margins (Hasan and Mohib 2009).

It is also difficult for low-income groups to fulfil the conditions for obtaining a loan, as many do not have the requisite formal employment, registered business, or income tax certificates. As a result of these restrictions, the majority of people seeking a home do not even consider applying for a loan with a banking institution.

The banks do not have a programme to facilitate group or community credit, although there are a number of successful community initiatives that the banks could support involving mutual saving groups.[8] These are particularly relevant in homogenous communities where there is some form of credible community leadership based on social or religious bonds. Another possible avenue would be to give employers guaranteed finance to enable lower grade employees to access such loans.

Surveys undertaken for this book[9] also show that people wish to become homeowners but do not think the existing schemes are appropriate to their income and savings status. About 15 per cent of the households surveyed live in rented accommodation due to the lack of suitable home ownership options, which are compounded by rising fuel costs, poor public transport options, and fluctuating fares.[10]

Developers have built numerous apartment blocks around the eastern and north-eastern edges of the city, but high prices and stringent loan

## Table IV

### Credit for Housing

| | Bank | Age limit | Interest rate | Preference | Minimum amount | Maximum amount | Minimum salary requirement | Loan tenure | Monthly instalments on Rs 500,000 over 15 years | For land purchases | For construction, house purchase and renovation |
|---|---|---|---|---|---|---|---|---|---|---|---|
| 1 | Bank Al-Islamic | 65 years BP and SP | Average 17% | Salaried class | | Rs 10 million | | 5–20 years | Rs 9500 | | |
| 2 | Dubai Al-Islamic | BP=65 SP=60 | Average 14% per cent | Salaried class | Rs 1,000,000 | Rs 30 million | Rs 40,000 | 3–20 years | Rs 6658 | | |
| 3 | HBFC (without KIBOR) | 18 to 59 for BP and SP | 3.47% for 15 years and 4.08% for 20 years | | | | | | Rs 4634 | | |
| 4 | HBFC (12% KIBOR) | 18 to 59 years for BP and SP | 15.55% for 15 years and 16.08% for 20 years | 35% of net income | | Rs 10 million | | | Rs 7134 | | |
| 5 | Meezan Bank | | 17% | | | | | 3–25 years | Rs 7170 | | |

**Legend**

| | |
|---|---|
| BP | Business person |
| SP | Salaried person |
| | Not allowed |
| | Allowed |
| | HBFC with KIBOR |

Meezan Bank called it Masharqa, claim to finance 20 to 50 per cent of the total value and term repayment amount as rent.

conditions make these a limited option. Developers and estate agents interviewed for the study indicated that levels of corruption in regulatory authorities like the KBCA (now SBCA) are such that people use estate brokers and other middlemen to deal with documentation issues. This increases costs and the chances of fraud. In fact, developers claim that their product prices would be 20 per cent lower if the KBCA and utility agencies were not corrupt. If this is true, it would represent a major saving for both lower and middle-income groups.[11]

The studies also show that it is important to establish the ability of the poor to pay for housing and the factors that contribute to this. Field surveys on the diverse geographical mix covered by this exercise revealed high levels of dependency, with just one earning member in most households. This makes proximity to the workplace a determining factor in deciding where to live.[12] Some form of security is needed to obtain loans for non-leased properties, and the availability of loans increases the incentive to get a lease. This is also important for people who are looking to buy land to build a house, regardless of whether it is serviced or has some kind of infrastructure on it.

# 5

# Land Related Conflicts – I: Findings from Secondary Sources

## INTRODUCTION

The previous two chapters presented a picture of the thirteen formal institutions that govern the land market in Karachi, and the finance options available for housing, which mainly cater for middle-income groups. The land situation is complicated by the political tussle between Karachi's city and provincial governments, which allows other forces of supply and demand in the land and housing market to exploit the weaknesses in its governance structure.

The land market differs from other markets because land is more than just a capital asset. It is the product of a number of site specific qualities, which means that land use and occupation in Karachi is coloured by political, ethnic, and corporate interests. This section uses secondary sources to identify the actors and processes that currently govern the development of land in Karachi. Secondary data were collected for two purposes. One was to gain more detailed knowledge about various aspects of land related issues that are not commonly known or understood. The other was to make this material available on the websites of Karachi's leading urban centres; specifically, NED University, the Urban Resource Centre (URC), and Arif Hasan's website. It was felt that this would be a huge resource for researchers, journalists, academics, students and politicians, and be helpful in redesigning courses in planning, architecture, public policy, and law.

The structure of Chapter 5 is determined by the nature of the data sources. The first part introduces information from news reports, films produced by NGOs and television shows accessed on YouTube. It is based on 35 videos, 83 per cent of which are television reports and productions[1] and 13 per cent of which were made by independent producers.[2] A synopsis of this material is provided in Appendix 2. The discussion on local media reports is supplemented by the portrayal of land markets in seven renowned feature films on land in India, Pakistan, and the United States.

The chapter also examines five case studies that describe the processes, actors, and legal and political issues involved in the land market in Karachi. These studies focus on the way that residents, the non-governmental sector, the corporate sector, and the law courts affect the environment and landscape of Karachi. It also outlines the massive land conversions that are under way along the coast of Karachi, with a brief description of the nature of these developments, the parts played by international capital and companies based in Dubai and Malaysia, and civil society opposition to these developments.[3]

The final section of this chapter (Synopsis of Data on Land from the Print Media) is based on 5,602 news clippings on land issues kept at the Urban Resource Centre Karachi. These are regularly compiled from the daily newspaper *Dawn*, *Jang* (Urdu), *the News*, and *the Daily Times*. These clippings were acquired from the URC and divided into six broad categories and further subcategories (shown in Table V), and analysed through a methodology which is described in **Appendix-3**, which also lists a number of unanswered questions. The synopsis of each of these categories and subcategories has been prepared in a fact sheet.[4]

**Table V**

Classification of News Clippings on Land Matters

| Land Acquisition | Land Development | Changes in Land-use | Land Disputes | Land Disasters | Money Matters |
|---|---|---|---|---|---|
| Allotment, encroachment, regularization, auctions, real estate, leases, and bookings | Construction, development, housing facilities and amenities, loans, leases, civic amenities, town planning, housing schemes and land-use | Conversion, reclassification of plots, auctions, demolitions, relocation, transfers, evictions, commercialization, illegal construction and heritage conversions | Court orders, land grabbing, legislation, murders, riots, katchi abadi and informal settlements, differences between actors | Demolition, collapse, disaster, and commercialization | Revenues, taxes and other monetary issues |

# DATA GATHERED FROM VISUAL MEDIA ON LAND IN KARACHI

These television news reports graphically illustrate the determinants and actors in contemporary conflicts over land in Karachi and the impact of land conversions and encroachment on the general public and the environment. In these videos reporters and interviewees (politicians, elected representatives, police officials, and citizens) repeatedly use the term 'land mafia' to describe powerful land grabbers in Karachi. They refer to influential, organized groups that systematically identify, capture, and develop land to sell at a profit. Often political patrons from a few key political parties that hold constituencies in Karachi and the surrounding areas provide security and backing for these land grabbing groups. At the other end of the spectrum are the squatters, who one government official describes as desperate, homeless 'encroachers'.[5] Case studies on the illegal subdivision of land in Karachi in the 1980s (M. Kool, et al. 1988; Hasan 1999) identified the *dallal* as informal developers with a key role in the division of land. They can no longer operate outside political affiliations, and have become cogs in the political land grabbing regime. As one former government official in the Master Plan office observed, 'Each informal developer, who previously would switch allegiances as he saw fit is now bound for his own safety and sustenance to one political party ... his lot is now tied to theirs.'[6]

Formal and informal estate agents and developers play an important role in land grabbing and conversion,[7] while political parties and government authorities are involved in encroachments (see Chapter 6 for primary evidence on the nature of state involvement).[8]

People who are employed to protect land at various sites are 'bought' by land grabbers and support them for a share in the development. *Nazims* who have tried to oppose land grabbing say that they are helpless because the police protect the encroachers;[9] a claim corroborated by serving ministers who maintain that the police cannot act as arbiters because they are firmly believed to be on the side of the land grabbers.[10]

Other stakeholders identified as breaking land rules and regulations include international and local business corporations, religious organizations, and the Pakistani military.[11] In many cases public landowning agencies have supported these actors even though they clearly ignored the express purpose for which the land was initially leased or reserved (see sections regarding the cases of Gutter Baghicha and Makro-Habib) as the offending commercial enterprises provide lucrative financial rewards for facilitators in these public sector bodies (see section on the role of the courts and NGOs in opposing illegal usage).

Different types of land have been encroached upon. Graveyards are flattened or flooded with sewage discharge to make them unusable for their true purpose, opening the way for subsequent illegal occupation.[12] In one case a neighbourhood public library was demolished and other incidents where Google images taken in 2004 and 2009 clearly show that parks have been converted into residential areas, even though it is technically not possible to change the use of amenity plots.[13] In the case of the demolished library, residents blame a court judgment that did not take public interest into account when upholding a claim.[14]

The land mafia reclaims coastal land by filling it with garbage, dividing it into plots and selling them informally.[15] Drainage channels are also being reclaimed for construction, which causes flooding during the monsoon season: in 2010 a four storey building illegally constructed on reclaimed land in Orangi Town collapsed, killing seven people. Residents hold a politician from a key political party responsible for the land reclamation and construction of this building.[16] The land mafia has also managed to prevent the government from beginning the construction of cottage industries on 468 acres (187.2 hectares) of land that belong the city government, which has had little success in combating land grabbers.[17] One independent production of a film shows that land grabbers in collusion with large industrial or political concerns are able to access trucks, tankers and heavy machinery for their operations.[18] Commercial imperatives seem to be more important than the vision of the city set out in a series of master plans.

Video evidence shows that the land mafia caters to commercial enterprises and interests, often at the expense of the city's citizens and their needs. The connivance of government officials and police officers in regularising and allowing land grabs in some areas, while protecting land or protesting about such grabs in other areas is indicative of the way that fractious relationships between different agencies allow them to act as both usurper and protector.

Meanwhile, the government has established a six member anti-encroachment cell under the authority of a provincial minister. Like the planning agencies discussed in Chapter 1, this cell has run into difficulties because of conflict between political forces, in this case the PPP (representing the Sindhi speaking population) and the Awami National Party (representing the Pashto speaking population). A number of videos show the extent to which land grabbing has been politicized.[19]

Resistance to land encroachment and conversion is fraught with danger, as guns have been readily accessible in Karachi since the Afghan war (see Chapter 1 for details). Violence enables encroachers to illegally settle people and industries on land, and resist those who strive to regain legal possession of land. This is often done by settling poor people on illegally occupied land, as reclamation projects lose public support if they result in homes being razed, violence and the arrest of dozens of people from lower-income groups, including women.[20] In the last ten years battles over real estate have escalated into turf wars, with gun battles between opposing groups who prevent the police and paramilitary forces from intervening by firing on them.[21]

Karachi's citizens and NGOs are constantly struggling against land encroachment and conversion. A number of activists have emerged on the scene, protesting at their own peril. Nisar Baloch opposed encroachment on the Gutter Baghicha amenity plot, was murdered the day after he attended a press meeting where he identified the political party that had threatened his life. No arrests were made for his killing due to lack of evidence and witnesses.[22] Other citizens fighting illegal conversions also receive death threats and consequently have withdrawn from the court cases they had filed[23] and news reporters covering land related conflicts face death threats as well. In 2011, a reporter for Geo News was killed after reporting on the political parties' involvement in turf wars over land and its repercussions.[24] Since then all the witnesses who came forward have been killed in targeted drive-by shootings, including members of the police force (Jawad, *The Express Tribune*, 16 April 2011).

The city's ecosystem has been unbalanced by these profit motivated land encroachments, which do not follow any plans or guidelines on adjoining areas or urban construction, and destroy farmland bearing fruit, flora, and fauna. Fishing communities and landowning agencies have been deprived of their land and livelihoods, and the city's natural drainage channels have been blocked. The reclamation of such channels and outfalls to the sea is not limited to low-income localities, as the federal government and defence authorities have also encroached on outfalls to obtain land to house the elite.[25]

Citizens from both middle and low-income backgrounds have been deprived of their legally owned properties,[26] and live in insecurity in areas where the land mafia operates. Intermittent gunfire and violent incidents regularly cause shops and neighbourhoods to close down, making groceries unavailable and social interaction impossible, and severely affecting the quality of life of residents.[27] There are numerous individual accounts of the inconvenience caused by the illegal activities of builders, the Karachi Electricity Supply Company (KESC), the police and the KBCA, which plague the lives of ordinary citizens seeking a piece of land or an apartment in Karachi.[28]

This chapter shows that the main demand for land in Karachi comes from commercial and business interests and ordinary citizens. However, the supply of land is controlled by politically aligned formal and informal developers who operate in association with state functionaries, police agencies and armed groups to ensure that land supply is geared towards commercial use, at the expense of housing. The connivance of state functionaries in land grabbing influences the land market's entry and exit procedures, making it more expensive for genuine buyers to acquire land. It appears that 'squatting' is rarely possible now; migrants coming into the city can no longer occupy a piece of land for housing or temporary accommodation without engaging with local political and land networks.

## OBSERVATIONS ON FEATURE FILMS ABOUT LAND ISSUES

Feature films that focus on India depict conditions very similar to those in Pakistan, showing situations that closely mirror reality and resonate with the background stories documented in the videos discussed in the previous section. Debt leads to the sale or confiscation (often by a bank) of a house or piece of land that may be the family's only asset, causing immense and often irrevocable harm to individuals and livelihoods.[29] Strong caste biases fuel opposition to the sale of land or its reservation for lower castes (in India)[30] or low-income communities (in Pakistan, where caste biases are not so prevalent). The courts frequently fail to adequately address the forcible occupation of homes, creating situations where victims feel obliged to take the law into their own hands.[31] Films like *Khosla ka Ghonsla* show how muscle power, connections with the establishment and an inadequate legal system enables those who encroach upon land or operate land scams to deprive people of land that they have paid for.

## DATA ON LAND IN KARACHI FROM FIVE CASE STUDIES

This part of the book is based on data on various cases documented by several NGOs that work on urban issues in Karachi. It builds on information garnered from five case studies, whose synopses follow. The data in these case studies reveal the relationship between land and the politics of ethnicity in Karachi, and the role of multinational corporations, their Pakistani partners, and the army in supporting illegal land conversions. They also show the struggle that NGOs and activists in Karachi are waging against illegal and environmentally and socially damaging land conversions.

These case studies were chosen to reflect different stakeholders, their impact on the land market and the way that it is managed in Karachi. The first case study looks at the role of residents in fighting demolition; the second shows how the planned efforts by an NGO to identify and safeguard the interests of *goths* to convert them into low-income residential areas has made the NGO an influential partner of the government; the third examines the way that the corporate sector interacts with landowning bodies in contravention of the city's master plan; the fourth case shows how land agencies and government officers get tempted by commercial interest and the high profits of residential plots and thus sometimes sacrifice land meant for parks and ancillary facilities, which are also necessary and the final case study shows the role that a court of law plays in managing land in Karachi.

## ZUBO GOTH

Zubo Goth is an old informal settlement situated on the outskirts of Karachi in Union Council Manghopir, Gadap Town. *Goths* were originally defined as rural settlements or villages, but as Karachi expanded its footprint grew to include adjacent *goths*. Decades ago many low-income households moved to outskirts like Zubo Goth as the cost of land in central Karachi became exorbitant. Settlers in Zubo Goth were granted land by the district commissioner, paying cash to purchase their plots and giving the police another Rs 5,000 per house 'for security' once the building was completed. Land values increased phenomenally after the construction of the nearby Northern Bypass, and numerous attempts have subsequently been made to demolish Zubo Goth. It has since survived three demolitions, one in 2007 and two in 2008 (Ismail 2009).

In 2001, the SLGO replaced the district commissioner system with elected mayors. In 2004, the MQM, the political party representing the interests of Urdu speakers, captured every level of local government in Karachi, obtaining the patronage to acquire valuable land where it could settle its supporters and thereby control an important route into and out of the city.

In July 2007, Zubo Goth was demolished under the supervision of the *nazim* of Orangi Town, who was an MQM candidate. The stated aim was to build a road (Shahrah-e-Gaddafi) that required 100 feet of land, which was already available. All that was needed was a further 7 feet strip of land, yet a 700 feet strip was identified and the houses on it razed to the ground. It is alleged that the demolition was carried out under the *nazim* of Orangi Town, despite the fact that Zubo Goth came under the jurisdiction of Gadap Town. It was not the only *goth* to be destroyed, as several others were bulldozed, their land taken over, divided into plots of 120 square yards and sold at Rs 45,000 ($445) per plot. This made them affordable to lower-income groups from the city who were looking for somewhere to live. The demolition of 'rural' villages thus allowed the urban poor to acquire land for housing themselves. Another demolition occurred in March 2008, supervised by the *nazim* of Orangi Town, officials from the land department, and the police.

After the first demolition, the residents of Zubo Goth organized themselves and took the matter to court, but found no relief from the judiciary. The *nazim* of Gadap Town supported the people in his area and advised them to form a committee, which received technical support and help from the OPP-RTI in obtaining people's land titles and relevant maps showing the settlement's boundaries. Some of these documents were supposedly 'lost' in government files, others were held by influential individuals from the *goth* who used them for deals with the land mafia. Thus the committee acquired maps and official records and reached out to political and social leaders, who in turn activated the media and focused public attention on the situation in the settlement.

The committee's cause was helped by changes at the provincial level when the 2008 elections put the PPP (which is mainly supported by the Sindhi speaking majority in the province) into government at the national and provincial level in Sindh. Residents of the *goths* in Gadap Town contacted the PPP leadership, which helped secure their settlements and mandated the BoR to grant them titles to their land.

The strategy in Zubo Goth succeeded for several reasons: because experienced activists helped mobilize the community; officials and *nazims* whose jurisdictional authority had been encroached upon by other elected officials became involved; residents set up their own committee chaired by the UC *nazim*; residents used their tribal, social, and political networks and contacted the media and other *goths* in similar situations; help from the OPP-RTI raised awareness of the need for the correct information on land demarcation and status and the affected had learned from other evictions where recourse to the official channels of justice had failed.

This case study demonstrates that political involvement is necessary to resist demolition, and that residents play an important role attracting the attention of the media. This is particularly useful if they are not closely linked to the local *nazim* and it is a means of gaining support in a city like Karachi where opposing political parties are always on the lookout for an opportunity to gain political points. Technical expertise from NGOs is helpful, but not sufficient in itself to stem incursions, particularly into low-income areas.

## THE DEVELOPMENT OF GOTHS IN KARACHI AND THE ROLE OF OPP-RTI

The second case study is based on an overview of the work done by OPP-RTI since 2008.[32] It identifies its core strategies and mechanisms for successfully developing and safeguarding the interests of low-income and poor areas in and around Karachi, with a particular focus on its work to regularize land titles in the *goths* of Karachi and achieve the status of *abadis* or regular settlements.

OPP-RTI focuses on several key areas:

i) *Advocating cases to secure land and land titles for low-income residents*: This involves initiating and maintaining regular contact with government officials from the BoR and the SKAA, related ministers and their teams, political parties, community groups, *goth* activists, and the media. Efforts in this field helped extend the cut-off date for informal settlements in Sindh to be eligible for land tenure from March 1985 to June 1997.

ii) *Bringing community activists together in the Secure Housing Group (SHG)*: These activists come from a number of towns, localities and informal settlements in Karachi. OPP-RTI has worked with them on mapping their areas and submitting the maps to the SKAA. The SKAA has accepted them and is using them to identify and notify *goths* regarding the provision of leases.

iii) *Mapping and infrastructure development*: OPP-RTI prepares plans for external (off-site) infrastructures, which are executed by the local government; and internal (on-site) infrastructures, which are executed by the concerned communities. Sewage and drainage is being designed and implemented in 133 *goths*.

iv) *Technical support to the Cooperative Housing Savings and Loan Programme:* This programme provides house building loans for residents in low-income areas. OPP-RTI supports communities by providing technical advice, supervising infrastructure and house building, and running workshops on housing design, construction techniques and technical guidance on proper ventilation and foundations. These are attended by young people from the *goths*.

## THE MAKRO-HABIB/WEBB PLAYGROUND

The third case study relates to corporate sector involvement in illegal land conversions in Karachi.[33] Steenkolen Handels-Vereeniging (SHV) Holdings is the largest private company in the Netherlands. It is one of the world's top liquefied petroleum gas companies and also runs the Makro chain of stores in Asia and South America. Makro is a cash-and-carry wholesaler that serves small and medium size retailers. Makro-Habib was formed as a joint venture between SHV Holdings and the House of Habib, a giant Pakistani company with broad commercial interests.

In 1938, the general officer commander-in-chief of the British Indian Army sanctioned a lease for the Webb Ground in Karachi to be used as a recreational facility by the Karachi Grammar School. In 1976, under an agreement between the Ministry of Defence, the provincial government of Sindh, and the KDA, the Webb Ground became part of the Lines Area Redevelopment Project, but retained its purpose as a recreational facility. However, in 2002 the ministry of defence laid claim to Webb Ground and violated the agreement by issuing a 99-year lease for the land to the Army Welfare Trust (AWT) for commercial purposes. In 2006, the AWT then leased the land to Makro-Habib Pakistan Limited for thirty years as a site for a cash-and-carry store.

The NGO Shehri contacted the mayor of Karachi in order to address this violation of the legal use of the plot. He responded by saying that the city government had a claim to this land. Shehri then wrote a series of letters to SHV Holdings in Holland, which went unanswered. Various article and protests in the print media drew attention to the illegality of the deal between AWT and Makro. Meanwhile, in 2007, a local resident filed a case in the High Court against the CDGK, the chief controller of buildings, the secretary of environment, the government of Sindh, AWT, and Makro, demanding a halt to construction and reinstatement of the Webb Ground as an amenity plot. The High Court responded by issuing a status quo order, which Makro openly defied by advertising and continuing the construction work within a week of the ruling.

The case developed by the residents of Webb Ground maintained that the land ownership and subsequent construction constitute legal violations: zoning violations (including illegal land transfers and unauthorized land conversion); defiance of court orders; violation of national environmental regulations and compliance procedures; environmental degradation in the locality and associated human rights violations.[34] As result of the publicity generated by the case, the Supreme Court of Pakistan took *suo moto* action and passed an order commanding Makro-Habib to move its premises to an alternative site on land belonging to the AWT. Despite this, Makro-Habib is still operating from the same site and shows no signs of relocating the store. In its documentation of this case study, Shehri notes that 'it remains to be seen if the Dutch giant would have been able to conduct itself the same way in its own country— or continent for that matter—where stores of this scale are limited to the suburbs and are consistently scrutinized under strict laws.'

It seems that the landowning authorities pay no heed to master plans or the limitations on land use that have been put in place in the interests of the city as a whole; and that law enforcement agencies are either unable or unwilling to carry out court rulings. This shows a huge lack of governance in Karachi's institutions, which are vulnerable to exploitation by powerful commercial interests.

The next two case studies highlight the role of the judiciary and the extent of its influence in controlling land management and the land market in the city.

## KIDNEY HILL AND AHMED ALI PARK

The fourth case study looks at successful efforts by the management of cooperative societies to convert amenity land into residential plots, and the role of provincial government ministers, local government, developers, NGOs, and concerned citizens in supporting or resisting their attempts to do so.[35]

In 1996, 68 acres (27.2 hectares) of land in KDA Scheme-32 were marked out as a park called Kidney Hill. This park is adjacent to the Karachi Cooperative Housing Society Union (KCHSU), Faran Society, Overseas Cooperative Housing Society (OCHS), and the Al-Riaz Cooperative Housing Society (ACHS). In 1997, the OCHS and ACHS reallocated Kidney Hill for residential development, in collaboration with officials in the federal Ministry of Works (MoW). Due to public hue and cry, the matter was referred to the president of Pakistan, and Kidney Hill was eventually handed over to the KMC to be maintained as an amenity. As a result of this decision, the allocation to OCHS and ACHS was cancelled.

The last two decades have seen multiple litigations between government agencies and land grabbing claimant societies and individuals (such as the minister of cooperatives in 1990) seeking to restore the land to OCHS and ACHS. OCHS also held meetings with the governor of Sindh and proposed the creation of 120 residential plots, which would generate approximately Rs 10 billion ($111 million) in revenue. Various attempts were made to reach a compromise between Shehri, the CDGK and residents who oppose the commercialization of Kidney Hill. The CDGK took a principled stand, stating that under law no amenity plot reserved for a specific use can be converted to or utilized for any other purpose.

In mid-2006, a settlement was finally agreed between OCHS, KCSHU, the MoW, the government of Sindh, and CDGK, allowing 20 acres (8 hectares) of Kidney Hill to be retained as a park. The Supreme Court disposed of the case by sanctioning the agreement in January 2007, regardless of the compliance issues, but gave local residents permission to seek separate remedy under the law within fifteen days. In February, the NGO Shehri and fourteen residents of Faran Society working in collaboration with OCHS filed a constitutional petition at the Sindh High Court, which conferred an interim order prohibiting the creation of third party interest in Kidney Hill. The fourteen residents subsequently withdrew from the case after they received death threats, leaving the NGO Shehri as the sole complainant apart from four concerned citizens who were not directly affected as they do not live in the area. The Kidney Hill case is still being debated in court as encroachments into the area continue; the park is 'inching towards assimilation with the adjacent housing societies with only a handful of people standing in between.'[36]

## GUTTER BAGHICHA

The fifth case study concerns encroachments on Gutter Baghicha (sewage farm).[37] This is the largest continuous open green space in the most densely populated part of the city, covering 1,017 acres (406.8 hectares). Since 1947, 55 per cent of the land has been encroached upon and developed for non-amenity use. Gutter Baghicha has had the KMC and then the CDGK as its caretakers. According to the case study, CDGK staff and politicians have cut down countless old fruit bearing trees to occupy land, and illegally burned garbage and dumped factory waste in the area. Only 430 acres (172 hectares) of the original 1017 acres (406.8 hectares) are left as open space. Large chunks of land have been built over due to fraudulent manipulation and backdating of documents by officials in the KMC/CDGK and government of Sindh.[38]

The main illegal leases concern:

i)   The KMC officer's housing society. In March 1993, the KMC (now CDGK) allotted itself 200 acres for plots for its officers, using a fake process that resulted in police cases being registered against two KMC/CDGK officials.

ii)  Ten residential plots.

iii) A petrol pump.

iv)  A local UC *nazim* occupied 50 acres of parkland in 2003. A case is in progress in the city courts and is to be taken up by the National Accountability Bureau (NAB).

v)   Ismailia Garden Cooperative Housing Society, which was allotted 7.2 acres (28.8 hectares) of land. The society has agreed to move from the plot if alternative space is provided.

In 2002, the president of Pakistan responded to pressure from the NGO Shehri and concerned urban activists by promising to establish a public park on the Gutter Baghicha site. However, local government officials managed to use their influence to reduce the size of the park from 430 acres (172 hectares) to 163 acres (65.2 hectares) to protect their illegal allotments. Many of these officials were members of the KMC/OCHS.

After the construction of the park began, the High Court issued a *status quo* order on all vacant areas of Gutter Baghicha. This order was violated in June 2009 when encroachers supported by the city and town governments occupied 30–50 acres of the park with armed guards, and constructed 100 homes without approved plans. It was difficult for officers of the judiciary to ascertain the extent and nature of the encroachment, as every time the court or civil administration sent inspectors to the site they were mobbed by hundreds of women brought in by vans and motorcycles, and were unable to examine the encroachments.

The battle to guard the land on Gutter Baghicha took a serious turn when two activists from the *Gutter Baghicha Bachao Tahreek* (Save Gutter Baghicha Movement), Nisar Baloch and Nadir Baloch, were shot dead in separate incidents. On the day before he died Nisar Baloch attended a press conference at the Karachi Press Club, where he identified the persons he felt were sponsoring the encroachment on the public park in Gutter Baghicha and appealed to the government and the Chief Justice of the Supreme Court to take action to preserve the amenity space.

Over the past 16 years, numerous cases concerning Gutter Baghicha have been fought in the Supreme Court and Sindh High Court. Suit 1484/2008, which was filed against CDGK/KMC-OCHS by Ardeshir Cowasjee, Abdul Sattar Edhi, Shehri, and local residents (including Nisar Baloch of Gutter Baghicha Bachao Tehreek), requires evidence to be recorded and is pending in Sindh High Court. None of these cases have resolved the issue in a satisfactory manner. Little or no action has been taken because the wrongdoers are affluent, able to hire expensive lawyers and often either include or influence the government officials concerned.

Taken together, these two case studies show the immense uphill struggle facing residents' committees, as there are few agencies that they can approach for recourse against the violation of land regulations. The most obvious agency—the landowning authority—is often complicit in the violations and the remaining agencies that could help, such as the courts and the media do not seem to have enough influence in the city to facilitate a simple resolution in accordance with the regulations.

## LAND CONVERSION ALONG KARACHI'S COASTLINE

The 1999 military coup in Pakistan brought a strong neo-liberal lobby to power. The military quickly promulgated the SLGO, which gave considerable powers to the elected *nazim* of Karachi. In 2002, the *nazim* of Karachi and the prime minister were very keen to attract direct foreign investment for real estate development. Between 1991 and 2006, Dubai-based companies with multibillion dollar portfolios entered into negotiations with the government of Pakistan and prospective private sector partners in the country. These international companies included Dubai World, Emaar, Limitless, and Nakheel.[39]

Three major projects were planned as a result of these negotiations. The first consisted of real estate development along 14 kilometres of coastline in the DHA by the world's largest real estate company, the Dubai based Emaar. This project also involved 74.5 acres (29.8 hectares) of land for a high end hotel complex that would make parts of the beach privately owned, a seven star hotel and 4,000 super luxury apartments with private beaches and lagoons.

The second project, Sugarland City, was initiated in 2006. This involved developing (privatizing) the city's public beaches at Hawksbay, Sandspit, Manora, and Cape Monze. Around 26,000 hectares of land was to be given to Limitless, a company owned by Dubai World, with US$ 68 billion invested in a 'new city' containing residential, commercial, recreational, and entertainment facilities 'in state of the art, master-planned communities'.

A memorandum of understanding was signed by the Pakistani minister of state for privatization and investment and the chairman of Dubai World. At a meeting chaired by the Prime Minister of Pakistan on June 24 2006, a number of directives were issued to different ministries in the country, including ports and shipping and defence, and the government of Sindh. It was decided that the leases issued to Pakistani citizens who had huts in the area would be cancelled prematurely, and that there should be a proper mechanism for shifting the navy and cantonment board facilities on Manora Island to navy land in Cape Monze, to make vacant land available to Limitless.

The third major project was a proposal to build Diamond Bar City. Port Qasim Authority (PQA) had decided to sell two of the islands under its control off the coast of Karachi (Bundal and Buddo) to Emaar. These islands cover a total of 4,800 hectares, and were to be sold for $42 billion. As they can only be accessed by boat, the federal government proposed that a $50 million bridge be constructed to connect the islands to DHA. A memorandum of understanding was signed by the PQA officials, Irfanullah Marwat (representing the Sindh government) and representatives from Emaar. The PQA also planned to develop a project in collaboration with Emaar, to create 15,000 housing units and commercial facilities in Defence Phase VIII (*Dawn*, 1 June 2006), and construct residential, commercial, and leisure real estate projects, an industrial park, free trade zones and port terminals at an estimated cost of $43 billion within thirteen years.

Civil society organizations opposed these projects on legal, environmental, cultural and social grounds, and because they would adversely affect the livelihoods of fishing communities by blocking their access to the sea. Work began on the illegal demolition of several villages to make way for the project, and people from Karachi were deprived of access to beaches that tens of thousands of them have traditionally used for recreation and entertainment. The media initially highlighted the negative aspects of the project but soon stopped focusing on it because, as one TV channel informally told the chairperson at URC, television channels were not in a position to criticize Emaar's projects since its advertisements were a major source of revenue.

The network of civil society organizations that opposed the projects included Sahil Bachao, which is composed of prominent citizens including two retired judges from the Supreme Court of Pakistan; Shehri for a Better Environment, a Karachi-based NGO popularly known as Shehri, which has a long tradition of struggling for better governance and the imposition of by-laws and building regulations pertaining to land use; the Pakistan Fisherfolk Forum and Mahigeer Tehreek (both of these are networks of fishing communities); Dharti, a civil society organization that promotes a better physical and social environment in Karachi and was created in response to the three aforementioned projects; and the Urban Resource Centre, which collaborated with OPP-RTI in collecting 5,000 signatures from low-income areas and schools that oppose the project.

Civil society opposition took the form of court cases, forums, demonstrations, walks, press articles, and various visual media productions. The projects were eventually suspended and the president of Pakistan presented the DHA beach to the people of Karachi as a 'gift'. However, Emaar has continued with its $2.4 billion project to develop 4,000 luxury apartments on reclaimed land in Crescent Bay.

The city government was working on the Karachi Strategic Development Plan (KSDP) 2020 during the debate on the beach projects, which naturally became an important issue in the KSDP—especially because some of people consulted by the KSDP team opposed the projects. The KSDP developed a number of strategies for the development of the coast, some of whose provisions are considered below.

Section 4.8 of the KSDP states that 'reclamation along any section of the sea front either on the landward side or the bordering sea would not be advised. The same restriction holds for the mud flats, marshes and back water creeks, which in no way (should) be allowed to undergo artificial morphological change detrimental to the existing hydrological environment.' Furthermore, 'the coastal sea and its back-water and creeks provide source of livelihood to fishing communities who live on the coast. The fishermen must enjoy free access to their traditional grounds in the sea, backwaters and creeks. For any development to be sustainable and acceptable, the historical rights of the communities to the sea and the coastal village land they occupy ought to be respected.'

The same section talks about environmental and socio-economic provisions, stating that 'the coast must be protected as an environmental asset, and environment quality, including reduction of pollution of the coastal zone must be improved. Green turtle sanctuaries and mangrove ecological system along the beach, in the backwaters and creek must be preserved and measures against its degradation should be urgently taken to control pollution.' Also, that 'the sea-shore and the beaches should be preserved and promoted as public assets. Public access to the beaches and the coast must remain free and unhindered, and to keep the enjoyment for the general citizens, no development should be allowed in land area up to 150 metres from the high water mark.' The KSDP-2020 also talks about 'a programme to promote the seashore and beaches as a public asset.' It accepts the concept of real estate development along the waterfront, but in these terms: 'together with the coastal development programme given above, the coastal area has a potential for development such as housing, business offices, commercial establishments and public amenities in suitable sites. However, any development scheme designed in the area must adhere to the above mentioned guiding principles.' Another important provision states that 'development plans should be finalized with public participation and be presented for soliciting public opinion.'

The city council approved the KSDP-2020 in December 2007. Under the provisions of the plan, none of the three waterfront projects described above can be undertaken. However, two of these projects do not come under the jurisdiction of the city government; they lie within military cantonments, which are not obliged to follow the provisions of the KSDP (see Chapter 3). While it is not obvious why the projects in the cantonments have been abandoned, it is clear that the protests against their inequities played a large role in their 'suspension'.

## SYNOPSIS OF DATA ON LAND IN KARACHI FROM THE PRINT MEDIA:

### LAND ACQUISITION

Control over the *allotment* of land extends beyond landowning bodies in the city. A number of individuals and authorities are involved in allotting land: various development authorities (see Chapter 2), the CDGK/KMC, the *nazim* of the city, the Board of Revenue, the judicial courts, foreign investors, companies providing services, the KBCA, the governor of Sindh, and the chief minister of Sindh.

Land allocation and acquisition is a key land management policy instrument. The nature of this process and the difference between its stated and actual outcomes show the need for a change of focus in public interest policies. The process of land allocation in Karachi lacks transparency and is characterized by nepotism, favouritism, political pressure, and financial interests. The decision makers who influence this process are senior board members on landowning bodies such as the Board of Revenue. In the political sphere, the chief minister of the province is authorized to allocate land. This power was devolved to the office of the *nazim* at the city level with decentralization, and has been disputed by the provincial and city tiers of government since the end of the decentralized system (*Dawn*, 30 July 2009).

Land is allotted without any preliminary dialogue, debate, consultation or participation by the stakeholders who represent public, legal, and landowning interests in the area concerned (Cowasjee, *Dawn*, 16 June 2002). Instead, the process takes place almost exclusively behind the closed doors of executive offices and plots for sale are carved out of land intended for civic infrastructures without consulting local residents or the civic bodies concerned.

Public infrastructure construction and improvement often results in residents of the site being allocated plots in new locations. The costing of such projects takes no account of the direct costs of relocation or the indirect costs of rehabilitating families that have been moved away from their jobs, schools, child care and social networks. An extreme example of this kind of venture is the construction of the Lyari Expressway (LEW), which was built in Karachi between 2002 and 2009, and led to the eviction of between 30,000 and 77,000 households along the Lyari riverbed (Gazdar and Mallah 2011: 4).

In some cases allotment occurs in the same way as land grabbing. Government sponsored housing schemes are a recurrent example of irregular allotments and these schemes regularly face delays because plots are often allocated before a survey, price, or master plan has been finalized.

Some claim that the time lag in housing schemes serves another purpose (*Dawn*, 24 August 2004; *Pak Tribune*, 14 August 2004; Aligi, *Daily Times*, 10 December 2009). 'After a scheme is announced publicly in newspapers and so on, applications are invited for balloting. People who want to purchase submit a completed application along with a down payment and they are not told when they will hear and when balloting will occur. Delays happen for a couple of reasons. They delay balloting sometimes so that the collected deposits in a bank accrue profit. Then in some cases, such as Taiser Town, officers in government organizations are told that their numbers will be guaranteed in balloting for an extra price.'

Relations between the allocating authorities, accountability bodies, developers, and the public often result in compromises that contravene established rules and regulations. When a compromise cannot be achieved, records are burned so that the allotments can be redefined, which means that ownership has to be investigated all over again. For example, the revenue records of the BoR were destroyed in a fire in the violence following the assassination of Benazir Bhutto, and had yet to been reconstructed in 2012, despite the existence of central records in Hyderabad. In view of this 'inefficiency', the Supreme Court froze the BoR's right to allot and convert land in Karachi until the record was reconstructed, finding that 'land belonging to a genuine owner was being mutated in others' names' by the BoR (Siddiqui, *Dawn*, 29 November 2012).

The administration has never tried to analyse or establish the effect of encroachment, and therefore lacks a functional approach to this issue. To date it largely consists of periodic anti-encroachment drives by landowning bodies in the city (Ghori 2010). The main course of action has been demolitions, which are brutal, highly insensitive to the capital invested by the encroachers and sometimes lead to violent retaliation. Encroachments take place on public space, *naalahs*, riverbeds, fire stations, school buildings, footpaths, graveyards and in the past, even the grounds of the Governor's House (*The News*, 31 March 2004). They are a perennial phenomenon, seemingly independent of any change in the city's governance. Encroachers are usually members of the working class, driven by commercial motivations to occupy land near bus stops, major shopping centres, rainwater drains, and apartments. While their main aim is probably to optimize their working space, the fact that they are voters adds a political element to this phenomenon.

Encroachers include individuals and institutions alike, ranging from grocery vendors, rag pickers, makeshift auto workshops and fast food outlets to police stations, transporters, and multinational ventures. At one time even the US consulate in Karachi was accused of encroachment (ibid.). Interestingly, no press reports were found on the encroachments by McDonalds and banking institutions—something that may well be due to the lucrative advertisements they place in the newspapers.

The encroachment by grocery vendors around apartment buildings illustrates an interesting dichotomy: residents view them as a nuisance but continue to buy goods from them as they are easily accessible and therefore save time and resources. Pedestrian lanes and footpaths are the main targets of encroachment; parks and playgrounds come a close second. Encroachers are generally insensitive to the ecology of an area.

When the government launches anti-encroachment drives against pushcart vendors and roadside sellers, the encroachers tend to move away until the campaign is over and then return to recreate the situation. This continuing pattern of encroachment, anti-encroachment drive, and re-encroachment makes these campaigns redundant, even though they are organized by some of the highest offices in the country. Politically, they serve to reassure the middle class, media, and car and motorbike users that government agencies are doing something about congestion in the city. Anti-encroachment drives are thus primarily dictated by and conducted against the commercial interests of the working class rather than the big businesses that encroach on parking spaces or other land set aside for amenities (See the section on land development).

The government authorities regard demolition as a legal necessity and inevitable element of regularization, even though it destroys the huge investments that people have made in their homes and the city's economy. Builders' associations are not usually in favour of regularizing structures in poorer areas of the city, but are prepared to 'regularize' illegal structures put up by corporate interests (Cowasjee, *Dawn*, 16 June 2002). Informal developers, on the other hand, do support regularization as illegal buildings need a completion certificate to qualify for regularization, implying that the KBCA has inspected the building to verify that it complies with approved plans. According to one newspaper, 'Constructions with 20 per cent violation of the approved plan will not be given the facility of regularization' (*The News*, 6 February 2008).

Only 20 per cent of existing illegal structures have been regularized, and a lot of poor localities have remained out of the regularization loop, despite being relatively old. There are also illegal constructions on government land, including land belonging to the BoR and excise & customs. There have been sporadic initiatives to regularize *katchi abadis*, illegal constructions, and *goths* in urban and peripheral Karachi, but they have been hampered by interdepartmental rows, the extremely slow pace of bureaucracy within the CDGK, and the cumbersome nature of the process.

In 2009, the provincial revenue minister called the entire process of regularization 'fake', implying that it was ineffective in the extreme (*The News*, 18 April 2009). One reason is that the officials involved in land acquisition stand to lose the income they receive from transactions that occur behind closed doors. Buyers and sellers would benefit from a more fluid land market and clearer and better regulated procedures for selling and acquiring land. Even so, many are put off by the lengthy procedures for regularization, which affect their entry into and exit and from the land market. It takes at least twelve steps to obtain a construction permit from the KBCA, and each of these has many phases involving different public agencies in the city.[40] Every landowning authority and public agency has its own regulatory requirements because regularization procedures are not centralized. This has an impact on the way that consumers operate and the implementation of master plans for the city.

The same cumbersome procedures infect the process for *land auctions*, which are said to be deliberately complicated in order to discourage genuine buyers and leave the field open to brokers and real estate speculators. In 2002, the city government auctioned off various portions of unutilized land in order to generate revenue for its development schemes (*The News*, 10 October 2002).

The real estate market in Karachi is linked to and thus influenced by the global market. Pre-9/11, the real estate market was experiencing a slump and predicted recession; post-9/11, increased remittances and tougher new immigration rules resulted in bullish trends. In 2008, the slump in the UAE market directed investors towards Pakistan, Malaysia, and Turkey, all to the disadvantage of the poor as land prices and speculative buying increased even in low-income areas. Karachi has seen a fivefold increase in land values in the last ten years or so (Qureishi 2010: 306–321), prompting proposals to form real estate investment trusts and enact a law to control the exponential price rises in Sindh. The launch of the trust is pending upon rules and regulations drawn up by the Securities and Exchange Commission of Pakistan (Rind, *The News International*, 4 December 2012).

*Leases* and security of tenure are important factors in the regularization of Karachi's informal settlements and *katchi abadis*, but are actually more of a political issue than part of the human rights agenda, as political parties capitalize on the situation by promising residents security of tenure in return for votes and a chance to gain power in the city (Van der Linden and Selier 1991).

Potential beneficiaries are disadvantaged by the lack of information about the procedures and cost of leasing, and unhappy about the disparity in lease rates between different authorities. The SKAA in Karachi and other landowning bodies with informal settlements on their land are responsible for leases for *katchi abadis*. The process is often delayed due to flaws in the lease policy, or disputes between different public agencies over ownership and the right to lease land. There have been periodic attempts to deal with these issues, but like the anti-encroachment drives, they have not had any sustainable impact.

The information that does exist on land acquisitions shows that much is left to the discretion of the officials involved in land allocation. Their control over land records and the lack of transparent procedures mean that that allotments, encroachments and regularizations go unregulated. The regulations on land acquisition fail as a policy instrument because they do little to control entry and exit from the land market, making the master plan subservient to interest groups that are able to influence landowning agencies. As the section on land development shows, their focus is generally on commercial interests.

## LAND DEVELOPMENT

Global construction is set to outpace growth in GDP over the next 10 years, with China and India accounting for 38 per cent of the $4.8 trillion increase in output by 2020 (*The Indian Express*, 5 March 2011).

Formal and informal developers are generally more interested in maximizing their profits and serving commercial interests than in pursuing land developments or housing projects in the social interest. Unknown parties offer financial incentives for residential units on the outskirts of the city, and regularization is used as a tool to 'facilitate' customers and promote the construction industry.

Megaprojects in Karachi are regularly preceded by demolition and displacement. This causes major disagreements between the political parties that represent the interests of different ethnic groups or constituencies in various localities, shifting the debate from arguments against demolition to discussions about which locality should be demolished and which should be safeguarded. Bearing in mind the relationship between the location and the land value of an area, one political party leader made the following argument during an anti-encroachment drive in 2010: 'Since the land in urban parts of the city such as Nazimabad, Mohammad Ali Society Park and that in Gutter Baghicha is costlier than the value of land in Baldia or on the outskirts of the city, anti-encroachment operations should be carried out in the centre instead of the peripheral localities inhabited by the poor people' (Ghouri, *Dawn*, 22 July 2010).

Individuals who pay their fees late or delay construction on recently purchased property are penalized with hefty non-utilization fees, but there is no accountability framework that allows the planning institutions to sanction those responsible for the frequent delays in completing megaprojects. The relevant authorities justify their actions against individuals as efforts to curb speculation.

Karachi's development is shaped by the fact that it is a melting pot for a multitude of foreign and national immigrants who add to the city's cultural and linguistic diversity. As a result, it lacks a singular socio-economic, administrative architectural identity, especially in terms of development.

The traditional lifestyles of indigenous communities are being suffocated by new trends in development politics, which are invariably driven by financial motivations, selective development and self-serving political priorities. Rampant, largely informal development continues along the city fringes, and the development of necropolises within the city is as yet a dormant issue (*The News*, 2 December 2012). It is essential that the institutions of higher learning in Karachi have research and legal departments that can take up the issues associated with their development.

Home ownership remains a dream for the millions of people who live in informal settlements and rented accommodation across the city. The situation has changed for the worse over the last 40 years, with the need for 4 million housing units in Pakistan identified in 2004 increasing by 570,000 units each year (*The News*, 5 May 2004). Building a house has become a difficult task, especially in the cantonment area. It carries considerable financial risks, as the down payments that interested buyers have to make—which often represent their life savings—will not be returned if the housing scheme is subsequently cancelled. The authorities' failure to resolve this issue causes stress, uncertainty and homelessness among lower and lower middle class social groups, and increases the disparity between the rich and the poor.

A decade or so ago, the country's economic performance was tolerably good. Today, the situation seems to have changed drastically: hordes of people now live on footpaths, under bridges, and in front of shrines and mosques. The city government virtually ignored the housing problem in 2003, allocating the sector just Rs 150 million in its annual budget, when it could have met much of the demand for housing with a hybrid solution of microfinance and funding for housing. Around 27,000 building permits were issued that year, against a need for 80,000 housing units. Successive governments have paid lip service to good housing policies and promoting a better housing industry, and the government continues to disassociate itself from its own housing schemes, both conceived and developed.

Lyari is regarded as an area where housing problems are rife. Many residents have lived there for decades, and there is a constant influx of new arrivals in search of housing even though the area reached saturation point years ago. Innovative pilot projects like *Khuda ki Basti* provide hope for the millions of citizens who do not own homes, but their replication by government agencies remains a dream.

The authorities do not seem to view the provision of amenities as a basic constitutional right. Many government projects to relocate informal settlements lack any infrastructure or amenities, despite the fact that residents have been moved to the new site. One example of this is the Hawks Bay site, where people were resettled as part of the Lyari Expressway Resettlement Project (URC 2004). This lack of services is not limited to social projects. The ship breaking industry in Gaddani on the coast of Sindh has no on-site medical facilities for workers who are involved in accidents; the nearest healthcare facility is an hour away in Karachi. In addition to this, the labour colony that services the industry currently has no water, electricity or gas (Rana, *Dawn*, 11 June 2009).

Reluctant service providers exhibit a blatant class bias in the provision of amenities, which benefits higher income and/or politically strong areas (Water and Sanitation Project Report 2010). Figure III shows that *goths* are the worst served areas; and cantonments and armed forces settlements the best served, although there are always a few exceptions to this general trend.

**Figure III**

Provision of Amenities in Different Areas of Karachi

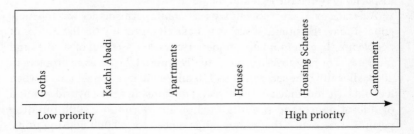

For decades, political leaders have filled the media with lofty but empty promises to provide uninterrupted services. They usually use market mechanisms to provide essential services, which consequently only reach those with sufficient finances and purchasing power. Meanwhile, the design and planning capabilities of city authorities leave much to be desired. They cannot even provide rainproof infrastructures: rainwater drains are usually laid parallel to the main arterial roadways, which are often significantly higher than the plinth level of houses. These roads are liable to flooding by the drains and sewage system, which then flows into adjacent homes and link roads.

There is some debate about the provision of amenities to high-rise buildings. Some argue that this would burden existing facilities; others that these buildings could be 'sustainable', with their own power generation, sewage treatment and water filtration plants. The Environmental Protection Agency remains sceptical about such ventures.

Town planning has changed. This is largely due to the United Nations, the World Bank, and the International Monetary Fund pushing the concept of 'Global Cities', an idea that has altered the parameters of urban planning. The focus has shifted from citizens' quality of life to the city as a site for events, *privatization*, investment-friendly infrastructure, and direct foreign investment (*The News*, 11 November 2009).

It is worth noting that the institutions that give practical shape to planning in Pakistan have been destroyed and replaced with an *ad hoc* approach to planning. Karachi is not well served by the architectural and planning professions, due to poor education in these disciplines, the culture among local representatives and decision makers, the mindset of the elite, and the state of its civic agencies. There is also excessive reliance on incompetent foreign consultants brought in to advice on housing and planning policies, who unintentionally turn a blind eye to the city's real functions and the need for sufficient parking spaces and transport services. Meanwhile, greedy developers misuse mandatory KBCA parking spaces for commercial purposes in order to maximize the return on their investment, leaving little room for local residents and business establishments to park. This has led to an unregulated 'parking mafia', which operates like a valet service, particularly in the central business district of Karachi (Hashim, *Dawn*, 8 December 2008). Each morning employees and workers in the area leave their cars with unregistered parking agents who then park illegally in side streets and nearby lanes, returning cars to their owners at the end of the working day.

Attempts to resist demolitions may result in settlements being burned and their residents losing all of what little they possessed. This is a serious problem in Karachi. The authorities have long turned a blind eye to the unauthorized mosques that have mushroomed all over the city. Building mosques is a well-known tactic for fending off demolition and anti-encroachment drives and encroaching upon amenity land, as public and private agencies are reluctant to be seen damaging religious buildings. For instance, in Sector 7-D/3 of North Karachi 11 mosques have been built on land that the North Karachi master plan had reserved for community centres, parks, and schools (Baloch, *The Express Tribune*, 19 April 2011). The Sindh home department responded to this situation in 2005 by banning the unauthorized construction of mosques.

Housing schemes are heavily promoted, with very mixed results. Unfortunately, builders across the city use these schemes to fleece potential homebuyers, luring them in with misleading advertisements for housing projects. Another problem is the rampant corruption in government sponsored housing schemes. The government has initiated thorough investigations into such malpractices and the National Accountability Bureau was investigating at least 55 housing schemes in 2011, but has not published the results of these exercises (*Financial Post*, 3 March 2011). Other issues that need to be addressed are the timely delivery of housing schemes, and refunds for unsuccessful applicants to the balloting process, whose financial woes are compounded by a long wait for their refund.

The public/private partnership between the city government and financial institutions spearheaded by the city's *nazim*s was envisaged as a means of providing housing for the poor. However, it has failed to meet its objectives, as the supposedly low cost housing is unaffordable for the stated target group. Foreign investors in the housing sector promise quality housing at exorbitant prices, and thus cater only to the needs of the elite.

The housing and construction industry could have a huge impact on direct and indirect employment and income generation, given its high employment potential and strong forward and backward linkages with a number of sectors and sub-sectors. Housing sector finance rose by 400 per cent in the fiscal year 2003, possibly due to remittances and more liberal government lending policies. Yet a sector-wise breakdown of consumer credit for the fiscal year 2003–2004 shows that investment in the housing sector was low: housing finance accounted for just 8 per cent of credit, compared with 35 per cent on car buying, 15 per cent on credit cards, 1 per cent on consumer durables, and 41 per cent on personal loans (*Dawn*, 25 January 2004).

Land surveys and resurveys are supposed to be undertaken to ensure proper land use. Unfortunately, they are often carried out in order to usurp state land rather than support socially and environmentally responsive planning. Experts fear that Karachi's 60 kilometre coastline is the most exploited stretch of the country's coastal belt, despite the desire of local and indigenous communities to preserve the natural landscape and boundaries of their habitat. Unplanned land reclamation has already started to alter the profile of the land, increase subsoil salinity and affect groundwater levels; while parks and amenity plots are used for private functions, in violation of constitutional provisions and zoning by-laws.

In 2007, it was observed that the city government's land auction department lay completely dormant: the department had not recorded a single instance of land auctions.

The data on land development shows a distinct bias towards commerce in the construction industry and the public provision of amenities. Town planning seems to be directed by commercial interests, while housing schemes that are supposed to provide homes and amenities in low-income areas are fraught with political pressure on residents to vote for certain parties. The situation is further exacerbated by the lack of help from government staff, who deal with commercial and political interests behind closed doors.

## CHANGES IN LAND USE

Unauthorized changes in land use are constantly taking place in Karachi, with legal and illegal conversions of libraries, residential plots, parks, government owned land, amenity plots, and footpaths. These conversions are instigated by schools, multinational food outlets, banks, religious authorities, and other commercial interest groups. A few attempts have been made to address this issue through conservation projects, but they have not able to prevent the *ad hoc* commercialization of the main arteries of the city.

Demolitions are common in Karachi (see sections on case studies and the visual media), but public agencies deal with illegal land conversions and encroachments in very different ways, showing a clear bias towards supporting commercial and profitable ventures over and above social housing and spaces, regardless of their legal status. This inequitable approach is illustrated in Figure IV:

**Figure IV**

Types of Land use Targeted for Demolition

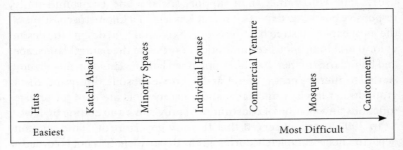

The process of survey-eviction-demolition is widely perceived as unjust and highly insensitive to people's cultural heritage and investment in the locality. These demolitions usually target informal settlements whose land is required for development and infrastructure projects, while formal settlements earmarked for these purposes are cleared under the Land Acquisition Act. There have also been accusations that many demolitions are initiated by the city government in support of the land mafia.

The lack of coordination between the state actors responsible for planning and implementing demolitions makes the process more violent and compromises the proper planning of resettlement. Relocation raises various issues: resistance by the affected population, which often leads to a breakdown in law and order, disagreements about land compensation and inappropriate resettlement sites. Little thought seems to be given to the social and economic consequences of resettlement, especially when the new site is far from people's workplaces.

It has become common practice to claim and transfer property titles through allotment letters issued to land purchasers by an authority, society, or developer. This raises the critical question of whether it is possible to create legal and equitable mortgages by depositing such allotment/transfer letters. It seems not.

Evictions are carried out to make way for megaprojects, clear encroached spaces and make elite and middle class residential areas 'secure'. Increasing demographic pressure within the city is also forcing indigenous communities off their native lands. Efforts to free encroached land are selective and fail to meet any goals, especially when the encroachers themselves happen to be state institutions.[41] In Pakistan, key issues in the eviction debate only emerge in public discourse after a controversial decision has been implemented. In the absence of any clear policy on evictions, the whole process is influenced by powerful lobby groups driven by the desire for personal financial gain.

It has been argued that changing land use to commercial purposes puts pressure on civic amenities and utilities, as it means providing a higher floor area ratio and changing land use from purely residential to office/retail. Unplanned commercialization is one of several manifestations of bad governance in the city, emerging as a severely problematic issue with far-reaching implications. The scale of commercialization can be gauged from the fact that in 2004 alone, the KBCA forwarded 800 commercialization cases to the city government's Master Plan Group for action (*Dawn*, 27 July 2004). It has been observed that land owned by minorities is a soft target for both encroachers and proponents of commercialization.

Illegal construction is common in Karachi. The city has 38,000 illegal buildings, including 259 frozen high-rise structures built in direct violation of building and town planning by-laws (*The Dawn*, 16 October 2001). Most of these structures have appeared in the last decade, many appearing on public utility and amenity spaces. Authorities such as the KBCA have initiated numerous surveys of illegal constructions, which have led to buildings being sealed and builders blacklisted (*Dawn*, 31 July 2005). Any plans to improve or rehabilitate the city's built environment need to start with an understanding of the scale and causes of this phenomenon, which is often ascribed to the gap between supply and demand for housing. Figure V illustrates the vicious cycle that contributes to illegal construction.

Like their anti-encroachment drives and periodic attempts to shake up bureaucracies, the authorities' attempts to report and seal illegal buildings have had little impact on the landscape of Karachi. Owing to inefficiency or connivance with the KBCA, only 116 illegal buildings were reported in 2008 in 3 of the 18 towns (Lyari, Saddar, and Liaquatabad). There were as many as 27 unreported illegal buildings on Shahrah-e-Faisal alone, one of the city major arteries (*The News*, 24 September 2008).

Karachi has numerous *heritage* buildings, listed in 2001 under the Sindh Cultural Heritage Act. Old buildings that reflect the city's multiple religions and multi-ethnic urban cultures are under serious threat from increasing religious homogeneity and the fact that houses planned in the old style are no longer considered feasible due to changing lifestyles, the rising cost of land and the introduction of new building materials and techniques. The constant increase in trade activities puts huge functional pressures on the old city and surrounding quarters where most of the heritage buildings are located. As a result, a substantial number of buildings in the area have been converted into warehouses to service the needs of the port and nearby wholesale markets.

Changes in land use by officials in landowning agencies result in losses to the city's exchequer (Sahoutara, *The Express Tribune*, 5 December 2012), encourage land grabbing, and violate master plans for the city.

**Figure V**

Factors in Illegal Construction

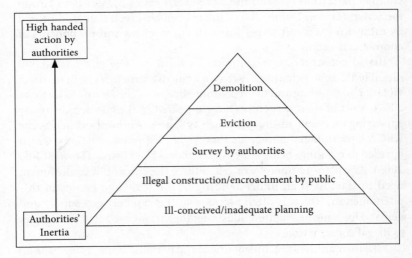

## LAND DISPUTES

Court orders are normally reported in the press. These cover a range of land-related issues, such as: (i) abuse of power by authorities; (ii) restoration of a plot's original status; (iii) restoration of land rights to someone whose property has been usurped; (iv) cognizance of illegal demolitions; (v) petitions against the commercialization of residential units; and (vi) refunds in housing schemes.

It has been brought to the courts' attention that the KBCA and KDA do not follow standard operating procedures for the demolition of illegal structures, and that demolitions are carried out before notices are issued. There are also cases where the authorities have illegally changed the use of plots that the court has classified as amenity land. Stern action is always taken against officials involved in the misuse of authority. Builders and contractors have also been charged for poor construction after their buildings have collapsed, but often manage to evade court orders for their arrest.

Land grabbing has been witnessed all across Karachi. This is often done by manipulating cooperative housing societies, grabbing land and then selling it off at nominal prices or under fake allotment papers. In the process, countless innocent citizens are deprived of their life savings and hopes of acquiring a home of their own; while the disposal of land at throwaway prices also robs the national exchequer of revenue.

Professional land grabbers blatantly encroach upon areas earmarked for graveyards or areas adjacent to graveyards. No action is taken against the land grabbers until local residents create a hue and cry, meaning that the burden of regulation comes to lie on the citizenry rather than the regulating authorities. The city government has been allocated huge budgets to construct boundary walls around these graveyards, but has yet to build them (*The News*, 7 May 2001). They therefore remain a vulnerable target, despite several warnings and operations in the Mororo, Khamosh Colony, Maula Madadd, and Gora Qabristaan graveyards; and graveyards in District West that were reportedly under illegal occupation for a long time. Schools and amenity plots are also regularly targeted, and continuous retrieval operations have had little effect as they are simply reoccupied when the operations end.

There have been many instances where members of the army, rangers, police, and revenue officials have been found guilty in land grabbing cases. For example, MDA officials conspired with the land mafia to grab plots and different sectors of Scheme 25-A in Shah Latif Town. There has also been mention of collusion between the land mafia and members of CDGK staff to grab plots belonging to former KMC employees.

Over the years numerous pieces of legislation and policies have been proposed to promote more uniform town planning and building by-laws; prohibit illegal construction activities and encroachments; sanction existing violations of the law; regularize and dispose of land and document changes in property ownership and high-rise developments. There has been talk of making the laws designed to protect cultural land and architectural heritage more stringent and implement them more strictly, but no real action has been taken in this respect.

Some of the policies that have been introduced over the past decade are summarized below:

- The Sindh government has amended the Land Grant Policy to allow agricultural land to be allotted to unemployed graduates. The Sindh Land Utilization department has duly advised all unemployed graduates to register with their respective deputy commissioners (2001).
- The Registration Stamps and Executive Property Wing of the Board of Revenue have strongly recommended that the Sindh government ban the right to delegate authority for the sale, mortgage, exchange or gift, etc. of all properties through Power of Attorney (2002).
- In 2003, the chief secretary of Sindh asked the local government department to simplify the procedure for mutating and transferring plots. Soon after this, having completed the first phase of investigations into the illegal disposal of amenity lands in the area, the CDGK partially lifted its ban on sales, purchases, mutations, and other land transactions in Gulistan-e-Jauhar. There is no mention of the ban being lifted in any other area.
- With the devolution of the KBCA to the city government in 2002, the Sindh housing and town planning department amended the Karachi Building and Town Planning Regulations 2002 with the approval of the authorities concerned. According to news reports, the CDGK approved a new commercialization policy in 2004 under these amendments, with six major roads to be constructed in the first phase of its implementation: Shahrah-e-Faisal, Tariq Road, Rashid Minhas Road, University Road, Shahrah-e-Pakistan (Super Highway), and Nazimabad 'A' Road. Sources in the cash starved KDA said that it expected to generate about Rs 3.6 billion through the commercialization of roads in the city, but was unable to do so because of reservations expressed by its governing body (*The News*, 25 January 2001). No area studies were undertaken to justify the policy, which was formulated to 'fill the pockets' of greedy officials and would eventually ruin the physical and social environment of the areas in which it was implemented.
- In 2004, the Governor of Sindh Dr Ishrat-ul-Ibad, urged members of the housing industry to launch low cost housing schemes to meet the growing needs of lower-income groups. In a review meeting with the Association of Builders and Developers (ABAD), he mentioned that foreign investors were interested in the sector, but nothing was done to follow this up. In 2006, the acute housing shortage was further aggravated by increasing land prices, the rising cost of building materials and higher interest rates on house-

building loans, which are hard to obtain because banks tend to prefer short-term loans that are not suitable for housing.

- The government implemented a number of measures to liberalize housing loans, but there is still insufficient finance available to service the housing industry, which is estimated to need between Rs 64 billion and Rs 70 billion ($711 and $777.7 million).

Over the years there have been a number of *murders* related to land disputes. They usually take place in the middle and lower-income areas of Karachi and are often dismissed as ethnic violence. Victims include estate agents who have been targeted in disputes with the politically backed land mafia over properties and plots in their areas of operation (Ayub, *Dawn*, 28 December 2009).

*Katchi abadis* are a direct indication of society's failure to integrate local-level planning into urban development. The authorities that do accept and publicize this fact have yet to provide a proper low-income housing solution. The All Pakistan Katchi Abadi Association estimated that 36 million people (25 per cent of the country's population) were living in 8,352 informal settlements across the country in 2003.

Many articles allege that *katchi abadis* are a haven for criminals, convicts, and prostitutes, and the best solution is to demolish them. Conversely, various housing experts and politicians argue that they are the homes of our future politicians and that every possible measure should be taken to improve them. This view is supported by visiting experts from international financial institutions and development agencies.

Work to upgrade *katchi abadis* is divided between the SKAA and the city government. This causes conflict between the two organizations, whose cost in terms of time, money and insecurity is ultimately paid by the supposed beneficiaries of the programme. There have been many plans (as in 2006) to follow the example of Mumbai in India, and build multistorey flats in the *katchi abadis* of Sindh with the aid of investors with newly acquired land. They were approved by the governor, but were still in cold storage in 2008, and have since gone unmentioned in the press.

The court tends to take a passive role in this area, as law enforcement agencies sometimes refuse to enact court orders. This is another factor that contributes to allowing unregulated commercial interests build wherever they want in the city, sidelining local residents and migrants and leading to an increasingly volatile social situation.

## LAND RELATED DISASTERS

There seems to be little press coverage of land related disasters in Karachi, perhaps because they are not seen as particularly important. However, in 2009, there were several reports on the collapse of buildings in densely populated low and lower middle-income areas of Saddar Town, Liaquatabad Town, and Mithadar.

Buildings in lower Sindh (including Karachi) have been classified as being unable to withstand earthquakes of moderately high intensity. Although it is alleged that most of them are not built according to their original design, or were not designed to resist earthquakes, these buildings, civic utilities, important installations and public places were hardly affected at all by the earthquake that struck Karachi in 2009.

## MONEY MATTERS

KBCA suffered a financial blow in 2001 and was unable to generate sufficient revenue to meet its needs. At the time the government of Sindh did not allow it to charge for the regularization of buildings, completion certificates, occupancy certificates, and permits for additional floors. This was because of the conflict between the province and the city over the SLGO 2001, which created the City District Government Karachi and its offices. In 2001, the government of Sindh lost the authority to collect property tax from almost a quarter of the city as the military authorities put pressure on civil institutions to transfer more areas to the cantonment boards. Their influence was substantially increased by the presence of a military government. Today, land continues to be transferred to cantonments whenever it is requested.[42]

In 2008, the charges for scrutiny fees for the approval of building plans increased for six main types of building on residential, commercial, industrial, and amenity plots. The KBCA made these increases without the public notification required by law, and also decided to levy infrastructure betterment charges on all buildings with more than four storeys above the ground floor.

The revival of housing finance can be mapped through news clippings from the past decade. On average, profit margins and recovery rates are higher for mortgage finance than for project and corporate lending. Many organizations have been involved in attempts to boost housing finance, such as the Pakistan Industrial Credit and Investment Corporation

(PICIC), the World Bank, the International Finance Corporation (IFC), and the House Building and Finance Corporation Limited (HBFCL).

In 2005, a major policy shift within HBFCL resulted in the initiation of a few schemes focusing on the lower and middle-income groups that constitute 95 per cent of the country's potential residents. The corporation also began projects aimed at the retail and wholesale housing markets in order to meet the annual demand for 1.2 million housing units, and designed the 'Sponsor a Shelter' programme in which philanthropists would finance underprivileged applicants for house loans.

In 2006, the National Bank of Pakistan planned to offer about Rs 2.5 billion ($27.77 million) over a four year period in loans for house-building and purchase aimed at lower-income groups. In 2008, senior bankers outlined a number of factors that were directly linked to the progress and expansion of the country's nascent primary mortgage finance market, ranging from the lack of documentation on the national economy to rising bank credit and land prices and the murky political scene.

## CONCLUSIONS

Contributors to the electronic and print media, members of research bodies, the legal profession, civil society, and activist community have identified a number of key land actors in Karachi. These include the armed forces, the national and international corporate sector, and local and provincial elected representatives. Rather than developing and implementing master plans, land use agreements and regulations, and providing easy entry into and exit from the land market, they facilitate land grabbing and land conversions, and have turned land in Karachi into a political and ethnic resource.

This state of affairs is due to increasingly weak governance. It began with the politicization of governance institutions during the Afghan war against the Soviets in the 1980s, when Karachi became the centre for war supplies for Afghanistan. This conflict and the following war of attrition were largely funded by the heroin trade from Afghanistan (Rasheed 2001). This went through Karachi, generating large sums of money that were used (legally and illegally) to acquire land and fund real estate ventures. Politicians and government agency officials were 'bought' to facilitate activities such as land grabbing, encroachment, and land conversion. This further weakened governance in a vicious cycle that created a powerful nexus of political, ethnic, and criminal groups that have become increasingly polarized along ethnic lines due to the complex politics of Sindh in general, and Karachi in particular.

Serving ministers and members of the provincial assembly claim that they cannot rectify the situation because the police are on the side of the encroachers, while the *nazim* might support violations of law in one case and actively condemns them in another (amid accusations of his personal involvement in this case). The lack of a unified stake in the city and its land means that those who seek to protect it by fighting encroachment on their site or jurisdiction often turn a blind eye to or facilitate the violation of rules, regulations and plans on another site. Such decisions are usually shaped by political pressure, demands for illegal favours, and nepotistic 'requests'.

There are numerous land related laws, but the rules, regulations and procedures are often unclear and subject to interpretation by officials with discretionary powers. As a result, conflicting interests are difficult to resolve and departmental rows are common. Attempts to reach a compromise through negotiations generally end with the stronger party dictating the terms, which often run counter to the law and principles of equity and justice. As higher income areas are politically strong, they benefit from this arrangement and the type of development it engenders, to the detriment of lower-income and minority groups.

The main victims of this poor governance are citizens who own or wish to purchase land and property, and the physical and social environment. The nexus between politicians, developers, and bureaucrats facilitates fake development projects and scams, and leaves the public with no protection from the extortion rackets run by developers and estate agents in both the formal and informal sectors.

Another result of weak governance and conflicts over land is that land records no longer depict the real ownership and tenure patterns. With no proper documentation, using legal processes to implement the law becomes a difficult, long, and expensive—if not impossible—process that rarely ends in justice being served. It also makes it hard for families to access credit for house building, which they should be able to obtain.

What Karachi needs is a major public sector reform that seeks to reconcile the differences between the different tiers of political offices and enable the enforcement and regulatory agencies to resist commercial and political pressures that violate the principles of good land management. This will only be possible if there is the political will for it; and if all the political parties and ethnic groups that are fighting over land and votes can rise above their party and group interests and reach a consensus that serves the wider interests of the city and its environment.

# 6

# Land Related Conflicts – II: Findings from Primary Sources

## INTRODUCTION

The first part of this chapter presents an account of the builder's mafia and the role of real estate agents and developers in Karachi. It is based on a set of interviews with developers, estate agents, real-estate lawyers, individual buyers and sellers of property, and people looking for a home to rent, which are summarized below. A summary of the interview transcripts is given in Appendix 5. This Appendix also contains a number of as yet unanswered questions about land related relationships and processes.

The second part of this chapter conveys the aspirations and motivations of consumers who live in different types of housing. They were investigated through questionnaire surveys of 25 people in each of the following categories: (i) middle and lower middle-income apartment buildings; (ii) lower-income housing built by developers; (iii) self-built middle-income housing; (iv) a notified *katchi abadi*; (v) an informal settlement not marked for regularization. Locations where these questionnaires were served along with the locations where interviews given in Appendix 5 were held, are shown in Map X. A list of the localities where the questionnaires were served is given in Appendix 6.[1]

## WHAT THE INTERVIEWS TELL US

The dominant theme that emerged from these interviews was the role of the builder's mafia in the informal land market. The next section considers how the mafia developed; describes the various stakeholders in Karachi's informal land market, and then gives an overview of their effect on certain low-income settlements.

## The Emergence and Role of a Builder's Mafia in Karachi

The Association of Builders and Developers (ABAD) became very active in the 1970s, when remittances from Pakistani nationals working abroad fuelled a big building boom in Karachi. The government responded by providing land and finance to enable builders to construct apartments. The KBCA set the 'moral' standards for this activity. It had strong ethics, everyone abided by rules and regulations, and any corruption that did occur was at the individual rather than the institutional level. At that time members of ABAD were professionals who could be said to belong to the educated elite. However, what they produced fell far short of the demand for housing.

The sale of cloth and yarn became extremely profitable at the end of the 1980s, which also saw the development of the garment industry. Stitcheries and their contractors paid high interest rates on instalments for their sewing machines, and cloth market traders and sewing machine dealers invested their profit in the construction industry. They were not professionals themselves, and because they were only interested in making a quick profit they did not hire professional staff but worked through petty contractors to minimize their overheads. This meant that they had to bribe various departments and utility agencies in order to register with the KBCA and get their substandard designs and construction approved—thereby creating the so-called builder's mafia that now shapes the architecture and physical environment of formally planned Karachi. Much of what the builder's mafia does today is made possible by the discretionary decision-making powers of a few high ranking officials and politicians. This leads to overbooked development schemes (which go unpunished); post-dated cheques being issued to buyers who wish to withdraw from development schemes (which are often not honoured); various hidden overhead charges and the illegal conversion of amenity land into housing estates. The Afghan war led to huge increases in contraband and transit trade, drawing contraband traffickers into the land market as they invested their profits in real estate. They then became part of the builder's mafia, further strengthening it and weakening the state agencies concerned with land and building affairs.[2]

All builders now have to pay the KBCA bribes to get their plans approved, obtain the necessary documents for approvals, and advertise their schemes in the print and electronic media. They also have to pay bribes for utility connections. All these illegal payments increase the customers' costs, to the extent that developers claim that projects would be 25 per cent cheaper for the public if they did not have to pay such bribes. Builders and developers also charge 19 per cent of the purchase price for the documentation needed to acquire an apartment and connect the utilities. Needless to say, the advertisements for such developments never mention these hidden costs.[3]

Vendors and buyers usually only see each other when their transaction is recorded at the registrar's office. Police corruption and the presence of armed gangs in the land business mean that developers have to cultivate good relations with the police by giving them money, plots, or apartments. The system is so convoluted that many land actors have to rely on the middlemen who arrange about 60 per cent of profitable transactions.

The absence of laws and regulations published in the national language Urdu or the regional and local languages of the area where they are implemented has already been noted in Chapter 2. The informal market also capitalizes on consumers' unfamiliarity with complicated procedures, giving developers the upper hand in disputes with clients or less well-connected rivals. This withholding of information increases transaction costs and impedes entry into the housing market for many.

Disputes over land related transactions between builders, estate agents, and their political patrons are settled through various manifestations of power—money, connections, the possibility of using the police to pressure other protagonists, and even killing and making an example of the opponent. A total of 14 estate agents were killed in 2010 and 2011 alone.[4]

## LAND IN THE INFORMAL DOMAIN—THE NEXUS OF BUILDERS, POLITICIANS, AND DEVELOPERS

Land is released through the BoR or may be allotted to a builder by the chief minister. These allocations are viewed as political and are often cancelled when the government changes, leading to disputes over ownership that often end up in court. In the Goth Abad Scheme, there are cases where villages that covered 0.8 hectares of land paid bribes to have their area increased by 30 to 50 times. When these irregularities were investigated, the building housing the BoR's land records was burned down to cover up the fraud.

There are a numerous fake housing and residential schemes in Karachi. They invariably have an office and some staff, but do not advertise in the print and electronic media as this is very expensive.

This is the giveaway for such schemes, which normally advertise through cable operators on movie channels like Star Plus, Sony, and Star One, but avoid the newspapers and hoardings around the city. Therefore, the best advice for the public is to stay away from poorly advertised schemes.[5] The situation in Karachi is such that people prefer to live with their caste and ethnic groups, which means that the majority of plots in these schemes are reserved for members of the developer's ethnic group or caste.

Some schemes fall through because the land is encroached upon by powerful interest groups with greater political or armed backing than the developer. One developer spoke of his experience in starting a housing scheme in Manghopir (the Mir Mohammed Housing Scheme). 'The first phase of the scheme was successful, but the second phase failed as the land mafia occupied the area. We fought the case for eight years and ultimately won but by that time development costs ran so high that the scheme didn't seem profitable anymore.'[6]

The legal process is so slow that even land that has been developed becomes inaccessible. This creates a manufactured scarcity of land that directly affects the residential market, especially because court cases are often about disputes in the informal market, as the court is the only recourse for low-income residents. There are a number of lawyers in the city who deal exclusively with issues related to land rights. Many of their cases involve rights that have been violated because somebody acquired property through pressure or by fraudulent means and pleading the cause of settlements that have been demolished in violation of laws. Because the courts take years to deal with these cases, people often prefer to settle matters out of court, even if the terms are unjust. Lawyers fighting these cases are frequently threatened and attacked by gunmen sent by the developers who have set up the offending scheme or the group interested in evicting residents and they resort to these tactics to dissuade the advocates from continuing with the case. As a result, lawyers now have their own guards and gunmen, and form networks with the informal nexus in the land market in order to buy police support for their own protection and to help their clients.

Some developers think that there are advantages to living on the periphery of the city: lower shopping costs, less socialization (which reduces expenses), and the ability to opt out of late night weddings due to the security situation. Living in the city centre, the poor are surrounded by rich residential areas where lavish lifestyles are the norm. This constant reminder of the gulf between social classes can cause great psychological distress to poorer residents, so it could be argued that there are some comparative advantages to developing schemes for low-income residents on the outskirts of the city, in addition to affordability. Approximately 1 to 1.2 million plots have been developed along the Northern Bypass, mainly through the Goth Abad schemes. Plots of land can be purchased and the necessary approvals obtained by bribing the relevant government agencies. Purchasers would save about 20 per cent if they did not have to make such payments to officials and utility companies.[7]

Builders acquire land from the KBCA and pay to obtain a lease. They carve out plots and sell them to buyers on a sub-lease, normally charging 150 per cent of the land price in development charges, which include utility connections and roads. A lot of invisible money is involved in this process. Buyers need six documents to purchase land, and have to pay bribes to obtain them. The simplest process is to hire an estate agent and get him to fulfil the necessary formalities. Getting a loan from the HBFC involves seven steps, each requiring informal payments. Here too, it is simpler and cheaper to do this through an estate agent or a middleman who charge fixed rates for their services.

Builders operate in partnership with the city's political leadership, who they pay informally to acquire utility services and basic amenities. They used to employ army officers to facilitate the approval process with the KBCA and utility departments; nowadays, this is done by political party workers.[8]

Typically a neutral lower level bureaucracy would have acted as a buffer in translating political pressure from both above (elected politicians) and below (workers supported by the politicians), but bureaucrats have been robbed of their power by police complicity in the nexus. Some interviewees claimed that before devolution bureaucrats used to follow the rules and regulations scrupulously; nowadays the political representatives who control the bureaucracy do not. Claimants stated that one reason why land and housing rights are increasingly violated is because politicians are corrupt and favour members or supporters of their political parties. As noted above, other contributing factors include the enormous capital generated by NATO supply trips, drug money, and the Afghan transit trade, and the combination of financial and muscle power.

Government land can only be acquired—legally or illegally—with the help of mid-level revenue officers, and allotted land can only be occupied with police protection. Sixty per cent of allotted plots in KDA Scheme-33 are occupied today. Land grabbers rent entire families to illegally occupy land and premises, paying them about Rs 15,000 ($167) a month to do so.

These families usually belong to the traditional 'lower castes', which have a semi-nomadic culture.[9]

People who rent out property have enormous problems because of the existence of rent laws that favour tenants, and the long legal process involved in getting rid of tenants. Great care is needed when renting, selling, or purchasing property because estate agents may turn out to be accomplices of aspiring buyers or renters. This means that property owners can end up losing their property or being landed with unmanageable tenants.

Buyers are not compensated for major delays in construction projects (which are very common), and have to deal with very rude and aggressive reminders and threats of cancellation if they are late paying their instalments. The builders who are considered the most reputable in the industry and deliver on time are those with sufficient funds to complete their projects in time—money that is usually acquired from the underworld.[10]

## House Prices and Market Mechanisms in Settlements

There are few property transactions in informal settlements in the city centre or on the main corridors of movement because these settlements are saturated. This applies whether or not they have been earmarked for regularization. House prices in these settlements have increased by over 1,000 per cent in the last two decades, compared with an increase of just over 200 per cent in the price of wheat (from Rs 17 per kilo to Rs 36 per kilo). Estate agents in these localities have little work, and think that big developers are unlikely to succeed in convincing local people to abandon their houses by paying them large sums of money, especially when a number of facilities are available on site and most residents work nearby. Most land in the settlement is bought and sold between residents, and homes are improved through *bisi* committees.[11] When transactions do take place, estate agents have to make informal payments to the relevant authorities to get them registered. These payments are charged to the seller.[12] If no estate agent is employed then the seller has to make the payments himself or find a middleman to do it on his behalf for an affordable fee.

Lyari Town is one of the oldest areas of Karachi. It has a large number of neighbourhoods that originally consisted of single or double storey stone houses, but are now filling up with five to seven storey apartment blocks. Developers buy a plot of land with a house on it, convert it into an apartment block and give the owner one or two apartments in addition to the payment for the land. Most of these apartments, which are two room affairs, are sold on *pugri* basis (i.e. with significant security deposit) for Rs 700,000 to 750,000 ($7,778 to 8,334), plus rent of Rs 200 ($2.2) per month, which increases by 5 per cent each year.[13] Without *pugri* the rent is Rs 3,000 ($33.4), increasing by 5 per cent each year. There are now so many apartment blocks that Lyari is becoming very congested and has almost no open spaces.[14]

Lyari was the starting point for Karachi, and is the home of the city's original Baloch population. They are now becoming a minority due to the trend for apartments, which are mainly promoted by Memon developers.[15] This creates resentment, and it is claimed that the current gang wars in Lyari are due to the increasingly multi-ethnic nature of the area and the availability of old warehouses whose leases have expired, which are targeted for real estate development.

Decisions were traditionally made by elders of the Baloch community, but are now made by *nazims* and councillors. Influential people carry arms to impress their influence upon the surrounding community. Baloch residents feel that the government does not want stability in Lyari because it is intimidated by the area's cultural and political affinity with Balochistan, where there is an anti-federal government insurgency.[16]

Under the Goth Abad scheme developers acquire land from villages that have been recognized as beneficiaries of the scheme. They often work with owners on the regularization process and pay the costs involved. They then pay the MDA informally so that they can claim to have its approval for a scheme, as this payment ensures that the MDA will not interfere or comment on any such claim. Every strip of land secured by developers has a set share of plots for local police officials who protect the development site. Villagers are relocated some distance away, and their land is sold on the market as affordable plots for low-income groups.

The players involved in developing land in informal settlements through the Goth Abad schemes and the land market in Karachi in general have changed. In the past, land acquisition and development was mainly financed by Pathans and people from financially strong and acknowledged backgrounds. Nowadays the main players are more likely to be Muhajirs and political activists backed by their parties.[17]

Interviews show that the urban poor who do not have the means to acquire formal or informal homes are constantly being displaced. They often find it impossible to pay the advances required to hire a space to live; and when they can rent somewhere they may be thrown out at a month's (or even less) notice because the rent laws do not apply to informal or unregistered transactions. Even where they do apply, tenants rarely have the capacity go to a court of law or to oppose their landlords who have strongmen to implement their decisions. As a result, they are constantly in debt because they have to borrow money for each advance. The lucky ones work as domestics or office boys, employed by influential families or establishments that provide them with accommodation or the means to acquire it on a temporary basis. However, this is not a permanent solution.[18]

## PUBLIC VIEWS ON HOUSING

The questionnaires confirmed the impression derived from our review of the laws in Chapter 3, that consumers and those who draft the laws see land and housing markets separately, even though land supply is crucial for housing developments. Developers and real estate agents in Karachi are driven by short-term profit goals and pressure from land lobbies with powerful political backing. The informal sector cannot provide adequate housing, whose key requirements include privacy, access to employment, and good schools, physical security, security of tenure, basic physical and social infrastructures, and local services. What is needed is integrated urban planning that considers housing in conjunction with the building industry.

The areas where the surveys were carried out are described in Appendix 6. Although the 125 questionnaires do not constitute a large enough sample to provide any definite conclusions (25 were administered in each of the five different types of housing and income group), they do give some indication of property values, family size, aspirations, place of employment, and the reasons for choosing the locality. The different types of settlement surveyed included: (i) middle and lower middle class apartments; (ii) self-built housing; (iii) housing built by developers; (iv) listed *katchi abadi*; and (v) an unlisted informal settlement. The first three are formal settlements, the fourth began as an informal settlement but is protected by being listed, and the fifth has a sizeable circulating population and no chance of being regularized. The differences between these settlements are determined by their origin and tenure status.

Residents of the formal settlements work far from home in the central business district and its surrounding and link areas, in formal and informal zones. Residents in the informal settlements work nearer to home or in the settlement itself. Families in the informal settlements can have up to 22 members, and are much larger than in the formal settlements where the largest families had 14 members. All children in the formal settlements and the listed *katchi abadi* go to school; on the other hand in the informal settlement that cannot be regularized most children do not. The formal settlements are homogenous in terms of ethnicity and religion, while the other two settlements have mixed ethnicity and different religions.

Despite these differences, there are similarities between the settlements surveyed. Almost all respondents chose the area where they live because it was affordable, and respondents in the listed *katchi abadi* and informal settlement said that family relationships and ethnic links also played a role in their choice. The majority of homeowners in the formal settlements bought their properties from developers and estate agents rather than owners. People there pool their resources, take loans from friends and family, and purchase or build their properties. Property prices have increased substantially everywhere apart from the informal settlement. The greatest increases seem to occur over a 10-year period. Some apartments have gone up by 400 per cent in a period of five years, while others purchased in the last one to four years have lost value. This is attributed to the deterioration of law and order in the area. The greatest property price increases have been in self-built housing and in the listed *katchi abadi*, for properties with the longest ownership tenure. Residents in the informal settlement do not know the land value or even the correct name of the place where they live.

A number of residents in the formal settlements said that they want to move to higher income residential areas because they are 'better' and cleaner. Others want to move to safer locations as they have experienced ethnic conflicts in their neighbourhoods or on the way to work, and claim that there is ethnically motivated crime in their areas. On the other hand, residents of the *katchi abadi* do not wish to relocate. Those in the informal settlement have nowhere else to go, although some do go back to the farmlands that they were 'evicted' from to provide labour during the harvest.

There are other trends as well. A sizeable number of residents in the formal settlements were dissatisfied with their children's schools. This is perhaps because they compared their neighbourhood schools to those in the more affluent areas of the city, whose advertisements and news items about their activities feature regularly in the media. Many households in the formal settlements prefer a one-window shopping facility whereby they can make best use of the time and money spent travelling. A good number of them also prefer malls and megastores to the existing neighbourhood shopping facilities, which do not provide the products they require. Interestingly, a majority of those who live in flats mentioned that they had moved there in order to separate themselves from the joint family system, which they see as a major impediment to their children's education.

All respondents were reluctant to state how many members of their household work, and a majority skipped the question about informal commercial activities in their homes. This may be because they are worried about the tax authorities or the KBCA taking punitive action against commercial activities in residential areas.

The survey enumerators made a number of observations based on the questionnaires and conversations with respondents during the survey process. These are presented in a paper produced by a member of the survey teams who visited all five settlements (Hussain 2012), and are summarized below:

People who live in the informal settlement do not see any upward social mobility. One person said that he feels he cannot have a house on his own because he lost his land in rural Sindh and has no assets. He and his family 'are living on day-to-day basis and barely make ends meet. If the government can do anything for us, fine, and if not, we will remain like this till our death.'

- Because of their high density, apartments provide opportunities for political parties to recruit members and secure a captive audience (observations from Rufi and Saima Towers). It is relatively easy for a political party to establish its influence in a densely inhabited apartment building rather than a settlement where households are more spread out. Furthermore, points of access and services in apartment buildings are under comparatively localized control, making them easier to influence and obtain bargaining power over residents.
- Community and clan based dwellings suffer from xenophobia and prefer to remain secluded. This tends to isolate them from outside influences. Fear of people outside the clan creates social and political ghettos, hampers understanding of other communities in the vicinity and creates volatile situations (observation from Rizvia-III).
- Respondents in under serviced settlements were more willing to spare time and express themselves than their counterparts in relatively affluent settlements. They were also more hospitable.

- Most respondents stated that they want to live in peaceful and affordable areas where there are livelihood opportunities. Planners do not provide for this ideal mix.
- Community and clan based mechanisms for the provision of housing are gradually emerging as an alternative to government mechanisms (observations from Ali Tower and Rizvia-II).
- Respondents were generally wary of taking loans from banks as they think that they will be financially entangled for the rest of their lives. They also think that they will be charged interest, which is against their religious beliefs.
- People want to live near their workplace to minimize time and travel costs. The distance between home and employment centres recurred as a key criterion for housing during interviews with members of the community, developers, and estate agents.
- Residents in informal settlements noted that the city government demolition squad demolishes minority places of worship first (although *imambargahs*[19] are an exception to this generalization).
- Unions and associations are of immense value in protecting residents' interests as they negotiate with authorities and political groups in the interest of the settlements (observation from Pahar Ganj).

## CONCLUSIONS

These interviews confirm many of the conclusions reached in the previous section, particularly with regard to the adverse effects of bureaucrats' and politicians' discretionary decision-making powers. They also reinforce the feeling that corruption has increased as a result of elected local government representatives replacing the old bureaucrat controlled system.

They also tell us that there has been a change in the actors and nature of formal development since the 1980s. The old professional elite that used to control the development of the formal sector has been replaced by traders and traffickers, and legally acquired funds are largely superseded by funds acquired illegally or through extortion. The availability of large amounts of money has helped 'informalize' formal sector processes. As a result, bribes in money and kind are used to bypass or bend government rules, regulations and procedures. This allows developers to make profits of over 150 per cent on land transactions alone, although they have to share some of these profits with others who 'help' them develop land. Informal payments can add up to 25 per cent to the price of the end-product, and make purchasers dependent on middlemen who can help them with the documentation and processes involved in purchasing, building, renting, or acquiring a loan for home. The purchaser pays for all the extra expenses, often through hidden charges that are only revealed after the purchase has been agreed.

Underworld involvement in property development has also led to land and property scams and forcible occupation of other people's properties. Although the 'informalization' of formal processes has given low-income residents access to a large number of affordable plots (something that the formal sector is incapable of doing), these are usually far from their workplace or from the city centre where better social facilities are available. The informal sector needs the protection of the police and elected local government representatives, because in this sector justice has been sacrificed to expediency and profit.

New informal settlements are developing all over Karachi, driven by a different impetus from their predecessors. Residents in the older settlements came to Karachi in order to improve their living conditions and educate their children. They made a conscious choice to move to the city, and were often better off than others in the poor segment of the population. People who live in the new settlements seem to have been pushed off their land by corporate farming or natural and manmade disasters such as wars and regional conflicts. These residents also tend to be more mobile.

As a result, old inner city areas that were originally ethnically homogeneous are becoming more densely populated and ethnically diverse. Both these trends are causing conflict and leading to the emergence of gangs and crime. Many residents in lower middle-income areas wish to move to areas that are free of conflict. Security is becoming an increasingly important criterion in deciding where to live, creating a preference for neighbourhoods dominated by the residents' own ethnic or religious group.

Planners and reformers need to take note of and address these issues. The legal processes used to resolve disputes and dispense justice need to be simplified and shortened. Planners and developers should recognize that lower middle-income and lower-income families want better education and shopping facilities in their neighbourhoods, and that rent laws that overtly favour tenants make it difficult to obtain rented accommodation through formal transactions. Another important consideration is the shift among more upwardly mobile families from living in joint family systems to more nuclear units.

# 7

# Karachi's Land Market: Support to Poor Communities, Affordability, and Location Issues

This chapter presents the views and opinions of non-state stakeholders in Karachi's land market. It starts by focusing on the role of NGOs and their influence on the land market, and then analyses the data on a cross-section of homeowners and tenants from different parts of the city.

## NGO AND CBO SUPPORT TO POOR COMMUNITIES

A number of NGOs support poor communities in Karachi, working to improve their physical and social environment. However, it is doubtful whether more than 15 per cent of the poor, who are estimated to account for over 50 per cent[1] of the city's 18 million residents, benefit directly or indirectly from their work. A major part of this outreach is the result of sanitation related work done by the OPP-RTI with local communities, and its advocacy work with the KWSB and the CDGK.

Most of the NGOs contacted for this paper operate through local community based organizations (CBOs) and other social activists. Many communities have their own local CBOs, which are often supported by NGOs. We interviewed a number of CBOs and NGOs in their survey areas and/or offices in order to understand what they do and the impact they have on the lives of poor communities. These interviews focused on bodies whose work was believed to relate to land and housing, or were interested in working on these issues. Some of these NGOs and CBOs also participated in group discussions during a workshop at the department of architecture and planning, NED University, Karachi. The methodology for the workshop, a list of the NGOs and CBOs interviewed, their areas of intervention and scope is given in Appendix 7. A synopsis of the interviews and workshop discussions and their conclusions is given below.[2]

## MAIN FOCUS OF NGO WORK

Most of work done by the NGOs and CBOs that operate in Karachi is issue specific. It may be based in one or more locations, and will depend upon (i) the organization's objectives; (ii) its leaders' professions; (iii) donors' funding directives; (iv) the available human resources and technical capabilities. NGOs do not necessarily link up with local CBOs, but when they do form alliances (as in Shah Rasool Colony, where the NGO HELP and the CBO Clifton Welfare Organization work together) they can achieve positive and concrete results in improving health indicators, literacy and social and physical conditions. Lack of interaction between the two types of organization is usually due to the NGO having difficulty in meeting its stated objectives or exceeding its budget.

Most NGOs and CBOs are run by professionals such as doctors, engineers, sociologists, lawyers and concerned citizens from various backgrounds. They tend to prioritize poverty alleviation, health, education, and social issues rather than physical improvements, which means that social indicators in an area often improve with very little change in the physical environment. This can limit the positive effects on health and economic programmes.

NGOs and CBOs also tend to be charity based rather than funded by the communities in which they work. This can lead to a lack of community ownership and empowerment, sometimes to the extent that communities become dependent on the NGO concerned and lose their former ability to act and organize themselves autonomously. This is a sign that the NGO does not have the vision, capability, or capacity to interact with poor communities and build on their existing strengths—often because NGOs and CBOs do not interact with each other or know about each other's work.

Of the ten NGOs and CBOs contacted for this report, OPP-RTI is the only one that trains community members and CBOs in building and survey related skills and promotes a savings programme related to housing. It also helps bring together diverse CBOs so that they can learn from each other's experiences.

None of the NGOs worked on land supply, apart from Saiban and the Aga Khan Programme for Basic Services, Pakistan (AKPBS,P).

Saiban works in collaboration with a body that provides land at a subsidized rate, planning the settlement and using a filtering process to identify beneficiaries. These beneficiaries have to move onto the new site immediately and construct a shelter. They pay for the land in instalments, and incrementally develop on-site infrastructures and their homes. Saiban helps develop off-site infrastructures and contacts NGOs to work on education and health facilities. So far, four such schemes have been developed. Although they have attracted international recognition, the methodology has not become government policy. Therefore, Saiban's intervention can be said to have had little impact in Karachi.

AKPBS,P works primarily for the betterment of the Aga Khan community. These are followers of the Aga Khan, who is the spiritual head of the Muslim Ismaili community. Cheap land is bought on the outskirts of the city; small affordable units are built on it and given to community members. This model does deliver, but is far too small to make a difference and would be too expensive to replicate on a large scale. During discussions at the NGO/CBO workshop, it became clear that the majority of poor communities access land through the informal sector. This is part of the expansion or densification of existing low-income settlements, and the creation of new settlements by a new breed of informal developers who operate with support from different political parties (see section *What the interviews tell us* in Chapter 6).

## ACCESSING CREDIT THROUGH NGOS

NGOs and CBOs may directly provide microfinance facilities for their communities themselves, or help them obtain it from commercial banks, the HBFC or local loan providers. Although loans are often given for small businesses, housing loans are rare and it is difficult to determine whether these enterprise loans help generate funds to improve housing or access land. Community saving schemes (*bisi*) do help with house improvements, but it is not clear whether they also help with land purchases. There is a need to better understand the role they play as informal credit providers, so that they can be promoted if they are found to be effective. However, NGOs and CBOs rarely provide direct loans; when they do these are usually given at low rates and on personal guarantees. A few NGOs and CBOs also help organize savings groups that can operate as revolving funds, but the scale of all these operations does not benefit more than 2,000 families per year.

## NGOs and Housing

OPP-RTI is the only NGO that offers technical guidance on home improvements and construction. Due to a lack of vision and expertise, none of the other NGOs and CBOs provides assistance in constructing sanitation and water supply systems. Poor communities often install these themselves without any technical advice or support, which leads to poor construction, wasted resources, and bad environmental conditions. Some NGOs and CBOs have contacted engineers and architects, but they are generally not comfortable working with low-income communities in general, and in low-income areas in particular. As a result, communities and individuals seek technical advice on housing design, alterations, and maintenance from the local builders' merchant (*thallawala*), whose services include house layout, providing materials on credit, and skilled labour.

OPP-RTI trains local youth as 'para-architects', who then set up resource centres that provide technical guidance and supervise house building and sanitation. The organization also trains local masons and has upgraded *thallas* by providing loans so that they can mechanize and improve their production. In addition to this, OPP-RTI has introduced new building materials and components that have helped reduce costs. Although its sanitation intervention has reached over 100,000 families in Orangi alone and influenced many other neighbourhoods in Karachi,[3] it has not made a significant impact on the overall provision of housing in the city.

## NGOs and Legal Aid for the Poor

NGOs like Shehri provide indirect benefits to the poor. This organization has been fighting encroachments on amenity plots, illegal land conversions, and violations of building by-laws and zoning regulations by builders, developers, corporate sector institutions, and the military. Its struggle for a better physical environment has benefited many poor communities and the larger urban environment in which they live.

Although the NGO/CBO sector does not have much to do with land and housing issues, it does help communities organize themselves in their struggle against evictions, and in negotiations with government agencies over access to infrastructure and development funds, government packages, and housing rights.

## CONCLUSION

The discussions at the workshop highlighted the need for NGOs and CBOs to replace their charity model mindset and recognize and build on the assets that communities have; thereby empower them. To do this they will need to upgrade their technical and social skills and cooperate on cross-cutting initiatives in order to increase their impact. This is currently limited to enabling residents in low-income areas to acquire the technical skills and information to improve their bargaining position with the state and the private sector. It was also agreed that NGOs and CBOs cannot and should not replace the state, which is the major landowner and has the potential to provide land and housing for poor communities. Their role needs to be defined so that they can help develop and implement more equitable land policies. At present their involvement is too sporadic and issue-based to have much effect on the land market.

## ISSUES ASSOCIATED WITH AFFORDABILITY AND LOCATION

In order to understand the issues associated with affordable land and housing and location preferences, four types of residents in low-income settlements were interviewed and asked to complete a questionnaire. 27 of the residents were tenants, 74 were homeowners, 52 had been resettled and 57 lived in settlements under threat of eviction. The interviews with tenants and homeowners were carried out in different types of settlement: regularized informal settlements, formally planned settlements and settlements whose status is undefined.[4] They include developed settlements, those that are undergoing development and those that are underdeveloped.[5] The surveys also covered two relocation settlements and two settlements under threat of eviction, as well as 30 informal businesses[6] and 27 hawkers in various locations, as they employ and cater to their needs of the poor, unlike formal sector shops and businesses. Details are given in Appendix 8. This Appendix contains a questionnaire analysis and profiles of the surveyed settlements.[7] The surveyors also interviewed local residents, informal businesses and hawkers. Their observations are included in the following sections.[8] Map XI shows the locations where these surveys were held.

## HOUSEHOLD SIZE

There are strong similarities between the residents of these settlements, the settlements themselves and their socio-economic situation. Overall, family size usually varies between 6 and 10 members, although about 20 per cent of families have more than 10 members and tenants tend to have between 5 and 7. A majority of respondents who are not tenants or have not been resettled have lived in their home for over 20 years. Around 44 per cent of tenants have rented their present accommodation for less than one year, and 33 per cent for between one and five years. This high turnover shows that tenants are vulnerable. Most of the residents surveyed (tenants and owners) have moved to their present location from other areas of Karachi; 17 of the 74 homeowners and 21 of the 57 resettled respondents moved to Karachi from rural areas over 20 years ago.

## QUALITY OF HOUSING

All the settlements surveyed have similarly constructed houses, irrespective of their tenure status, with load bearing concrete block walls and corrugated iron or asbestos roofs or T-iron and precast concrete roofs. There was some variation among the 74 homeowners, 14 of whom have reinforced concrete roofs. The vast majority of homes are built on plots measuring 50 to 80 square yards, and most are single storey (apart from 24 of the 74 houses belonging to homeowners, 6 of the 27 rented homes, and 25 of the 57 homes in settlements threatened with eviction). A substantial number of houses are one or two room affairs (22 of the 27 rented homes, 16 of the 72 owner occupied homes and 28 of the 57 homes in threatened settlements). Most of the rest have three to four rooms (4 of the 22 rented homes, 42 of the 72 owner occupied homes and 19 of the 57 homes in threatened settlements). Fifty per cent of homeowners have documentation of their ownership, and resettled residents have proper leases, but the other respondents have no 'legal' ownership papers. Only 10 of the 74 homeowners have obtained formal permission to build their homes; the rest were either unaware that permission was required or do not need papers because they live on encroachments—although the latter keep their utility bills as proof of tenure because this can help their case in any subsequent regularization process. All respondents expressed a preference for single-unit houses on a plot that they own rather than an apartment.

## EMPLOYMENT STATUS

The survey revealed other similarities and differences between different groups. Tenants are for the most part skilled and unskilled workers, while homeowners included rickshaw drivers who own their vehicles and a small percentage of white-collar workers and shopkeepers. Most members of the households surveyed walk to work, except those who have been resettled far from the city centre, and home owning households with white-collar jobs in the city (9 of the 74). Those who do not need transport to get to work save a good deal of money. There has been a phenomenal increase in property prices across the survey sites. Homeowners have seen average values rise from Rs 100,000 ($1,100) to Rs 1–10 million ($111,110) since their property was purchased, while property values in threatened settlements have increased from Rs 30,000 ($333) to Rs 500,000 to 1 million ($5,555 to 11,100). Tenants and respondents from other settlements chose to live where they do to be near their workplace, because the area is affordable or because their relatives live nearby. Resettled residents had no choice in the matter. Respondents said that they heard about their properties through relatives and friends, who helped them, strike the deal. They did not use estate agents or market mechanisms to purchase properties because it is expensive and they do not trust market operators.

Most tenants earn between Rs 7,000 and Rs 15,000 ($78–156) per month. The majority (14 out of 27) pay Rs 2000 to 4000 ($22 to 44) per month to rent two rooms, and 18 pay less than Rs 2000 ($22); while 13 of the 27 tenants surveyed rent a single room, living with 5 to 7 people in very cramped conditions. Contracts with landlords are verbal and can be terminated at a month's notice as a month's rent is paid in advance. Written contracts are not required because the properties are owned by people who have clout in the locality. Almost all the tenants surveyed (20 out of 27) thought it highly unlikely that they would ever own a house themselves; 10 of the 27 have never even considered it; and 21 of the 27 said that they would not want to move to a non-regularized informal settlement where they might be able to own their home because it would be illegal and insecure. Therefore, they prefer to rent. Although 15 tenants said that they could raise the down payment of Rs 10,000 to Rs 30,000 ($110 to 330) needed to buy a house, this would not help them obtain a formal loan and they have no assets to secure a mortgage. In any case, they would not be able to pay more on loan instalments than they currently pay for their rent; 17 of the 27 tenants surveyed said that they cannot save any money at the end of the month.

The group of homeowners contains some upwardly mobile and better-off households. As noted above, they include white-collar workers, and 38 out of the 74 homeowners surveyed have plots of more than 80 square yards. They have also raised the funds to build their homes—from savings (38 out of 74), loans from relatives and friends (19 out of 74), selling assets (16 out of 74), and loans from the HBFC (2 of the 74). Most of the people that had taken out loans (14 of the 19) did so without mortgaging their assets or properties. Only five of them purchased their properties through estate agents. Most of the houses/plots were bought through cash deals, and only 13 of the 74 homeowners purchased their property on instalments. Of these, 5 had to make down payments of around Rs 10,000 ($110), while 7 paid between Rs 50,000 and Rs 100,000 ($555 and $1,100). Instalments varied between Rs 1000 and Rs 10,000 ($11 and $110) each. None of the tenants surveyed could purchase a house on these terms.

## LEGAL STATUS

As mentioned earlier, 50 per cent of homeowners have documented ownership. Most of the papers relating to their property (45 out of 75) are sale deeds on paper stamped by the court. Banks that offer housing finance do not accept these documents, requiring a proper lease from the landowning authority before they will issue a loan. Only 11 of the 74 respondents have lease documents. It is worth noting that about one-third of these respondents live in formally planned or regularized settlements, hence the large number of ownership documents in their possession.

When asked how long it took to build their homes, 52 of the 74 respondents said that it had taken between one and ten years. Only 15 of the 74 respondents completed construction in one year. In all, 56 of them bought materials from their local builders' merchant, and 21 obtained materials on credit from him. This shows the importance of incremental development and the merchant's role in providing materials, technical assistance and credit for house building.

## ISSUES ASSOCIATED WITH RELOCATION

The survey also covered 52 residents from two settlements that had been displaced by the construction of the Lyari Expressway along the Lyari

River Corridor. The Expressway relocation began in 2002. Residents were given a plot in the resettlement site measuring 80 square yards (meaning that 32 out of them moved to smaller plots), Rs 50,000 ($556) and asked to move as soon as their homes had been demolished. One of these sites is about 20 kilometres from the original settlement; the other is about 12 kilometres from the original site but is in an underdeveloped area that had no public transport until recently. Most of these residents (38 out of 52) built one to two room houses, using the same construction materials and roofing as their former homes.

There are two advantages to moving to the current sites. Firstly, residents that did not have a lease before are now formal property owners; secondly, the area is planned, with more open spaces and the potential for a better physical environment. As 28 of the 52 resettled respondents were tenants before they moved, they have benefited by becoming homeowners and saving on rent.

However, there are many disadvantages to this relocation, both in terms of the moving process and in the comparative quality of life in the two settlements. People were unable to move off the original site immediately because there was no accommodation on the new land. Therefore, 28 of the 52 respondents rented a house while they constructed a shelter on their new plot. This was expensive because the construction process took an average of about five months. Getting to and from work from the new settlement is more time consuming and expensive than it was from the original settlement, and 47 of the 52 families have been adversely affected by this. They used to be able to walk or take local neighbourhood transport to reach their workplaces, markets, and education and health facilities, but can no longer do so. And although primary school facilities are available in the new settlements, college and hospital facilities are not.

The ethnic, clan, and neighbourhood affiliations of these residents were also badly affected. When they moved to the new sites they were unable to obtain food items on credit from the local shops. This is a common practice in most low-income settlements, where the customer pays at the beginning of every month. Now, one decade on, it is possible to make some purchases on credit, but 38 of the 52 respondents said that they could not get credit from the local *thalla*. In addition to this, 39 of them said that the *bisi* system has declined since the move because the close ties of mutual trust on which the system is based have been ruptured. The most serious problem for respondents is their inability to find part-time jobs in the area (47 out of 52 are affected by this).

Previously, jobs were not only available but also they were situated in the neighbourhood or near workplaces in the city; now they are not worth having because it takes too much time and money to reach them. Some 50 per cent of respondents said that their income had fallen because of this.

There are also administrative issues associated with relocation. The new settlements were to be developed, monitored and maintained by the Lyari Expressway Rehabilitation Project (LERP), which set up its offices on site. Respondents and local residents claim that once the new arrivals had moved in and settled, LERP staff started illegally subdividing the green belt and amenities and selling them as plots on the open market. Water supply tankers disappeared, and so did teachers in the newly constructed schools. Local communities have constantly petitioned officials and politicians about LERP staff activities, but have not had their concerns addressed. Respondents believe that this is because the LERP staff share the proceeds of this illegal activity with their superiors and local politicians, and therefore enjoy political patronage. The administration's lack of interest in addressing the petitions is also ascribed to the fact that the community's relationship with the town *nazim* and higher government officials has declined since the move out of the inner city. The relationship with ward councillors has improved, but they are not very effective in dealing with larger issues.[9]

Just over 4600 households in settlements along the city's existing circular railway are to be relocated as a result of the KCR Rehabilitation Project (according to a project estimate). A survey was conducted with 57 residents from four informal settlements along the circular railway track that are threatened with eviction. The circular railway passes through densely populated areas of the city. Most respondents are labourers and hawkers (15 of the 57 have office jobs), many walk to work as 34 of the 57 work within the settlements, and most of their children's schools are within walking distance (40 out of 57). In all, 32 of the 57 have utility connections, and 39 have sale agreements with the persons from whom they purchased the land recorded on court stamp paper.

While the majority (25 out of 57) did not express their views as to whether the KCR should be built or not, they did agree that it might be beneficial for the city. A total of 19 respondents said that they did not think it should be built at all, and that they were not willing to vacate their land at any cost; 32 said that they do not wish to be part of any government scheme to move them out of the city, but that they would be willing to move if the government compensates them for their property at the market rate. This would give an average value of Rs 600,000

($6,667) per property,[10] and a total of Rs 2.76 billion ($30.66 million) for the 4,600 properties concerned. The government could explore this option, saving itself from a politically unpleasant task and the residents from life in an inhospitable location that they have not chosen.[11] It is also worth noting that 34 of the 57 respondents claimed that they will continue to live in the vicinity of their settlement even after they have been evicted. This shows the importance of place and its relationship to work and social facilities.

## INFORMAL BUSINESSES AND THEIR LOCATIONS

The survey covered 30 informal businesses and 27 hawkers in different locations. In addition to the survey, the researchers and their supervisors also held conversations and interviews with the respondents and their neighbours. Informal businesses were surveyed in five settlements: two were low-income settlements surrounded by affluent areas; two were developed low and lower middle-income settlements with cottage industries on the site; and one was a poor underdeveloped settlement with a large minority of migrants from Bangladesh.

Many businesses in the settlements that are surrounded by affluent areas cater to their wealthy neighbours, working as domestic staff, producing handicrafts and utensils like wooden spoons, clay cooking pots and flowerpots, paintings by artists who live in the settlements and even fake medicines in one settlement. Other businesses include eateries for local residents that sell food prepared by local women.[12]

Businesses in the settlements with cottage industries include weaving, thread production, and the manufacture and sale of leather goods such as slippers, wallets, and jackets. These are supplied to the Karachi wholesale markets. The main informal business in the underdeveloped settlement supplies prawns and shrimps to be cleaned and fishing nets to be repaired by local families. In some cases, businessmen have built shacks where this work can be carried out instead of in people's homes.[13]

In all, 28 of the 30 respondents live near to their businesses and 11 of them walk to work. Most of the 30 businesses are located on plots of 10 to 60 square yards. Only 2 were acquired through estate agents; 12 businesses own the property they operate out of, and 18 are rented. It is interesting to note that rents have hardly increased over the last decade. Only two of the 30 businesses pay regular *bhatta* (bribe extracted through coercion), but unofficial payments are made periodically to political parties as a part of their unofficial fund raising campaigns. The main complaints made by informal businesses relate to power outages, irregular water supply, growing insecurity because of crime and the lack of affordable credit to expand their businesses.

Hawkers were also surveyed and interviewed in five different settlements. One is near an affluent area and has become a centre for fresh fish, which is bought by residents from wealthier localities. Another settlement is next to a formally planned and developed middle-income area. The majority of hawkers here work along the footpaths, selling meat products, vegetables, and fruit to local residents. They have established a union, collectively purchased an electricity generator whose running costs are shared and collectively dispose of their waste and keep their operating area clean. The city government has 'regularized' them. They pay Rs 30 per day as tax to the union council. Some doubt that this goes to the union council, suspecting that the money is pocketed by officials and that this scheme is fake. However, it provides them with the protection they need.[14]

Saddar is an important location for hawkers. It is in the centre of the city, and most intra-city transport passes through it. Hawkers have been in Saddar since Independence when refugees flooded the city. They have since grown to occupy footpaths and even road space, resisting all attempts to relocate them. They service the commuting public, the vast majority of which is poor, selling old shoes, second-hand clothes, caps, trinkets, and cheap cooked and uncooked food. They come from different ethnic groups and are protected by their ethnic political parties in return for protection money. The researchers conducting the survey had to seek permission to do so from these political parties, as the hawkers were not willing to cooperate without their permission.[15]

Hawkers in the other settlements surveyed, mainly sell food to the local population—apart from newspaper hawkers, who deserve special mention. They exist in all settlements and have a city-wide union. Because they have the backing of powerful media houses, they have not been affected by the periodic campaigns to evict hawkers launched by successive local governments.[16]

Of the 27 hawkers surveyed, 21 work and live in the same locality and 19 walk to work. The majority of them (14 of the 27) say that the best location for business is near markets as a lot of people go there. Hawkers who have a permanent space or a cabin collectively employ watchmen (13 of the 27) to look after their site and stored goods at night and on holidays. Some do not take their pushcarts home, leaving them chained together where they work. These pushcarts owners also employ watchmen.

Yet watchmen alone cannot ensure that their goods are safe or protect their sites. This is guaranteed by paying *bhatta* to the local government, police, or political parties that control their work area.[17] Some respondents refused to discuss the topic; 3 of the 27 claimed that they will be tortured if they do not pay *bhatta*; 7 said that they would not be able to work in the area and 2 said that they would be 'relocated'.

## CONCLUSIONS

A number of conclusions and policy directions emerge from the discussions in these two subsections with regard to the role of NGOs, physical planning and housing credit. NGOs and CBOs serve a small segment of the population in the provision of housing. They are mostly involved in social sector issues such as education, health, and microcredit for income generation. Discussions with these organizations suggest that most of them are unlikely to make a difference to the existing gap in housing demand and supply. This means that the state needs to play a more appropriate role. While individual NGOs are unlikely to be able to change state policy on their own, a network of NGOs pushing for change can make a difference. It has also emerged that architects do not wish to work with low-income settlements, and that incremental housing improvements in these areas will be largely at the mercy of untrained architects until this attitude changes.

The surveys on affordability and location point to a number of ways that housing and land policies could benefit low-income communities. These surveys show that all low-income settlements are built in the same way, irrespective of their tenure status, with precast concrete block walls and in the initial stage, metal or asbestos sheet roofs. Almost all houses are built incrementally, and homeowners are heavily dependent on local builders' merchants (*thalla*) for technical advice, purchasing materials, and often for credit as well. These findings support the work done by the OPP-RTI housing programme in upgrading the *thallas*' products and technical capacities, providing training for 'para-architects' and support through OPP-RTI resource centres.[18]

The surveys also make it clear that low-income groups prefer informal deals in property matters, even when formal processes are available. This is because they do not trust market operators or government officials and are uncomfortable dealing with them. It is also hard to obtain information about formal processes. Officialdom needs to develop a poor-friendly culture to overcome this, making market information easily available in accessible formats. The HBFC website is a step in the right direction in this respect.[19]

People prefer one unit houses rather than apartments, as this allows them to increase their homes incrementally and use them for economic activities.[20] They also prefer to live in affordable locations near their work place and relatives. Living near their work saves time and money on travel, and being near their relatives strengthens their social, physical, and economic security. It is interesting to note that the majority of people with informal jobs work in or near their settlements, while those with formal office jobs travel considerable distances to work.[21] People also prefer to rent rather than live in settlements that have insecure tenure.

The surveys of relocated settlements show that displacement has various adverse effects on the communities concerned: their transport and utility costs increase, job opportunities diminish and community support systems are destroyed. They also lose the social facilities that were available in the original settlement. Another major issue is the time lag between being evicted and building a home in the new settlement. This causes immense problems with their children's education, and is expensive because residents have to rent accommodation while building their new homes and frequently have to move into unfinished houses. In addition to this, office staff in relocation project sites is often inefficient and corrupt and illegally indulge in subdividing and selling amenity plots. This could be resolved if residents affected by such projects set up organizations to negotiate the eviction and rehabilitation process.[22]

Low-income groups need to be able to live near their workplace or the city centre, but have been forced to survive on the outskirts of the city since the Greater Karachi Plan and Greater Karachi Resettlement Plan of 1958 ordained that land and housing for low-income residents should be far from the key manufacturing areas and city centres where employment opportunities are found (see section on Review of Land and Urban Master Plans in Chapter 3). The 2011 federal government task force report on urban development recommends that state land in or near the city centre should be used for low-income settlements,[23] with planned high density settlements that can grow incrementally near residents' work places. Densities could be increased to more than double housing provision in the resettlement areas surveyed, while reducing development costs and the amount of land required.[24]

Tenants are the most vulnerable group surveyed, as they are unable own formal or informal housing in affordable and appropriate locations. Housing census statistics show that the number of tenants in Karachi

is increasing.[25] Many live in extremely cramped conditions, with five to seven family members crammed into one room. The survey shows that they cannot feed themselves and their families if they have to pay both rent and transport. With low-incomes and no savings, they have no prospect of owning a house at any time in their lives. Any serious policy must address the problems of this most vulnerable of all groups.

Renting is a highly pertinent issue because the last decade has seen development literature urge governments to shift the focus from home ownership programmes to rental programmes (UN-Habitat 2003; The World Bank 2010), which are seen as a neglected area of housing. However, while rented housing does need attention and regulation, it should not replace the drive for homeownership. The interviews conducted for Chapters 6 and 7 show that people aspire to home ownership and only live in rented abodes because they feel disempowered by the formal market.

The *pugri* system used to rent residential and commercial properties (discussed in Chapter 6) reflects the inaccessibility of land. Under this system, the landlord lets a 'tenant' use his property in return for a sum that is less than the market price (which the tenant cannot afford). The tenant pays rent each month and operates from the premises without any fear of eviction. The property remains in the name of the landlord, who pays taxes on it. None of this is reflected in a written agreement.

Almost all the informal businesses covered by the survey link into the skills available in the locality, and are run by people who live in or near the settlement. These businesses are important because the majority of jobs in Karachi are in the informal sector, but they require better utilities, informal credit, and improved skills to expand and create more jobs. The surveys also showed the importance of hawkers, not only for low-income settlements, but also for middle and high-income areas. Proper by-laws and zoning regulations need to be put in place to provide secure sites for hawkers in new public and private development projects. They should also include rules and procedures to safely accommodate hawkers in existing public spaces without disrupting the flow of traffic or pedestrians.

# 8

# Towards a More Equitable Land Policy

The findings presented in this study establish the existence of laws and statutes that could support the development of equitable land policies in Karachi. However, they require simplified rules, regulations and procedures to ensure that they are applied in a more equitable manner, with proper monitoring to identify problems in their implementation and help develop more appropriate rules, regulations and procedures. The situation in Karachi is detrimental to its citizens, planning processes, and land and housing market. These are also adversely affected by conflicts over governance and turf wars between different political parties and ethnic groups, which often involve criminal gangs.

Evictions in Karachi continue to cause considerable suffering. This could be reduced if the processes set out in certain portions of the law were followed, such as giving adequate notice; agreeing resettlements on suitable land and addressing resident's grievances through the proper channels. Agreement on these rules and criteria is hampered by a lack of coordination between different agencies, from landowning entities and individuals to local government, cantonment board officials and politicians, and the communities themselves. Due to pressure from bureaucrats, politicians and landowners, the police often act on their own without notifying the community thirty days before demolition, as required by law.[1]

The notification process, whereby informal settlements and *katchi abadis* are formally accepted as legal settlements, is hampered by conflicts between the SKAA, the CDGK, and landowning agencies. Resolving such disputes can take well over a decade as it is not a priority for the protagonists. This creates considerable insecurity for the communities that live in these settlements, which may be notified for regularization and then have their notification withdrawn when it is discovered that the land titles are unclear. Even though they are the most important stakeholders in the system, most communities do not properly understand the processes for leasing and regularization because little information is available or accessible to them.

The problems with both the eviction and the regularization processes can be only overcome if they are recognized and analysed, and the necessary rules, regulations, and procedures established to oversee their implementation.

The ballot system for allotting plots is also problematic because the advance payments submitted by unsuccessful applicants stay tied up in the system, sometimes for well over a year, and retrieving them involves a number of time consuming formalities.[2]

In order to resolve the issues raised by hawkers, the link between commuters, poor communities, and hawkers needs to be accepted and their importance to the city's economy recognized, before the necessary zoning regulations can be developed to give them space. One of the real challenges in implementing a reform agenda is acknowledging these issues and the need to address them in order to improve poor communities' living and economic conditions and their physical and social environment.

Land for 'public good' is acquired under the Land Acquisition Act 1884. According to the law, all legal property owners should be compensated at the market rate for the demolition of their property, and for any additional damage that they may suffer as a result of their relocation. Those with proper leases and freehold documentation are considered for compensation, but are not always given proper redress by 'priority' projects, so often they find themselves forced to go through long and expensive court processes. Some communities that have lived in rural and urban areas for centuries without any legally documented ownership have to fight long battles to establish their ownership rights. The government has also started offering compensation and relocation plots to residents without ownership documents, who are technically encroaching upon the land. This *ad hoc* compensation is not given in accordance with any law. The Land Acquisition Act needs to be amended and properly implemented in order to address these issues.

The market also faces a number of constraints in functioning freely and effectively. The land allocation processes used by local governments and landowning agencies lack transparency, and the auctioning of public land by government agencies is also manipulated. Politicians and government officials flout the prescribed rules and regulations, using their discretionary powers to allot land to friends and family members or for political purposes. This undermines the confidence of more scrupulous developers and entrepreneurs and opens the way for speculation.[3] Discretionary powers over land allocation need to be reviewed, as they are a major impediment to the smooth functioning of the land market.

Rental laws are strongly in favour of tenants. Because of this, there is no formal development of rental accommodation even though it is in great demand. It is being developed in low-income settlements, however, where tenants have little or no security.[4] The federal government task force on urban development has recommended changes in the rent laws to make this market more attractive to developers and individuals. Developing 'formalized' low-income rented accommodation could also improve informal rental conditions in low-income settlements.

The lack of information and established processes means that tenants have to be careful who they rent from, landlords mindful of whom they rent to and both parties wary of estate agents and property dealers. Karachi's reform agenda contains proposals to establish a network of property dealers who follow the rules and regulations. Such an association does exist, but it mainly consists of agents who work in elite and middle class areas and is too small and ineffective to have much impact. There are constant conflicts due to bad relationships between owners and tenants, forced evictions of tenants and occupancies that end in violence and court cases.[5] Many people go to court, but legal processes are long and expensive, and lawyers involved in these cases have been threatened with violence and death. Those who get fed up with the court system and seek out-of-court solutions find that they are dictated by the party with the strongest connections and greatest muscle power.[6] There is a need for special courts that can dispense justice quickly and have the power and capacity to enforce their judgments.

The market also functions poorly in other respects. It does not address the housing needs of the poor (who are potentially its largest target group), and has difficulty in providing appropriate locations for commercial and industrial development. There are no incentives for poor and lower middle-income groups, who cannot afford market prices or obtain affordable credit to access the market. Developers are not comfortable working with low-income groups because the Pakistani elite and middle class are strongly biased against the poor. In addition to this, market operators pay bribes to obtain land, utilities, and approval for construction (which add 18 to 25 per cent to the cost of their end product),[7] and get away with fleecing the public. This nexus between developers and official planning and building agencies makes it hard for 'good' developers to function. The interviews in Chapter 5 reveal that well established developers have opted out of the business because they could not stomach the corrupt practices that dominate today's real estate and development business.

Another constraint to the market is the inability of most low and lower middle-income groups to obtain loans to purchase land and housing or improve their homes. There are three reasons for this. First, strict banking rules and regulations require applicants to be credit worthy, which means that they need a regular job or proper registered business. The vast majority of low and lower middle-income groups do not have either of these. Second, banks do not lend money to buy land, which is what most low and lower middle-income groups want to do. They lend to individuals who have leased properties, something that poorer people can rarely afford. Third, interest rates and repayment schedules are too expensive for families and individuals who earn less than Rs 15,000 ($167) a month.[8] NGOs and microcredit organizations have demonstrated that poor and lower middle-income groups are credit worthy even though they have no assets to mortgage. The housing related banking sector needs to be reformed to provide incentives for the market to cater to the needs of low and lower middle-income groups.

In the meantime it is important to recognize that the formal residential market in Karachi does not work well for the majority of its inhabitants. Access to land and housing, need to be based on the kind of non-exploitative informal mechanisms traditionally used by the poor.

The other major issue facing the market is the unavailability of land for development in appropriate locations. This problem could be overcome, as the landowning agencies have hoarded large amounts of notified urban land for speculation or to create housing estates, facilities and commercial developments for their current and previous employees, often in violation of official land use plans. In order to address this serious constraint to the market, an effective system for surveying and registering land needs to be considered and a tax levied on unutilized land.

There are also broader planning issues that need to be addressed. Each of the numerous landholding agencies in Karachi has its own building by-laws, zoning regulations and allotment and development processes. With no mechanism to encourage them to work together, they protect their own interests rather than promoting the social and physical environment of the city as a whole. Thus, while the power of the military has led to better governance and processes to prevent land related frauds and scams in cantonments, they are strongly anti-poor and have the *de facto* power to evict poor people (including hawkers) from their area, in violation of state laws. They are creating elite settlements on land near the city centre whose proximity to the city makes it ideal for low or lower middle-income settlements,[9] and have exacerbated problems of flooding by encroaching upon the city's drainage outfalls. Meanwhile, political patronage has played a large hand in shaping the development of land controlled by the city government (including the illegal conversion of amenity plots into residential and commercial areas), with highly adverse effects on the built environment.[10]

One way of tackling this serious problem with coordination and planning would be to establish the Karachi Division Planning Agency, as proposed by the Karachi Development Plan 2000 in 1989. This body should represent all the landowning agencies, establish consensus between them and work in the larger interests of the city. Creating this kind of mechanism to coordinate multiple land actors within the law would minimize the room for discretion and political patronage, although care will need to be taken to ensure that the agency is not dominated by the most powerful group. This will require a strong and informed civil society that can exert pressure on the agency and monitor its proceedings and decisions. In order to do so, civil society groups and academics will need access to official information, which they are currently denied. If this state of affairs continues, it will greatly hamper the transparent functioning of any such agency. Karachi is lucky in having a very active civil society and well researched literature on its problems and their possible solutions. Both have the potential to counter the reluctance that state institutions have shown in promulgating information about procedures. However, civil society needs to use this research and information more effectively in order to help build more equitable relations between the different actors involved in the city's land and housing drama.

One of the major constraints to implementing these proposals is the ethnic conflict in Karachi, which has turned land into an instrument of power. The turf wars between ethnic groups exploit the discretionary powers of politicians and government officials, unclear land titles, and the inability of the justice system to deal effectively with land and property related issues. They manipulate the market through pressure, coercion, and the targeted killings of estate agents and property dealers. Moving forward on this agenda will require consensus on the need to resolve these ethnic conflicts and a willingness among the leaders of ethnic groups to rise above the politics of 'constituencies' and 'votes' and behave as statesmen, acting in the larger interests of the city and the province. However, the recent ethnic conflict in Karachi has sapped the political will for reform and change, leaving the city undecided about its governance system.[11] At the moment, it is torn between a highly decentralized system proposed by the MQM and the bureaucratic system supported by the PPP, which has been provisionally imposed upon the province.[12]

# Notes

## Introduction

1. Definition in, Informal settlements created through squatting or informal subdivisions of state or private land, A. Hasan and M. Mohib, Challenge of Slums: *Global Report on Human Settlements (2003)*, 195–225. http://www.ucl.ac.uk/dpuprojects/Global_Report/cities/karachi.htm
2. Definition: This is the Karachi interbank rate set by the State Bank of Pakistan. It is the rate of interest charged for short term loans made between banks. Banks borrow and lend money in the interbank market in order to maintain liquidity or meet requirements placed on them; Investopeadia [Online encyclopeadia for investments]: http://www.investopedia.com/terms/i/interbankrate.asp

## Chapter 1: Karachi: The Context

1. Defined as a metropolitan area with a population of 10 million or more. In MPGO, Karachi Strategic Development Plan-2020 (2007).
2. 'Karachi's population explosion is far greater than experts' calculations' (2011), *Pakistan Today*, 6 Dec.
3. Ibid.
4. S. Hossain, *Karachi Strategic Development Plan-2020* (2006), 2.
5. Henry L. Stimson Centre, *Case study Lagos: Growth without infrastructure* (2010).
6. According to S. Qureishi, 'The Fast Growing Megacity Karachi as A Frontier of Environmental Challenges: Urbanization and Contemporary Urbanism Issues' (2010). *Journal of Geography and Regional Planning*, 3(11), 51: 18 per cent of Karachi's residents were literate in 1972, rising to 55.04 per cent in 1981 and 67.42 per cent in 1998. Qureishi also reported that 45.02 per cent of women were literate in 1972, compared with 48.84 per cent in 1981 and 62.88 per cent in 1998.
7. A. Hasan and M. Mohib, *Urban Slums Reports: The Case of Karachi, Pakistan* (2009).
8. Ibid.
9. Asian Development Bank, *Karachi Megacities Preparation Project Volume 1* (2005).
10. Hasan and Mohib, *Urban Slums Reports.*
11. Ibid.
12. Chishti, 'The Political Economy of NATO Trucks' (2011), *Friday Times*, 15 Sept.
13. MPGO, *Karachi Strategic Development Plan-2020.*
14. Calculated on the basis of Government of Pakistan, Census Reports (1998).
15. MPGO, *Karachi Strategic Development Plan-2020.*
16. A. Khan, 'Pakistan's Sindhi Ethnic Nationalism: Migration, Marginalization, and The Threat of 'Indianization'' (2002). *Asian Survey*, 42 (2), 213-229.
17. Calculated from Government of Pakistan, Census Reports (1998)

18. In Karachi 'the economic base is increasingly shifting from manufacturing to services. Manufacturing growth is slowing due to security problems, inadequate electrical power supply and high informal payments required to establish and maintain a business. As a result, manufacturing's share of metropolitan output has decreased from 37 per cent in 1985 to 18 per cent today. In the meantime, the service industries have been growing recently at about 8 per cent yearly and now represent a substantial part of gross metropolitan product. Growth has been particularly strong in trade (wholesale and retail) and banking and financial services; the latter has witnessed the arrival of a large number of international banks, the emergence of exchange companies, and a boom in the stock market and consequently in stock brokering, investment management and financial advice. ICT businesses, such as back office support functions and to a lesser extent software development, are also growing and have the potential to become cornerstones of the future economy of Karachi.' In MPGO, *Karachi Strategic Development Plan-2020*, 6.

19. A. Hasan, 'Sindh local government: The Real Issues' (2012b), *The Express Tribune*, 10 Jan.

20. T. Khan, 'Ethnic Violence Rules Karachi Politics' (2010), *The National*, 29 Dec.

21. A. Humayun and A. Jafri, Karachi's Ethnic Tinderbox (2010). *Small Wars Journal*, 2 Dec.

22. S. Das, *Kashmir and Sindh: Non-convergence in the Third World: Nation-Building, Ethnicity and Regional Politics in South Asia* (2001); S. Shah, 'Karachi, Pakistan's Biggest City, On Edge of Gang-led Civil War' (2010). *McClatchy*, 17 Nov.

23. Karachi is not alone in seeing a boom in real estate driven by Gulf States. See L. Moreno, *The architecture and urban culture of financial crisis* (2008) on its effects on the London landscape; V. Desai and A. Loftus, 'Speculating on Slums: Infrastructural Fixes in Informal Housing in the Global South' (2012) on the real estate boom in the wake of the financial crisis in Mumbai; and T. Ngwane, *Xenophobia in Bottlebrush: An Investigation into The Reasons Behind The Attacks on African Immigrants in An Informal Settlement in Durban* (2010) on South Africa.

## Chapter 2: Karachi: The Land

1. MPGO, *Karachi Strategic Development Plan-2020*.
2. H. Javed, interview with Asiya Sadiq (2011).
3. Pakistan Railways official website. <www.pakrail.com>
4. CDGK (2005); Karachi Strategic Development Plan 2020.
5. Karachi Port Trust official website. <http://www.kpt.gov.pk>
6. MPGO, *Karachi Strategic Development Plan-2020*.
7. Defence Housing Society Karachi official website. <http://www.dhakarachi.org>
8. S. Akhtar and M. R. Dahnani, *Industrial land use and land value pattern in Karachi City* (2011).
9. ARCOP/CK-NBBJ, *Sindh Education City Master Plan* (2011).
10. Port Qasim Authority official website. <http://www.pqa.gov.pk/>
11. Malir Development Authority official website. <http://mda.com.pk/>
12. Dr N. Ahmed, interview (2012).
13. Lyari Development Authority official website. <http://ldakarachi.com.pk/>
14. ARCOP/CK-NBBJ, *Sindh Education City Master Plan*.

15. R. Arsalan, interview (September 2011).
16. Enormous sums of money have been generated through heroin, arms and the Afghan transit trade as a result of the Afghan war. Much of this money has been invested in real estate and in supporting forcible land grabbing. Transporters supplying the NATO war efforts from Karachi port have also invested heavily in land with the proceeds of their trade.—Author.

## Chapter 3: Land Management in Karachi: Review of the Laws, Statutes, and Regulations

1. Applications for land parcels are submitted to the landowning authorities with a cash deposit, and processed through a computer ballot. Those whose number comes up get a plot of land. Well-to-do individuals often submit multiple tickets through their servants or dependents, and hold the land for speculation if they obtain more than one plot.
2. In 1988 a group of concerned citizens formed the group Shehri-Citizens for a Better Environment under the Societies Registration Act XXI of 1860. It is based in Karachi city, and operates as a non-political, non-commercial NGO that aims to provide citizens with a platform where they can effectively voice their concerns; determine their future; take action to prevent the further deterioration of their living environment and initiate proper reforms to improve it.
3. For details of densification in Karachi, see International Institute of Environment and Development's (IIED) report on urban density, [online report]: <www.urbandensity.org>
4. The committee consists of eight members. It is chaired by the governor of the province, co-chaired by the chief minister, and the chief controller of SBCA is the secretary. The other five members are the minister for local government and housing, the town planning department, the chief secretary of Sindh, the secretary for local government housing, the *nazim* of the district, the executive district officer and the MPGO or head of master plan for the district concerned. NO.PAS/Legis-B-14/2010.
5. A hearing on the Karachi elevated expressway project EIA was held 3 April 2007. It was inconclusive but the project has been shelved due to strong public reservations. The EIA hearing for Bahria Town Icon Towers, a 60 storey building, was held in April 2010 and major changes to the design were agreed upon. The EIA hearing for Noman Castello Tower, a 20 storey building, was held on 14 October 2010, and permission for construction was not given for social and environmental reasons.
6. S. Badiuzzaman, interview (2012).
7. Y. Baloch, *Forced Evictions in Karachi: Socio-economic and Political Consequences*, (2010). <http://www.urckarachi.org/Eviction%20watch%20report%20Sept%20 2010%20draft%202.pdf>
8. Khalid Siddiqui, interview (2011).
9. The FAR for residential areas is normally between 1:1 and 1:2, depending on their location. It can be as high as 1:5.5 for commercial areas, which include markets, offices and related functions. If an area is converted from residential to commercial use, its existing residential units can be used for commercial purposes.

10. A backlog is the gap between the number of housing units required in the city at six persons per unit, and the existing number of housing units. It is calculated from the most recent population and housing census and/or its projections.
11. H. Javed, interview (2011).
12. Riaz un Nabi, interviews (2011-12).
13. The SKAA has a head office in Karachi and separate field offices in Karachi, Larkana, Sukkur, Hyderabad, and Mirpurkhas.

## Chapter 4: Land and Housing: Credit for Purchase

1. These interviews were conducted by Samia Shahid and Madiha Salam, researchers at the Urban Research & Development Cell, NED University, Karachi, between 25 June and 30 November 2011. A list of persons interviewed is given in Appendix-1.
2. State Bank of Pakistan official website. <www.sbp.org.pk>
3. House Building Finance Company official website. <http://www.hbfcl.com/nc_eligibility_criteria.html>
4. Riazul Haque, interview (2011).
5. Based on forms obtained from the HBFLC Offices at Civic Centre, Karachi.
6. Nadeem Hussain, interview (2013).
7. See Chapter 3.
8. See Chapter 7.
9. Survey analysis can be requested on demand from Arif Hasan on arifhasan@cyber.net.pk
10. See Chapters 6 and 7.
11. See Chapter 6.
12. See Chapters 6 and 7.

## Chapter 5: Land Related Conflicts – I: Findings from Secondary Sources

1. Broadcast on various TV channels, such as Samaa TV, Geo News, ARY News, Express TV, and CNBC.
2. Apart from two videos filmed and uploaded by independent users, the independent productions were made by the NGO Shehri-CBE, which focuses on urban issues.
3. Details are given in Appendix-4.
4. These fact sheets can be acquired on demand from Engr. Mansoor Raza at <mansooraza@gmail.com>
5. M. Salahuddin, ARY News. <http://www.youtube.com/watch?v=LMiKWwZsEtM&feature=related>
6. I. Siddiqui, interview (2013).
7. Interview with estate agents and scam victims in Gulistan-e-Jauhar on Geo TV. <http://www.youtube.com/watch?v=FhfF5STy1fo#>
8. MNA Sufyan Yusuf on program 'Aap Ki Baat,' Samaa TV; Qudsia Kadri on program 'Agenda 360,' CNBC.
9. Report on land grabbing: M. Salahuddin, ARY News. <http://www.youtube.com/watch?v=LMiKWwZsEtM&feature=related>
10. A. Bhatti, Geo FIR, Geo TV. <http://www.youtube.com/watch?v=bR-1sYSz8tg>

11. H. Khan and A. Jameel, Samaa TV. <http://www.youtube.com/watch?v=KJLY9rJxfPE>

12. S. Lodhi, special report, ARY News. <http://www.youtube.com/watch?v=x_FEjocw9I8>

13. Film on the land mafia's takeover of Karachi city parks, The NGO Shehri-CBE. <http://www.youtube.com/watch?v=NHVll_QXaxg>

14. Reports on the operation against park encroachments initiated by a Supreme Court order: A. A. Khan, Samaa TV; M. Salahuddin, Geo News: <http://www.youtube.com/watch?v=eREsRxd8MY4>

15. A. Bhatti, Geo FIR, Geo TV. <http://www.youtube.com/watch?v=bR-1sYSz8tg>

16. Report on the collapse of a four storey building in Orangi Town during the flood season: Q. A. Shah, Samaa TV: <http://www.youtube.com/watch?v=vUvsPEjC4Rw&feature=related>

17. Report affirming the City Government allotment of 468 acres of land in Baldia's Ittehad Town for Cottage Industries on Samaa TV. <http://www.youtube.com/watch?v=_hCVWgoAtUE&feature=related>

18. Karachi Land Grabbing at Sohrab Goth <http://www.youtube.com/watch?v=_iXbV5pP9JE&feature=related>

19. Report on land grabs in Karachi on ARY News. <https://www.youtube.com/watch?v=-ho9hocHeYY>

20. Report on a police operation against the land mafia on National Highway on Express News: <http://www.youtube.com/watch?v=QdIgWTQ58hA&feature=related>

21. Report on a land ownership dispute: Z. Haider, Geo News. <http://www.youtube.com/watch?v=3If_Ixc9opU&feature=related>; Report on the forced encroachment of rooftops on residential flats in Gulistan-e-Jauhar (Rabia City Block 11 & 13): on Express News. <http://www.youtube.com/watch?v=hubBd2LOWrY&feature=related>; also the case of Katti Pahari.

22. The story of Kidney Hill/Ahmed Ali Park/Faluknuma: H. Khan, Samaa TV <http://www.youtube.com/watch?v=TWcJpSoJY7E&feature=related>

23. Film on the land mafia's takeover of Karachi city parks: NGO Shehri-CBE <http://www.youtube.com/watch?v=NHVll_QXaxg>

24. Report on Pehlvaan Goth: W. K. Baber, Geo News. <http://www.youtube.com/watch?v=sML_DYGUac8>

25. M. Omar. Film on Gutter Baghicha. NGO Shehri-CB <http://www.youtube.com/watch?v=PJXSg7WkhFY> and <http://www.youtube.com/watch?v=OokvKHrVRos>; and M. Omer. Getz Pharma and NGO Shehri-CBE. <https://www.youtube.com/watch?v=kzI80WqAzB0>

26. Report on Karachi's land scams: Qazi Hasan, Geo FIR, Geo TV: <http://www.youtube.com/watch?v=U3rIHlZDY-g#>

27. Report on Pehlvaan Goth: W. K. Baber, Geo News. <http://www.youtube.com/watch?v=sML_DYGUac8>

28. Episode on builder's 'mafia' in Karachi: *Benaqab*, Aaj TV. <http://www.youtube.com/watch?v=6CXb7afR8yQ> <http://www.youtube.com/watch?v=YFGnYFlK2Rs&feature=related> <http://www.youtube.com/watch?v=JDuut4ODcmI&feature=related>

29. See the films *'Do Bigha Zameen'* (1953); and *'Peepli Live'* (2010).

30. See the film *'Aarakshan, (2011),'*

31. See the film *'Lagay Raho Munna Bhai'* (2006).

32. OPP official website. <http://www.oppinstitutions.org/>

33. Shehri-CBE official website. <http://www.shehri.org/>

34. Details of these various violations, see Shehri-CBE official website. <http://www.shehri.org/>
35. Ibid.
36. Ibid.
37. Ibid.
38. Ibid.
39. A profile of these companies is given in Appendix-4.
40. See World Bank Group, *Dealing with construction permits in Karachi—Pakistan* (2014). <http://www.doingbusiness.org> for more on Pakistan's economy and construction permits
41. Politically powerful communities are not evicted. Evictions often take place on land with a high commercial value, through a nexus of government agencies, developers and politicians.
42. Dr. N. Ahmed, personal communication (2013).

## Chapter 6: Land Related Conflicts – II: Findings from Primary Sources

1. A detailed analysis of the results of the questionnaires can be had on demand from Architect Saeed Uddin Ahmed at <architectsaeed@yahoo.com>
2. Nuruddin, interview (2011).
3. Ibid.
4. List of murdered estate agents for 2010 and 2011 and the location where they were killed can be had on demand from Arif Hasan at <arifhasan@cyber.net.pk>
5. R. M. Mazahar, interview (2011).
6. S. Moinuddin, interview (2011).
7. J. Khan, interview (2011).
8. M. Hussain, interview (2011).
9. S. Moinuddin, interview (2011).
10. F. Zaidi, interview (2011); and A. R. A. Jaffery, interview (2011).
11. Community saving schemes.
12. Sohail, interview (2011).
13. F. Sadiq and R. Sadiq, interview (2011).
14. Hasan, A., Sadiq, A., and Ahmed, S., *Planning for High Density in Low-income Areas: A Case Study from Karachi* (2010).
15. A Sindh-based trade community now active in formal real estate development.
16. N. Khan et al, interviews (2011).
17. Shahid, interview (2011).
18. Janti, interivew (2011); and Bilqees, interview (2011).
19. A gathering place for Shia Muslims.

## Chapter 7: Karachi's Land Market: Support to Poor Communities, Affordability, and Location Issues

1. MPGO, *Karachi Strategic Development Plan-2020*.
2. These interviews were conducted by Associate Professor Asiya Sadiq, Assistant Professor Saeed Uddin Ahmed, Research Assistant Madiha Salam and Research Assistant Samya Shahid. The workshop was held on 1 Dec. 2011.

3. OPP official website. <www.oppinstitutions.org>
4. Regularised settlements include former *katchi abadis*; formally planned settlements were planned by development agencies; and those with undefined status are *katchi abadis* that have not yet been notified.
5. Developed settlements have local government supported infrastructure; developing settlements are in the process of acquiring it; underdeveloped settlements have yet to acquire it.
6. Businesses that are not registered in land use plans or tax registers.
7. Detailed tabulation can be obtained from Architect Saeed Uddin Ahmed of UDRC at NED University, Karachi, by emailing him at <architectsaeed@yahoo.com.>
8. Y. Khan and A. Iqbal, interview by Arif Hasan (2012).
9. Ibid.
10. Based on the average market value of respondents' homes.
11. The cost of rehabilitating 26,071 families affected by the Lyari Expressway Project would be PKR 8.7 billion. The government is considering a similar package for those affected by the KCR project (see Lyari Expressway Resettlement Project and Karachi Circular Railway Rehabilitation Project official websites).
12. Y. Khan and A. Iqbal, interview by Arif Hasan (2012).
13. Ibid.
14. Ibid.
15. Ibid; see also A. Hasan, C. Polak and A. Sadiq, *The Hawkers of Saddar Bazaar* (2008).
16. Ibid.
17. Ibid.
18. OPP-RTI official website. <http://www.oppinstitutions.org/Rsearch%20and%20training.htm>
19. HBFC official website. <http://www.hbfcl.com/>
20. Hasan, A., Sadiq, A., and Ahmed, S., *Planning for High Density in Low-income Areas: A Case Study from Karachi.*
21. This is also borne out by the survey results in Section *Public Views on Housing* in Chapter 6.
22. Similar to the National Slum Dwellers' Association and support from SPARC for communities that are being relocated by the World Bank funded improvements to Mumbai's suburban railway system.
23. Planning Commission, *Task Force Report on Urban Development*. Government of Pakistan (2011).
24. Hasan, A., Sadiq, A., and Ahmed, S., *Planning for High Density in Low-income Areas: A Case Study from Karachi.*
25. Government of Pakistan, *Census Reports.*

## Chapter 8: Towards a More Equitable Land Policy

1. For an example of this, see section on *Data on Land in Karachi from Five Case Studies* in Chapter 5.
2. For details see Chapter 6.
3. For details see Chapters 5 and 6.
4. For details see section on *Issues related to Affordability and Location* in Chapter 7.
5. For details see section on *What the Interviews Tell Us* in Chapter 6.

6. Ibid.
7. Ibid.
8. For details see Chapter 4.
9. For details see section on *Land Conversion along Karachi's Coastline* in Chapter 5.
10. This is discussed throughout the book.
11. For details see section on *Views of the Provincial Government and the CDGK on the Karachi Strategic Development Plan 2020* in Chapter 3.
12. For details see section on *Views of the Provincial Government and the CDGK on the Karachi Strategic Development Plan 2020* in Chapter 3.

# Appendices

# Appendix 1

## Persons Interviewed and Profile of Financial Institutions that Fund Housing

PERSONS INTERVIEWED:

1. House Building Finance Company Limited:
   Riazul-Haque, Assistant Manager
   Website: <www.hbfcl.com>
2. Tameer Micro Finance Bank:
   Shahid Mustafa, Group Executive Director,
   Product & Risk Management
   Website: <www.tameerbank.com>
3. Meezan Bank:
   Wise-ur-Rehman, Vice President Business,
   Manager Easy Home
   Website: <www.meezanbank.com>
4. Dubai Islamic Bank:
   Syed Raheel Haider Rizvi, Relationship Manager
   Website: <www.dibpak.com>
5. United Bank Limited:
   Mr Kashif Islam, Product Manager
   Website: <www.ubldirect.com>
6. Askari Commercial Bank Limited:
   Website: <www.askaribank.com.pk>
7. Muslim Commercial Bank Limited:
   Zeeshan, Consumer Banking
   Website: <www.mcb.com.pk>
8. National Bank of Pakistan:
   Khurrum Tanveer, Credit Manager
   Website:<www.nbp.com.pk>

Profile of Financial Institutions that Fund Housing:

Micro-credit Banks

| Institute | House Building Finance Company Limited | Tameer Micro-Finance Bank Limited |
|---|---|---|
| Types of Loans Offered: | | |
| Construction | With this convenient plan the customer can construct a residential property on already owned land or add onto an existing residential unit. HBFCL will facilitate up to 60% of total projected cost of construction (land cost + cost of construction).<br>• Finance Limit<br>→ Up to Rs. 10,000,000 | Micro Mortgage—Tameer Makaan<br>• Product and service promise:<br>→ Urdu: '*Makaan Hamara Banay Sahara*'<br>→ English translation: 'Our Property (House) Is Our Support'<br>• Product advantage<br>→ Loans from Rs. 50,000 up to Rs. 500,000<br>→ Lead time (availability of finance) 15–21 days<br>→ Loan Tenure up to 3 years<br>→ Imbedded Life Insurance |
| Purchase | The customer can live their dream of owning a house as quickly as possible,<br>• Finance Limit<br>→ Up to Rs. 10,000,000 | |
| Renovation | For renovation on an existing house, apartment or bungalow financing up to Rs. 2.5 million is available pertaining to urban cities. For other rural cities, maximum investment limit is Rs. 0.5 million.<br>• Finance Limit<br>→ Up to Rs. 2,500,000 | |

| Institute | House Building Finance Company Limited | Tameer Micro-Finance Bank Limited |
|---|---|---|
| Terms and Conditions, Eligibility Criteria | • Pakistani citizen between 18–60 years for salaried individuals<br>• Up to 18–65 years for business/self-employed person/professionals<br>• In case the customer does not have sufficient income, a guarantee of a blood relation will be accepted.<br>• The customer should be employed or self-employed and have adequate repayment capacity to meet the investment obligations.<br>• Proof of income should be presented in the form of salary certificate, affidavit & tax return.<br>• Legal documents, utility bills, bank statements, employment proof, etc. in order to take home finance. | • Any customer whose income is Rs 20,000 but less than Rs 50,000.<br>• Proof of income should be presented in the form of salary certificate, affidavit & tax return.<br>• Legal documents, utility bills, bank statements, employment proof, etc., in order to take home finance. |
| Mark-up Rates | • 3.6%service charges + KIBOR<br>• For salaried persons: Last available one year KIBOR offer rate + 3.25 %<br>• For business persons: Last available one year KIBOR offer rate + 3.50 %<br>• (Note: Insurance premium @ 0.463 paisa per thousand per month) | • Tameer microfinance bank follows a flat rate, e.g. if 1 lakh loan has been given for a tenure of 3 years. Loan returned would be 19% per annum. The internal interest rate is 36%. |
| Minimum and Maximum Amount of Loan | Maximum 10 million as per rules of State Bank Pakistan | Minimum Rs 1 lakh and maximum Rs 5 lakh. |

| Institute | House Building Finance Company Limited | Tameer Micro-Finance Bank Limited |
|---|---|---|
| Mortgage Requirements | HBFCL equitable mortgage is available in the leasehold residential properties in urban cities on the following basis:<br>• High market value with memorandum of deposit of title deeds.<br>• Red entry on record of rights.<br>• General Power of Attorney in lieu of HBFCL Requirements:<br>• The maximum age of the house having 'A' Class construction should not exceed 45 years (from the date of approved building plan)<br>• Investment may be made at all coastal areas except for the front row of Sea View Township and Darakhshan Villas, Clifton Karachi.<br>• House purchase product is available in urban areas at district quarter & *tehsil*, on the basis that construction should be 'A' Class & all basic amenities should be available. The value of the house as per existing policy has been evaluated from the PBA approved evaluators.<br>• Sale agreement, title deed, valuation and soundness certificate from an approved architect will be required. Investment shall be released in one instalment. The cheque will be delivered in the presence of sub-registrar at the time of execution of Islamic Housing Finance Agreement | • If a person can pay instalments of the loan of 50% of his monthly salary he is eligible. In very rare cases, with very small loans, up to 60% is acceptable. Other than that the person must have a genuine salaried job or small business with a certain amount of monthly revenue. |

| Institute | House Building Finance Company Limited | Tameer Micro-Finance Bank Limited |
|---|---|---|
| Minimum/ Maximum Period of Loan Return | 20 years standard, depending on applicant's age | 5 Years |
| Additional Details | • HBFCL has financed around 456,256 houses to the tune of PKR 47.82 billion.<br>• In 2010 the annual disbursement was PKR 679 million, and recoveries were PKR 3.4 billion.<br>• In December 2010 the total work force was about 951, and the loan portfolio stood at PKR 14.6 billion. | |

Commercial Banks

| Institute | Meezan Bank | Dubai Islamic Bank | United Bank Limited | National Bank of Pakistan | Muslim Commercial Bank | Askari Commercial Bank |
|---|---|---|---|---|---|---|
| **Types of Loans Offered** | | | | | | |
| Construction | Finance for up to 70% of the appraised value or Rs 40 million. | | Home building | Finances up to Rs 35 million over 3 to 20 years. Maximum debt to equity ratio of 85:15. | House building on land owned by borrowers should be disbursed in tranches. | House building with *halal istisna/ musharakah* finance specifically tailored to match the client's cash flows and needs. |
| Purchase | Finances up to 85% of the appraised value of a new home or a maximum of Rs 40 million. | House Purchase. | United Bank Limited finances up to 70% of the appraised value for house purchases. | Finances up to Rs 35 million over 3–20 years. Maximum debt to equity ratio of 85:15. | Purchase ready property. | Finances 85% of the cost of the property up to Rs 50 Million.* Other terms apply. |
| Renovation | Finances up to 30% of the appraised value. | Purchases undivided share (home renovation). | Renovation | Finance of up to Rs 15 million over 3–15 years. Maximum debt to equity ratio 80:250. | Renovation of existing home with documented end use; should be disbursed in tranches. | Facilitates house renovations. |

| Institute | Meezan Bank | Dubai Islamic Bank | United Bank Limited | National Bank of Pakistan | Muslim Commercial Bank | Askari Commercial Bank |
|---|---|---|---|---|---|---|
| Terms and Conditions, Eligibility Criteria | • Salaried customers must have minimum gross income of Rs 20,000 per month.<br>• Businessmen must have a minimum gross salary of Rs 50,000 per month.<br>• Requires legal documents, utility bills, bank statements, employment proof, etc.<br>• Primary customer is 25 years old and co-applicants must be over 21.<br>• Applicants must be residents of Pakistani nationality. | • Pakistani and non-resident Pakistanis as per policy.<br>• Age 25–65.<br>• Minimum monthly net income of Rs. 15,000.<br>• Copies of utility bills.<br>• Professional degree (for self-employed professionals only).<br>• Salary certificate/ proof of profession.<br>• Latest salary slip.<br>• Bank statements for the last 12 months and bank certificate. | • Minimum monthly income: Rs 50,000.<br>• Age: 23 to 65 years.<br>• Resident Pakistani.<br>• Self-employed businessman/ professional or salaried individual.<br>• Minimum loan: Rs 500,000.<br>• Employment certificate confirming last 12 months work experience.<br>• Tax documents for the past 24 months.<br>• Current salary slip<br>• Bank statements for the last 12 months. | • Must be resident Pakistani national aged between 21 and 65 year.<br>• Minimum income requirement Rs 5,000 for government employees, Rs 10,000 for other salaried persons and Rs 15,000 for self-employed and businessmen.<br>• Requires legal documents, utility bills, bank statements, proof of employment, etc. | • Applicants must be Pakistani national.<br>• Salaried, self-employed businessmen (SEB) and-self employed professionals (SEP) are eligible to apply.<br>• Requires satisfactory verification and bureau checks, estimated income, property valuation and legal opinion. | • Pakistani nationals aged 21 to 65 years.<br>• Permanent employment, at least six months with present employer.<br>• Self-employed individuals need at least 3 years business track record.<br>• Requires legal documents, utility bills, bank statements, proof of employment, etc. |

| Institute | Meezan Bank | Dubai Islamic Bank | United Bank Limited | National Bank of Pakistan | Muslim Commercial Bank | Askari Commercial Bank |
|---|---|---|---|---|---|---|
| Mark-up Rates | For salaried customers including SEP, NRP and merchant navy: <br>• Fixed 1st Year … K * + 3.00 % p/a. <br>• Annual re-pricing: K ** + 3.00 % p/a. <br>• (Floor 8.00% p/a and capped at 30% p/a.) <br>For business-en: <br>• Fixed—1st Year … K * + 4.00 % p/a. <br>• Annual re-pricing: K ** + 4.00 % p/a. <br>• (Floor 8.00% p/a. and capped 30% p/a.) <br>* For first year fixed rate, 'K' denotes KIBOR (Karachi Inter Bank Offer Rate), announced on 1st working day of each calendar month. | Applicable Profit Rate = Relevant KIBOR + margin. <br>* Based on the arbitrary 12 month KIBOR and bank's rate. <br>** In year 2, the KIBOR is increased by 3% from year 1; the bank's margin remains constant. <br>*** In year 3, the KIBOR is reduced by 5% from year 2; the bank's margin remains constant. <br>The bank's margin is 4.00% <br>Amount financed: Rs 10,000,000. | For salaried customers: <br>• Applicable mark-up rate = KIBOR + 3.5%. <br>For SEB/SEP: <br>• Applicable mark-up rate = KIBOR + 4.5%. | Variable rate option: <br>SBP discount rate + 2% with12 months re-pricing (with life insurance). <br>SBP discount rate + 4% with 12 months re-pricing (without life insurance). | Salaried <br>1 Year KIBOR (offer) + 4.0% SEB/SEP. <br>1 year KIBOR (offer) + 4.5%. | Salaried <br>KIBOR + 4.0%. <br>SEB/SEP KIBOR+ 5.0%. |

| Institute | Meezan Bank | Dubai Islamic Bank | United Bank Limited | National Bank of Pakistan | Muslim Commercial Bank | Askari Commercial Bank |
|---|---|---|---|---|---|---|
| | ** For annual revision, 'K' denotes 90 days average of 12-month KIBOR announced for each calendar quarter by the bank. | | | | | |
| Minimum and Maximum Amount of Loan | Rs 5 lakh to Rs 40 million. | • House purchase Rs 500,000 to Rs 50 million.<br>• Home renovation Rs 500,000 to Rs 10 million.<br>• Finance transferred from another bank Rs 500,000 to Rs 50 million. | Rs 5 lakh to Rs 30 million. | Maximum amount for all products except home improvement is Rs 35 million; maximum amount for home improvement is Rs 15 million. | Minimum loan of Rs 500,000; maximum loans:<br>• HP: 20 million.<br>• HC: 10 million.<br>• HR: 5 million. | Minimum amount is Rs 300,000; maximum Rs 30 million. |

139

| Institute | Meezan Bank | Dubai Islamic Bank | United Bank Limited | National Bank of Pakistan | Muslim Commercial Bank | Askari Commercial Bank |
|---|---|---|---|---|---|---|
| Mortgage Requirements | • Compliance with eligibility criteria.<br>• Profit margin charged by Meezan Bank equal to convention mortgage market trends.<br><br>• *Shariah* allows any market factor to be used as a benchmark to determine the profit rate of a particular product. | Compliance with eligibility criteria. | Compliance with eligibility criteria. | | | • Must be a taxpayer.<br>• Must have a valid computerized National Identity Card (CNIC).<br>• Must have a mobile phone. No landline required.<br><br>at current or potential residence for house purchases or construction; any mobile or wireless connection at residence is acceptable for home renovations if there is no PTCL landline. |
| Minimum/ Maximum Repayment Period | 3 to 20 years | 3 to 20 years | 3 to 20 years | 3 to 20 years | 2 to 20 years | 1 to 20 years |

| Institute | Meezan Bank | Dubai Islamic Bank | United Bank Limited | National Bank of Pakistan | Muslim Commercial Bank | Askari Commercial Bank |
|---|---|---|---|---|---|---|
| Additional Details | • The bank developed a finance product based on the concept of *'wakalah'*, to encourage the development of financing partnerships between Islamic banks and Microfinance banks. | • Caters the middle income groups with a minimum gross monthly income of Rs 20,000. <br>• Up to Rs 3.5 to Rs 4 billion has been dispatched. Loans not given in areas such as F.B. Area, Gulzar-e-Hjiri, Orangi, Baldia, Surjani. | | • Islamic banking has seen deposits increase 356% and finance and investment by 148% over the last year. The bank has total assets Rs 1.035 trillion at the year-end, representing a 9.6% increase on the year-end in 2009 | | |
| | • The bank demonstrated robust business growth in 2010, closing the year with deposits of Rs 131 billion and Rs 143 billion in import/export business. | *100% shariah* compliant. | | and appreciable growth in a challenging economic environment. <br>• Pre-tax profits increased by 15% from Rs 21.3 billion to Rs 24.4 billion. | | |

# Appendix 2
## Review of Land Related Videos

1. Land Grabbing in F. B. Area Karachi
   <http://www.youtube.com/watch?v=HFn-lykk3VA#>

This clip is taken from the program *Aap ki Baat* on Samaa TV, where correspondent Irtiza speaks to MNA (MQM) Sufyan Yusuf in public. The discussion revolves around the matter of encroachment on parking space meant for flats in Block 7, F. B. Area, where a number of people, owning lease documents, claim to have lived for 59 years. Sufyan Yusuf disproves them with a copy of the master plan map of 1986 showing the land marked as parking, adding that the encroachment occurred in 1998 under governor's rule.

2. Fake Housing Projects/Spread of Land Mafia across Karachi
   <http://www.youtube.com/watch?v=U3rIHlZDY-g#>

Qazi Hasan reports on Karachi's land scams for the program *FIR* on Geo TV. The clip illustrates the issue through the stories of Mohammed Abbas and Kaneez Fatema—both of whom are over 60 years old and spent their life savings on acquiring a plot (in Gulistan-e-Jauhar) only to have it occupied by life-threatening land-grabbers. Further Mohammed Irshad, an estate agent took the Geo team to various sites around Gulistan-e-Jauhar, pointing out places (marked with related political party flags) occupied or illegally constructed on by the land mafia and potentially worth billions of rupees.

The *FIR* reporters also go with a hidden camera to the office of a fake housing society near the Super Highway that offers its own lease, as opposed to that of the Sindh Government.

3. Land Mafia in Machhar Colony Keamari, Karachi
   <http://www.youtube.com/watch?v=bR-1sYSz8tg#>

The report by Amir Bhatti for the program *FIR*, Geo TV shows how the land mafia is selling government land/waters in an area called Taapu, near Machhar Colony and Keamari. This coastal land, considered highly profitable, is reclaimed by land filling with garbage (adversely affecting marine life) and divided into about 400 plots: each plot is sold at Rs. 80,000. The clip includes footage of provincial minister for *katchi abadis*, Rafiq Engineer explaining how the new *katchi abadi* on land owned by KPT cannot be regularized without a NOC and Minister Babar Ghauri claiming the Sindh cabinet and the president have been informed of the rampant land grabbing and that the police are on the land grabber's side.

4.  Massive Land Grabbing in Gulistan-e-Jauhar
    <http://www.youtube.com/watch?v=FhfF5STylfo#>

This report is similar to video 1: Geo TV produces it and it is about land-grabbing/
scamming issues; Mohammed Abbas (victim) and Mohammed Irshad (estate agent)
are interviewed. The latter states that lease files worth 5–6 million are being sold for
400,000 rupees in Gulistan-e-Jauhar. The police station refused to comment and other
victims were too scared to come on camera. Plots belonging to thousands of people have
been illegally occupied in Ehsanabad, on either sides of the Northern Bypass and Super
Highway, Gulistan-e-Jauhar and Gulshan-e-Maymar.

5.  ANP Terrorists raping girls and land grabbing in Karachi
    <http://www.youtube.com/watch?v=_kSI44_YRjk>

The clip is from the talk show *Agenda 360* on CNBC, where guest speaker Qudsia Kadri,
Chief Editor of the Daily Financial Post and President, MWPJO, relates the story of
distressed women living in Mikasa Apartments at Civic Square, who have approached
her to complain about members of the ANP Students' Wing who took control of their
building and physically harassed them; consequently the women were forced to give up
their apartments and relocate.

6.  Karachi's Graveyard land grab mafia- a special report
    <http://www.youtube.com/watch?v=x_FEjocw9I8>

Salman Lodhi gives a special report for the ARY News channel from a graveyard at SITE
Town. Here the land mafia has been flattening graves and selling the land and houses
have started mushrooming in the vicinity regardless of the locals' consistent complaints.
The new residents also tend to direct their drainage and throw their garbage to other
parts of the graveyard.

7.  Library Demolition and spread of Land Mafia in Sindh
    <http://www.youtube.com/watch?v=eREsRxd8MY4>

This clip is a montage of 3–4 separate clips relating first to the demolition of a public
library and later to the land mafia in Sindh. Amer Ahmed Khan of Samaa TV and
Mohammed Salahuddin of Geo News report on the operation against park encroachments
initiated by an order of the Supreme Court. The 22nd of 164 listed demolitions was a 20
plus year old, double storeyed public library in Azizabad, in the Jauharabad Football
Club. A number of on-site interviews with locals and library users unanimously signalled
dissent towards carrying out the SC order in the case of the library, claiming that it was
an educational facility, regularly in use and should have been granted protected status in
light of national interest.

The second half of the clip is a report by Tariq Moeen Siddiqui for Geo News,
highlighting an unsuccessful attempt at grabbing land directly belonging to the Ministry
of Defence's Pakistan Meteorological Department Headquarters' Karachi Camp Office
in Gulistan-e-Jauhar. The attempt was made in the name of Zulfiqar Mirza (PPP Sindh
home minister) who later, in the Sindh Assembly aligned the MPA/DPO with the land
grabbers and named a number of Sindhi politicians directly involved with land grabbing.

8.  Land Mafia in Karachi at large- Makro etc
    <http://www.youtube.com/watch?v=KJLY9rJxfPE>

The clip is part of a short, twelve-minute film produced by Hussam Khan and Asif Jameel for Samaa TV. The film discusses the growth and spread of land grabbing in Karachi, expounding on evidence from interviews with:

- Mustafa Kamal Mayor of Karachi, who states that the constant land grabbing is supported with police protection;
- Roland DeSouza a member of a NGO, who elaborated on the major culprits behind the land grabbing:
  1. Politicians,
  2. Big Business Corporation, and
  3. Religious Outfits.

  Desouza illustrates his argument with the example of the incident Makro-Habib. This corporation has illegally occupied an amenity plot, the Webb Playground, in the Lines Area in Karachi with no consideration for and adversely affecting residents of the local community. Although the courts have passed judgments in favour of the residents, Makro-Habib remains functional whereas the Sindh High Court declined comment/discussion on the subject when approached by Samaa TV; and,

- Ardeshir Cowasjee, a prominent columnist, who stresses on the importance of law and order.

9.  Massive Land Grabbing in Karachi: Babar Khan Ghauri MQM
    <http://www.youtube.com/watch?v=-ho9hocHeYY>

A report for ARY News says that protocols followed in actions taken against Karachi's land mafia resulted in differences between political parties PPP and ANP. ANP Sindh leader Shahi Syed claimed that encroachments in Baldia Town had not been considered, whereas PPP's Rafiq Engineer stated that Sumar Jokhio Goth was not to be considered an encroachment. Consequently a six member anti-encroachment cell was created under the authority of Agha Siraj Durrani, who remarked against the unprecedented land grabbing in Sindh and its politicization.

10. ANP leader Ameer Nawab's land grabbing held responsible for death of seven innocent people in roof collapse
    <http://www.youtube.com/watch?v=vUvsPEjC4Rw&feature=related>

In a clip from Samaa TV, Quaid Ali Shah reports on the collapse of a four storey building in Orangi Town during the flood season. According to the KBCA and residents of the area there was a natural rainwater channel running below the building that had weakened its foundations and two of its four floors had been illegally constructed. Three heavy machines and people of the area were sorting the rubble for dead: seven were reported dead including two little girls and two rangers, whereas others were still missing. The neighbouring building was evacuated. A citizen at the hospital blatantly held Ameer Nawab of the ANP responsible.

11. Karachi Land Grabbers: A Special Report
    <http://www.youtube.com/watch?v=LMiKWwZsEtM&feature=related>

Mohammed Salahuddin of ARY News reports on the consistent land grabbing and encroachments enveloping Karachi as millions of rupees are spent in efforts to beautify and develop it. Kamran Akhtar, a town *nazim*, recounted his fruitless efforts to get in touch with the governor, the police, and the land grabbers themselves. He is convinced of the latter having police protection. Masood Alam, ED Municipal Services made a distinction between the desperate encroachments of the homeless and the brazen encroachments that result in large, profitable plazas. He further elaborated on the heightened encroachments along the majority of rainwater channels in the city where heavy machinery cannot be used to clean out the drainage lines and also the rainwater channel, therefore manual cleaning is the only option, and people were in danger of facing 2'–3' deep flooding within their make-shift homes.

12. Wali Khan Baber's last report on Pehlvaan Goth
    <http://www.youtube.com/watch?v=sML_DYGUac8>

This is the last report submitted by Wali Khan Baber for Geo News, who died in a target killing in Liaquatabad receiving four gunshots soon after submitting it. He narrates the situation in Pehlvaan Goth in Karachi where two, allegedly political groups, had set up barriers and had exchanged heavy gunfire for a number of days. The police and rangers arrived at the area on the third day, conducted a six hour-long search operation for illegal possession of arms or ammunition. The SSP in charge of the operation, Naeem Shaikh, reported that the culprits had been arrested and contraband confiscated, but provided no further details. The people complained that they were scared of stepping out of their houses and all the shops in the vicinity, including basic grocery shops, were shut down for days. Wali Baber mentioned how the general public was trying to push for peace and they were the ones who had to pay for discord between political parties.

13. Navy Land Grab
    <http://www.youtube.com/watch?v=LHE3RY-SwbY&feature=related>

The host of a TV show, *Centre Stage* on Express News, elaborates on a dispute pertaining to transfer of land along the coast: The Gwadar Master Plan allocated 581 acres of land of the navy (Pak Bahria) land to the Gwadar port authority. The Pak Bahria, however, was unwilling to part with ownership of the land or even follow the Balochistan government's directive to instead transfer an equivalent amount of land elsewhere in the area to the port authority. Babar Khan Ghauri Minister for Shipping, notified the Prime Minister of the case and created a committee to resolve the issue; the Baloch Minister of Treasury Mir Asim Kurd told the host that the matter was a longstanding issue—the chief minister of Balochistan had been informed of it long ago, the land was prime for port and trading activities and currently the lease file was missing from the navy annals.

14. Land Mafia Grabbing Billions Worth of Land from Cottage Industries
    <http://www.youtube.com/watch?v=_hCVWgoAtUE&feature=related>

The clip is from Samaa TV. It affirms that the city government's allotted 468 acres of
land in Baldia's Ittehad Town, for cottage industries. Once construction work began on
site, the land mafia protested, created havoc and began illegal construction, in response
to which the city government launched an operation and razed the structures. However,
the mafia began construction once again and this time carried on through the night
and now apparently the city government is hesitant to stop them and has yet to launch
another operation.

15. Land Grabbing Proof: Sohrab Goth and surroundings are grabbed by ANP
    <http:/www.youtube.com/watch?v=_iXbV5pP9JE&feature=related%3e>

This is a silent video taken while driving through Sohrab Goth and surrounding areas,
showing areas that have been grabbed with examples of illegal construction; and also
showing the trucks, tankers and heavy machinery that contributed to the land grabbing.

16. Police Operation Against Land Mafia on National Highway
    <http://www.youtube.com/watch?v=QdIgWTQ58hA&feature=related>

The report on Express News cites the police operation against the land mafia and
reclamation of land from the mafia along National Highway near Soomar Jokhio Goth
police station, where there are numerous encroachments. More than 24 people including
women were arrested as a result. The police managed to rid the land of encroachers and
razed illicit structures to the ground and in response the people became violent and
attacked the police.

17. Land Grabbing in Pak Colony Using Arms Against Police/Rangers
    <http://www.youtube.com/watch?v=3If_Ixc9opU&feature=related>

Zille Haider of Geo News reports on a land ownership dispute between two groups and
the consequent exchange of fire in Pak Colony, near the Old Golimar/Gutter Baghicha in
Karachi. Members of the two groups forcefully occupied the roofs of apartment buildings
in the area, whereby they exchanged fire on each other and also shot at the rangers and
police when they attempted to enter the area.

18. Terrorists Land Mafia of Karachi Supported by ANP
    <http://www.youtube.com/watch?v=hubBd2LOWrY&feature=related>

The clip from Express News reports on the forced encroachment on the rooftops of
residential flats in Gulistan-e-Jauhar (Rabia City Block 11 & 13) that was responsible for
gunfire that lasted throughout the night leaving one dead. The police in the area declined
to comment whereas residents were too scared to leave their homes. The area has faced
consistent violence over the past year. The residents have complained to all levels of the
government and claim that the government and the assembly are not giving the issue
enough attention.
    The DG of Karachi, Javed Hanif, encountered firing in Sohrab Goth a few days prior
to the report whilst the reporter claims that often gunfire continues throughout the night

in Gulistan-e-Jauhar, Orangi, Landhi, Korangi, Hasan Square, and North Nazimabad, only to pause for the day.

19. Gutter Baghicha, Parts 1 and 2
    <http://www.youtube.com/watch?v=PJXSg7WkhFY;>
    <http://www.youtube.com/watch?v=OokvKHrVRos>

Filmed by independent filmmaker Mahera Omar for the NGO Shehri-CBE, this is the story of colonial amenity plot Gutter Baghicha originally spanning over 1,000 acres. It was a sewage/fruit-bearing farm, more than half of which has been progressively encroached upon and polluted by its own caretakers (the KMC/CDGK and the SITE Town administration) for illicit housing, factories and *katchi abadis*, as well as by a peripheral graveyard. The film expounds on evidence gained from interviews with Amber Alibhai (Shehri-CBE), Mir Husseyn Ali (environment and alternate energy department), Roland De Souza (Shehri-CBE), Liaquat Ali (EDO, CDGK), Saeed Ghani (opposition leader, CDGK), the late Nisar Baloch (prominent social activist, head of NGOs Alliance and Gutter Baghicha Bachao Tehreek) and residents of the area.

20. One man stand against MQM the Real Land Mafia of Karachi
    <http://www.youtube.com/watch?v=SNN0_NqxmSU&feature=related>

The video, uploaded by an independent Youtube user, is a montage of the events leading to and the circumstances of the death of prominent social activist Nisar Baloch, head of NGOs alliance and Gutter Baghicha Bachao Tehreek on 7 November 2011. It illustrates evidence through news clippings, showing Baloch to have held a press meeting the day before his death, clearly stating that the MQM would kill him. It was MQMs Burns' Road unit that had been delegated the responsibility of Baloch's assassination. He was shot dead riding his motorbike the next morning. He played an active role in protesting against the illegal encroachment of Gutter Baghicha, a colonial amenity plot.

21. Land Mafia in Karachi (Kidney Hill)
    <http://www.youtube.com/watch?v=TWcJpSoJY7E&feature=related>

The report submitted by Hassam Khan of Samaa TV narrates the story of Kidney Hill/Ahmed Ali Park/Faluknuma. The Karachi Union Cooperative Housing Society, government of Pakistan, government of Sindh and the CDGK divided the park into five parts whereby 35 of the 60 odd acres were granted to the Overseas' Cooperative Housing Society, roughly a few acres to the intended park and of the 18 acres originally marked out only 1 acre was allotted for the water reservoir. Opposition to the case received serious threats and they eventually backed away. In an interview, the managing director of the Water Board has accepted the new land allotment. The partisan case of Kidney Hill is further illustrated through interviews with Mustafa Kamal (the then mayor of Karachi), Sharif Baijee (OCHS Incharge), Roland De Souza (Shehri-CBE), and the case lawyer.

22. The Take Over of Karachi City Parks by the Land Mafia
    <http://www.youtube.com/watch?v=NHVll_QXaxg>

This is a slide show compiled by Shehri-CBE outlining the reality of Karachi's ever growing parasite: land grabbing, its key factors and players, as well as Shehri's own involvement in the case along with possible solutions to the problem. The research on the subject is largely supported by Google Earth/satellite images of parks in North Nazimabad that have been encroached upon by the land mafia between 2004 and 2009.

23. Gutter Baghicha—Paradise Looted
    <http://www.youtube.com/watch?v=8DsDalsL81c>

This is a slide show compiled by Shehri-CBE outlining the story of Gutter Baghicha: its history, its importance, the multiple abuses, the encroachments and the consequential struggle to re-establish this vast amenity plot dating back to the colonial period. Solutions to the issue as well as possibilities for the future are also delved in to.

24. Benaqab Builder Mafia, Parts 1, 2 and 3
    <http:/www.youtube.com/watch?v=6CXb7afR8yQ>
    <http:/www.youtube.com/watch?v=YFGnYFlK2Rs&feature=related>
    <http:/www.youtube.com/watch?v=JDuut4ODcmI&feature=related>

This is an episode from a series called '*Benaqab*' on Aaj TV, a show that aims to expose the frauds that Pakistani citizens have to deal with. This episode addresses the issue of land grabbing in Karachi and focuses on the case of Mehmood and Amber Anwer's story. The couple paid a total of Rs. 825,000 to Al-Asar Builders for a flat in Sanober Heights, located in Gulshan-e-Maymar. Regardless of additional payments made outside the set schedule time and again, they faced an FIR charge based on the last illicit payment not being made. Al-Asar scammed them on paper and insofar has managed to get away with it. The reporters for *Benaqab* have clearly shown clauses that have been blatantly violated. The builders even went so far as to steal the couple's kitchen and toilet fittings.

KBCA's Qazi Mumtaz denied giving the TV team an interview and claimed there was much illicit activity on the part of both the builders and the buyers, although they are meant to provide full assistance to any party interested in buying/making a home in the city. Officers at the KBCA are caught on camera stating that citizens almost always end up getting scammed, yet to date KBCA allows advertisements of illegitimate, uncertified buildings in the media, thus facilitating scams on the general public.

It was further deduced that the KESC is connected with the building scams: Ashraf Hassan, Estate Manager KESC North Nazimabad, says KESC favours the builder in cases where the buyer has not signed an agreement for the builder to provide electricity: thus saving money for the builder as they needn't connect meters and consequently the KESC comes down harder on citizens for stealing electricity via *kundaa*.

25. City by the Sea: The Future of Karachi's Coastline
    <https://www.youtube.com/watch?v=kzI80WqAzB0>

Filmed for Getz Pharma and Shehri-CBE by independent filmmaker Mahera Omar, this is the story of the environmentally and also otherwise damaging development along Karachi's 75 km long coastline and those that it affects. The issues are illustrated with the help of 3d animations and interviews with Fehmida Firdous (Sindh wildlife department), Arif Hasan (Architect), Parween Rahman (Director, Orangi Pilot Project), Abdul Ghani (Councillor Kakapir Village), Tahir Qureishi (World Conservation Union, IUCN), Ahmer Ali Rizvi (Birdwatchers' Club of Pakistan), Durriya Kazi (owner of a Beach hut), Mohammed Ali Shah (Chairperson, Pakistan Fisherfolk Forum), Aziz Agha

(Conservationist), Mir Hussain Ali (Sindh Environmental Protection Agency), Babar Ali (WWF Pakistan), and Mohammed Hussain (Mahigeer Tehreek).

The film discusses the urban sprawl and rampant land reclamation projects being carried out by the DHA and government agencies that block natural drainage channels of Karachi and negatively affect oceanographic communities, whilst being in direct violation of the law. These are spurred on by corruption and greed whereby the flora and fauna, the fishing communities, the general public, and land owning agencies are the ones to pay for it. The mass deforestation of the mangroves is leaving the coast vulnerable to tsunamis and cyclones whilst destroying homes of migratory birds; settlements along and the narrowing of the Malir and Lyari Rivers (along with the enormous waste load of 400,000 strong dairy farms in Landhi) add to the industrial and urban pollution being emptied in the sea, the huts along the beaches eat away breeding places of already endangered turtles and other marine life whereas one-dimensional corporate skyscraper developments, some of which have been successfully sidelined (such as Sugarland City), further marginalize the fishing communities living along the coast and islands; all this whilst Karachi's three sewerage treatment plants are grossly underutilized. The late Parween Rahman, of the OPP, claims a long-term, highly affordable solution for Karachi's drainage/sewerage problems is available—one, which the government is not yet willing to pursue.

# Appendix 3

## Methodology of Compiling and Analysing Press Clippings (Land Research)

The press writings in Pakistan often contain reports, stories and editorials about urban development related issues in Karachi. The electronic media also gives great importance to such issues. The media is a major opinion builder not only for the public but also for the federal and provincial establishments. Therefore, it was considered necessary to mention the land related issues raised by the media in the last ten years in a coherent form.

The Urban Resource Centre (URC) Karachi is one of the leading resource and urban knowledge management institution of Karachi. It was been compiling news items since 1989 from *The News* (English), the daily *Dawn* (English), the *Jang* (Urdu), and the *Daily Times* (English). It was decided to acquire land related news items from the URC for the years 2001–2010. These news items consist of five thousand and sixty-two (5062) news clippings.

After collecting the above-mentioned news clippings together, they were numbered year wise and each one was read. Subsequently, a date wise Excel sheet of those clippings was constructed. The columns, in the Excel sheet were developed to encompass i) Serial number; ii) Date; iii) The name of the newspaper; iv) Caption; v) Punch line (meaning essence of the news item); and vi) Key words representing the subject/main issue of the clippings.

Those key words were filtered into the Excel Sheet as a result of which different categories of the news items were clubbed together. After which the news items were read again subject wise. As a result 72 categories were identified. That was too large a number for making a reasonable analysis. To overcome the constraints six main categories were identified. Those are given below:

1. Land Acquisition
2. Land Development
3. Land Use Changes
4. Land Disputes
5. Land Disasters
6. Money Matters

On further reading of the main categories, subcategories against each were identified. The main categories with subcategories are given below:

1. Land Acquisition

   1.1  Allotment
   1.2  Encroachment
   1.3  Regularization
   1.4  Auction
   1.5  Real Estate
   1.6  Lease
   1.7  Booking

2. Land Development

   2.1  Construction
   2.2  Development
   2.3  Housing facilities/amenities
   2.4  Loans
   2.5  Lease
   2.6  Civic amenities
   2.7  Town planning
   2.8  Housing schemes
   2.9  Land utilization

3. Land Use Changes

   3.1  Conversion
   3.2  Reclassification of plots
   3.3  Auction
   3.4  Demolition
   3.5  Relocation
   3.6  Transfer
   3.7  Eviction
   3.8  Commercialization
   3.9  Illegal construction
   3.10 Heritage conversion

4. Land Disputes

   4.1  Court orders
   4.2  Land grabbing
   4.3  Legislations
   4.4  Murders
   4.5  Riots
   4.6  Katchi abadi/informal settlements
   4.7  Conflict between actors

5. Land Disasters

   5.1  Demolition
   5.2  Collapse of buildings
   5.3  Disaster
   5.4  Commercialization

6. Money Matters

   6.1  Revenue
   6.2  Taxes
   6.3  Other monetary issues

After that the colossal work of reading each and every clipping and writing the summary was undertaken. This produced an enormous amount of paper work running over 400 pages. This was considered unpublishable and so an exercise was undertaken to identify trends and club the trends together in fact sheets under the relevant, respective heading as listed in the six main headings above.

Questions raised by the Researchers:

The persons working on the clippings project have also expressed their view that proper reporting on Karachi is difficult because of a lack of easily available information for use by journalists. To make better sense of the clippings, the researchers felt that the following issues need to be addressed through more and better data.

A. Statistics

1.  Percentage comparison of people in owned houses as compared to people living in rented houses, in Karachi. Comparative land configuration: Goths, residential, commercial, apartments, cantonments/DHA.
2.  Water, sewerage, electricity and gas supply provisions at a glance—according to the spatial and economic stratification of city.
3.  A time line of increase in land price, and rentals and what relation it has with a) the rise of the middle class, rural urban migration, 9/11, increased women mobility, nuclear family system, and remittances.
4.  Average distance and time travelled for middle, working, and upper classes to the job place?
5.  How many residential units are converted to *madrasahs* (religious seminaries)?
6.  The official criteria for demolition of an area?
7.  List of relocations over the last ten years.
8.  How much government land has been transferred to private hands in the last ten years?
9.  List of major evictions in the last ten years.
10.  Names of police stations that have occupied public land.
11.  List of regularized buildings over the last ten years.
12.  List of heritage building

B. Policies

13.  What is the national policy on *katchi abadis*?
14.  What is the land allotment policy?
15.  What is the retrieval (encroachment) policy?
16.  What is the land commercialization policy?
17.  What is the policy for green belts?
18.  What is the national housing policy?

C. Laws and Legislations

19.  What is the Colonization of Government Land (Sindh) Act 1912?
20.  What is the Sindh Regularization and Control Ordinance 2002?
21.  What is the Sindh Public Property (removal of encroachment) Bill 2010?
22.  What is the Illegal Dispossession Act?
23.  What is the Disposal of Urban Land Ordinance 2002?
24.  What is the Quaid-e-Azam Mazar Protection and Maintenance Ordinance?
25.  What happened to the idea of Real Estate Investment Trust for real estate exponential hike control?
26.  What is the Sindh Katchi Abadi Amendment Bill 2009?

D. Housing Programs

27.  What was the HBFC 'Sponsor a Shelter Program'?
28.  What is the Peoples Housing Scheme?
29.  What is the Mera Ghar Scheme of Nawaz Sharif?
30.  Can we develop a list of housing schemes in last 10 years?

E.  What happened to the following cases?

31.  Anwar Shah Goth
32.  Rasool Shah Colony
33.  Jhoojhar Case
34.  GM Village Ghagar Phattak
35.  Jumma Goth
36.  Liaquat Colony
37.  Zakaria Jokhio Village Gadap Town
38.  Mullah Essa Brohi Goth
39.  Gulshan-e-Mazdoor
40.  Mubarak Village
41.  Mororo Graveyard

F.  What are the details of the following troubled schemes/projects?

42.  Scheme-33
43.  Hawksbay Scheme-42
44.  Malir Housing Scheme
45.  Saima Trade Towers II Chundrigar Road
46.  Medina Gardens
47.  Sabzi Mandi
48.  Bhopal House Case
49.  Hindu Gymkhana
50.  Khadija Manzil Tragedy
51.  Dolmen Mall—SEPA reservations
52.  Forty Villages at Bin Qasim
53.  Al-Najeebi electronic market case
54.  Clifton Cross case
55.  Oak Towers Case
56.  Army Housing Scheme over the land that belongs to National Stadium

G.  How do the following factors affect land-use?

57.  Functional pressures
58.  Variance in land price
59.  Change in population
60.  Gender relationships
61.  Environmental factors
62.  Trade/commerce and commercial activities
63.  Class immobility/mobility
64.  Incoming foreign investment
65.  Variance in religious expression
66.  Change in relationship between various sects and ethnicities and other religious groups
67.  Law and order and security situation
68.  Priorities of governance

It is envisaged that if information on the above issues is easily available then a more informed reporting and opinion can be expressed in the national print media.

This clippings work was conceptualized and supervised by Engr. Mansoor Raza and was carried out by Fatima Zaidi, then a student of Mass Communication Department at University of Karachi. Engineer Mansoor Raza can be contacted at <mansooraza@gmail.com> for further details and item wise soft copies of the Fact Sheets can be acquired from him on demand.

# Appendix 4

## The Gentrification of Karachi's Coastline
### (Paper for London Workshop towards an Emerging Geography of Gentrification in the Global South, 23–24 March 2012)

by Arif Hasan

### 1. Background

Karachi has a 27 kilometre long coastline in addition to numerous creeks and mangrove forests. Most of this coastline is dotted with ancient fishing villages. More than half of it is visited by hundreds of thousands of Karachiites every week for recreation and entertainment. After 1999, attempts at its gentrification through global capital and Dubai and Malaysia based real estate companies have been made. There is a background to this.

In 1999, through a military coup, General Musharraf dismissed the democratically elected government in Pakistan and became the country's chief executive. He appointed a chief vice executive of the Citibank as finance minister who in 2004 was appointed prime minister. He also appointed a very senior economist of the World Bank as the governor of the State Bank of Pakistan whose additional job was that of chairperson of the National Commission for Government Reforms. Another important World Bank person was appointed as the minister for finance, planning and development in Sindh province. In 2002, he was made federal minister for privatization and investment.

One of the first acts of the Musharraf government was to initiate local body reforms, replacing the old colonial system by elected mayors at the level of the district, sub-districts and city districts. The process known as 'devolution' led to the implementation of the provincial Local Body Ordinances. In Sindh, the province in which Karachi is located, the Sindh Local Government Ordinance (SLGO) was enforced and Karachi became an autonomous city government in 2001.

Its first mayor initiated a major signal-free road-building programme, complete with flyovers and underpasses. During his time, the federal government backed Lyari Expressway was also initiated, displacing over 200 thousand people. Civil society organizations and also the city planners had serious concerns regarding these initiatives. However, unlike earlier, the city planners were not the decision-makers. The programme remained modest due to the conservatism of the mayor.

With the election of the second mayor, things changed. He was 'dynamic' had international links and represented Karachi's main political party. The road building programme was expanded and projects for 'beautifying' Karachi were developed aggressively. New terms, seldom use before (such as world class city, investment friendly infrastructure, direct foreign investment, cities as engines of growth, privatization, golden handshake, 'build, operate and transfer', 'build, operate and own') entered the development and planning vocabulary. In addition, foreign companies started visiting Karachi and missions from IFIs also increased substantially. Due to all these new developments, projects replaced planning.

During the period of 1991–2006, Dubai based companies having multibillion dollar portfolios entered into negotiations with the government of Pakistan and other prospective private sector partners. These companies included Dubai World, Emaar, Limitless, and Nakheel. A profile of these companies and their work in Pakistan is given in their websites. As a result of the new culture that was projected, many beach development projects were proposed and some were carried out. In the following sections a brief description and civil society response to them are given.

2.  Defence Housing Authority (DHA), Waterfront Development Project

The DHA began as the Pakistan Defence Officers Housing Society. It consists of 3,530 hectares and is the most elite area of the city. It contains luxury apartments and homes, schools, colleges, clubs, posh shopping centres with designer boutiques, and five and six star hotels. Functioning of the Authority is vested in two bodies: the governing body, headed by the secretary of the ministry of defence and the executive board headed by the Karachi Corps Commander of the Pakistan army. The housing society also contains about 18 kilometres of coastline and creeks.

In 2002–3, the DHA built a promenade along a stretch of beach. It came to be known as Sea View. It was a major addition to recreation for the city of Karachi. As a result, people shifted from other beachfronts to it. Hawkers, jugglers, animal performers, camels and horses for riding, invaded it. The DHA was horrified for it wanted its beach to be used by 'decent people'. So, it banned all hawkers, performers and other persons serving the poorer sections of the population from the beachfront. It set up expensive food outlets along this stretch of beach. As a result, poor people stopped coming here. This stretch came to be known as the rich man's beach and a beach adjacent to it in the jurisdiction of the city government, where all activity was permitted, as the poor man's beach.

The Urban Resource Centre (URC) took up this issue by articles and letters in the press and the media also made it an important issue. Finally, the DHA resident society interviewed and made the DHA management relax the conditions they had imposed. Meanwhile, the city government developed the poor man's beach as a park and turned away all the hawkers and performers from there as well. However, they have come back at least as far as the entrances to the park and in the lanes next to it by informally paying the city government staff and officials.

However, in 2004, the DHA initiated another project. Its promotional literature described the project: 'In Karachi, DHA has a virgin, unspoiled waterfront of nearly 14 kilometres ready with full potential for development. ... The residents of Karachi will soon see a qualitative change in their lives and their concept of relaxation, style and fun. Fire of creativity and imagination is promising to make Karachi beachfront a much sought-after tourist destination in the foreseeable future. Entirely practical and wholly realizable projects will have a deep impact on the lifestyle of the people of Karachi whose perception of enjoying the sea at present consists of riding a camel or a horse or just taking a walk on the wet sand and watching the waves crash on the shore. They will soon have access to multiple recreational activities within their reach.'

The project also involved the 'reclamation of 74.5 acres of land for a high-end hotel complex', '5-star hotels owning private segments of the beach' and a 'private beach with lagoon for hotel and residential blocks'. It also included Emaar's 'Crescent Bay Project' with a 7-star hotel and 4,000 super luxury apartments with private beaches and lagoons. Civil society organizations argued that as a result of these developments, 20% of the beach will not be available to the public but even the remaining 80% that is meant to be available is beyond the disadvantaged and the poor's economic power to access.

Furthermore, civil society organizations had a number of other objections. They pointed out that the DHA project was a clear violation of the Doctrine of Public Trust principle, which guarantees public access to beaches even if they are privately owned. It was also a violation of Section 12 of the Environment Protection Act 1997 and also of the Pakistan Environment Protection Agency Regulations 2000. It was also a violation of the Sindh Government Notification of May 1975 which prohibits the leasing of land within the area of the ports or seashore limits. A project of this magnitude must also undergo environmental assessment under the laws (as beaches are included as 'sensitive areas'). And then, Article 9 of the Constitution about promoting the quality of life of all citizens is also violated as the project only promotes the wellbeing of those who can use and afford the facilities it is offering.

A number of environmental issues also surfaced, such as, development between the coastal roads and the Karachi beach comes in the way of the preservation of biodiversity as well as the natural environment. As a result, people will no longer be able to access the beach in its natural condition and will no longer be able to see the wildlife (especially during the winters).

Socio-economic issues also surfaced, such as, fishing communities will be deprived of their income and livelihoods; hawkers/jugglers/performers, etc. have already gotten replaced by expensive food outlets and after further development, the lower middle income groups will be further marginalized; and people with plots and houses along the beach will no longer be able to view the sea.

The DHA argued that the project will provide employment. Civil society organizations argued that a project of a different nature could also bring in profits and employment. The DHA also argued that *katchi abadis* would develop along the coast if this project was not initiated. Civil society organizations pointed out that this was unlikely as not an inch of land can be occupied without the connivance of the development agencies.

The media initially gave prominence to the negative aspects of the project but soon stopped focusing on it. Informally, one of the TV channels informed the chairperson URC that since Emaar's ads were a major source of revenue, they could not criticize Emaar's projects.

The civil society organizations involved in opposition to the project worked as a network. They were: Sahil Bachao, an organization consisting of prominent citizens including two retired judges of the Supreme Court of Pakistan. Shehri for a Better Environment, is a Karachi based NGO, popularly known as Shehri and has a long tradition of struggling for better governance and imposition of by-laws as well as building regulations pertaining to land use. Pakistan Fisherfolk Forum (PFF), it is a network of fishing communities. Mahigeer Tehreek, it is a network of fishing communities. Dharti, it is a civil society organization formed for promoting a better physical and social environment for Karachi and was created as a response to the three projects listed above. And Urban Resource Centre, which also collected 5,000 signatures opposing the project from low income areas and schools.

Civil society opposition consisted of court cases, forums, demonstrations, walks, and writings in the press and making of films. Finally, the project was suspended and the president presented the DHA beach as a 'gift' to the people of Karachi. However, Emaar's 2.4 billion dollar Crescent Bay project of 4,000 luxury apartments on reclaimed land continues.

## 3. Sugarland City

Sugarland city was initiated in 2006. It involved the development (privatization) of the city's public beaches at Hawksbay, Sandspit, Manora and Cape Monze. Around 26,000 hectares of land (size of Washington) with total investment of US$ 68 billion was to be given to Limitless, a Dubai based company launched by Dubai World. The 'new city' was to contain residential, commercial, recreational and entertainment facilities 'in state of the art, master-planned communities'.

A Memorandum of Understanding (MoU) was signed between Pakistan's minister of state for privatization and investment and the Dubai World chairman. At a high level meeting chaired by the prime minister on 24 June 2006, a number of important directives were given to different ministries including those of ports and shipping, defence, as well as the Government of Sindh. It was decided that that a premature cancellation of leases would take place as individuals have huts located there, which are given to them on lease. It was also decided that there should be a proper mechanism for shifting the navy and cantonment board's facilities located at Manora to the navy land at Cape Monze to make vacant land available to Limitless.

The main opposition to the project came from the Pakistan Mahigeer Tahreek (the Movement of the Indigenuous Coastal Fisherfolk Communities of Pakistan). They produced a position letter referring to the project as 'Development to Destroy Nature and Displace People' (September 2007). The letter was an outcome of consultations with various stakeholders especially local communities. The letter pointed out that the project posed a threat to the ecosystem since Hawkesbay, which was being built over, was a major breeding point of the green turtle. In addition, the Sandspit back waters contain mangroves (which the project would destroy) and which are the resting place to migratory birds and serve as a nursery for shrimp and several fish species. Also, mangrove products are used as fodder and fuel by local fishing communities.

The letter also pointed out that fishing communities have been living on the coast for centuries and that the project will have far reaching impacts on their livelihood since their survival is dependent on subsistence fishing and beach related leisure activities. More than a hundred villages were coming within the project area and their future had not been even mentioned in the project proposal. One thing was certain that even if these villages survived, they would have no access to the sea. In addition, the letter pointed out that no details have been given regarding compensating and benefiting the affected local communities and that given past records one cannot expect the government for fulfilling its promises.

The letter also mentioned that lower and lower middle income Karachiites will no longer be able to go to the beaches in search of recreation and entertainment and this will increase the divide between the rich and poor in the city.

The letter and consultations were followed up by public demonstrations and a systematic press campaign. Meetings were also held with the chief secretary Sindh, in which various land departments who had been asked to surrender their lands to the project were also invited along with prominent civil society individuals. The URC's position that the interests of the four stakeholders in this dispute should be respected was also endorsed. These stakeholders were the flora and fauna of the coast and its creeks, fishing communities, lower and lower middle income groups who use the beaches for recreation and entertainment, and the land owning individuals and agencies.

Because of opposition from all segments of society, Limitless backed out of the project in 2009.

4. Sale of Islands for Development of Diamond Bar City

The other mega project was the proposal for the building of the Diamond Bar City. Port Qasim Authority (PQA) had decided to sell two of the islands under its control (Bundal and Buddo) to Emaar (one of the world's largest real estate companies). The islands measure about 4,800 hectares and were to be sold for US$ 42 billion. Access to the islands can only occur by boat. At one point a US$ 50 million bridge was proposed by the federal government connecting the islands to DHA. A Memorandum of Understanding was signed between PQA officials, Irfanullah Marwat (representing the Sindh Government) and Emaar representatives. PQA planned to develop a mega project in collaboration with Emaar which aimed to develop 15,000 housing units and commercial facilities. The project also involved the construction of residential, commercial and leisure real estate projects, industrial park, free trade zones and port terminals at an estimated cost of US$ 43 billion within 13 years.

This project drew the strongest response from the Fisherfolk Forum, World-wild Life Fund, and fishing communities from all over the province. The WWF pointed out that the Indus delta is the fifth largest delta in the world and these islands are protected under international commitment as Pakistan since 1976 has been a signatory to the Ramsar Convention, which is focused on the conservation of Wetlands. Wetlands were also described by WWF as being 'environmentally sensitive' zones and any development in them should be subject to assessments under the Pakistan Environmental Protection Act of 1997. The other issues raised by WWF included the fact that the Pakistan Poverty Reduction Strategy Paper and the Sindh Government Medium Term Development Framework talk about a commitment to improve natural ecosystems by increasing forest cover but the contrary will happen as the islands are developed and that the sea is already polluted with 300 MGD (million gallons daily) of the city's untreated waste and construction of the new city would further pollute the waters, causing great threat to marine life.

There was also a general agreement between all stakeholders that the destruction of the mangroves on the islands would have seriously repercussions for fishermen since most of fish life that they exploited was born in these mangroves. Statements that man-made forest plantation would compensate for the destruction of the mangroves were ridiculed by the ecologists.

Heritages issues were also raised. The 10th century tomb of Yousuf Shah, the patron saint of the fishermen of Sindh, is located on one of the islands and there is a huge gathering with music and dancing at his tomb every year. Thousands of fishermen with their boats from all over Sindh gather on the occasion.

The islands lie on the mouth of Korangi Creek near the open sea and the fishing villages lie further inland along the creek. Fishermen use the passage between the islands to the open sea for their fishing trips which number hundreds within a day. They feared that this movement would be disrupted depriving tens of thousands of persons of livelihood. In addition, the two islands form a joint property where thousands of fishermen dry their catch, clean their nets and camp during the fishing season.

The Korangi Creek fishing villages also receive boat hands and fishermen from all over Sindh who come seeking employment during the fishing season. As such, the opponents to the project claimed that the development would result in poverty and hunger among 8 million members of the fishermen community, who have been historic inhabitants of the coast and traditionally earning their livelihood along the coast.

The PFF convened a number of meetings to discuss the sale of the islands and invited the media, prominent citizens, academia and NGOs to them. It also observed hunger strikes at the press clubs of Sindh cities. It also convened an All Parties Conference (inviting representatives of all Pakistan political parties) and presented its findings and concerns to them. In January 2007, the PFF observed a black day and a shutter down strike throughout Sindh in collaboration with political parties and civil society organizations.

It is not clear why the project did not go through. However, in private conversations politicians and bureaucrats say that they were afraid of a province wide agitation by the fishermen community against the project.

## 5.  Port Grand Karachi

The Native Jetty Bridge was built by the British in the 1850s. It linked the island of Keamari where the port is, to the Karachi main line. In the decade of the 1990's, a new bridge (Jinnah Bridge), linked to a number of flyovers was built parallel to the Native Jetty bridge, which as a result, was abandoned.

From the time the Native Jetty Bridge was built, it served also as a place for gatherings and various cultural activities. 'Common' people sat at the edge and watched the water. Boys jumped off it to swim. Older men fished while sitting at its edge. The water catered to a number of religious superstitions; fish were fed, birds were released from cages, trysts were consolidated and many religious processions terminated at the water edge. Old religious manuscripts were also ceremoniously given to the water. After the construction of the Jinnah Bridge these activities continued at the Native Jetty Bridge.

However, in 2003, the bridge was taken over by the Grand Leisure Corporation. As a result, all the popular activities shifted to the Jinnah Bridge. Meanwhile, the Grand Leisure Corporation have constructed Port Grand Project on the Native Jetty Bridge. 'The project is a food, shopping and entertainment complex which has been built with over Rs. 1 billion investment by Grand Leisure Corporation. Port Grand project is a 13-acre world-class facility that has been designed and built in collaboration with top international architects and designers who employed the latest technology and building techniques to deliver a state of the art facility. About 40 outlets are being made operational at this stage while more outlets would be opened soon. The entry fee for the Port Grand would be Rs. 300 per person out of which Rs. 200 would be redeemable at different food outlets and shops inside the project. The native jetty bridge has been entirely rebuilt to ensure a world-class tourist destination and a source of pride for Karachites that would ultimately attract millions of people from all over the country and beyond. Visitors would come to Port Grand not only for food and entertainment but for over a hundred different concepts at port grand that includes free wifi, port bazaar, bookstore, florist, art lane, gift and antiques etc. Parking for over eight hundred cars with complimentary valet service, and pristine public restrooms and plenty of pedestrian friendly walkways are additional attractions at the project. Port Grand is also one of the first projects in the city that has been dedicated to building an open eco-friendly environment, with special focus on urban regeneration. Port Grand is going to be a model for lot of good to be followed in the city.' (Source: <*forum.xcitefun. net/port-grand-karachi-food-street-t63136.html*>Cached)

Politicians, middle classes, elite and the media are all full of praise for Port Grand. Various Karachi websites are very appreciative of it. However, Jinnah Bridge looks down onto Port Grand. As a result, poor people on the bridge while carrying on their various 'cultural activities' could look into Port Grand which also hosts fashion shows. It was felt that Port Grand should be protected from such voyeurs and so barriers were built on either side of Jinnah Bridge making the populist activities that took place there, impossible. So far, no protests against this discontinuation of popular activities have been registered.

## 6.  Role of Architects

Architects and planners have played an important role in developing a very large number of anti-poor projects. I have advocated (without success) an oath for architects and planners, something similar to the Hippocratic oath for the medical profession. The theory being that the Council of Architects should be deregister anyone that violates this oath. In 1983, I took such an oath.

'*I will not do projects that will irreparably damage the ecology and environment of the area in which they are located; I will not do projects that increase poverty, dislocate people and destroy the tangible and intangible cultural heritage of communities that live in the city; I will not do projects that destroy multi-class public space and violate building byelaws and zoning regulations; and I will always object to insensitive projects that do all this, provided I can offer viable alternatives.*'

I have kept my words. I feel that if 20 other prominent architects had taken a similar oath in 1983 and stuck to it, Karachi would have been a different city.

# Appendix 5
## Interviews with Persons Involved in Real Estate Business and Transactions

**INTERVIEW—01: JUNAID KHAN (DEVELOPER)**

Director Al-Adil Builders, project: Momal Pride. Interviewed in his site office on 21 July 2011.

*New Karachi Town is in the northernmost part of the Karachi, located between the Lyari River, Mangho Pir Hills and two major roads (Surjani Road to the north, Shahrah-e-Zahid Husseyn to the south). Gadap Town lies along its north and west boundaries and Gulberg Town and North Nazimabad Town on the south. In the 1998 census the population of New Karachi Town was estimated to be more than 680,000 people, 99% of whom are Muslim Muhajirs.*

1. Momal Pride is a seven storeyed residential project located near the Power House, New Karachi. The project was approved by the Karachi Building Control Authority (KBCA) and Rs. 150,000 were paid as a bribe to the KBCA to obtain the approval letter. Junaid mentioned that the project would be 25% cheaper if it weren't for the invisible money he was obliged to pay the relevant government agencies.

2. Junaid claims that the land was allotted to his grandfather by the court as compensation. Khan ran a business of earth moving equipment and to prove his financial credentials mentioned that his earth moving equipment is involved in the Reko-Deq project in Balochistan, though some of the equipment was blasted by Baloch separatists.

3. Momal Pride has a total of 52 flats. The flats are categorized according to covered area and are specified as Super Classic and Ultra Classic. Super Classic flats offer two bedrooms (11.0' x 13.6' each) and a living room (11.0' X 16.6'). Ultra Classics cost Rs. 8.5 million and their covered area is less than that of Super Classics.

4. Although only three floors have been constructed thus far, all the flats have been booked—except for a few on the 5th Floor. His emphasis on this fact illustrated the roaring demand for flats in the area.

5. To book a flat, the requirements are a copy of the buyer's NIC and upfront payment of the booking amount. The buyer is required to pay Rs. 1.1 million with a flexi payment schedule (HBFC loan) of Rs. 1.0 million: a total cash payment of Rs. 2.1 million. There are additional hidden charges pertaining to documentation and facilities equivalent to Rs. 400,000 whereby the amount comes to Rs. 2.5 million. There are extra charges for specificities: a flat with a corner location, a flat open to

the west whereas the flats facing the road are the highest priced. After the payment of four instalments, an allotment order is to be issued to the buyer and the lease granted after full payment is received.

6. Buyers can apply for a loan from the (HBFC). All payments are made in the name of Al-Adil Builders, the ultimate recipient of most loans connected with this project.

7. The interest rate is 13% and approval for the loan depends on the age of the applicant and the loan repayment period.Buyers are required to pay additional sums of money for water, electricity and gas connections, amounting to Rs. 150,000. Al-Adil Builders will be responsible for the provision of utilities. Economies of scale affect the business: Junaid claims if there were 500 flats in the project, the current amount would be reduced to one tenth of the total Rs. 150,000 for each buyer.

8. It was mentioned that it would take another two years to complete the project.

Further Discussion:

1. Why is there such a huge demand for flats? The issues connecting the demand for flats to the nucleus unit family concept; increased consumption; emerging middle class/gender *glasnost* and the aspirations of today's youth need to be established.

2. Why is this particular belt of the Power House area ridden with flats?

3. What are the terms and conditions for buyers? Are they open and transparent or hidden for future manoeuvring? None of the builders shared any substantial information concerning terms and conditions with the researchers.

4. What made people trust those builders?

5. Money is the connecting chord amongst all the players. What is the percentage per player? Is it possible to make a pie chart of the findings?

## INTERVIEW—02: MR NURUDDIN

Ex-developer now Adviser to Chairman, Institute of Engineers Pakistan, Karachi. Interviewed on 15 August 2011.

Mr Nuruddin, advisor to the Chairman of the Institute of Engineers Pakistan, was one of the founding members of the Association of Builders and Developers (ABAD). He graduated from college in 1956 and started work with a German company in Karachi. In 1974 he began work as a developer.

Development of Pakistan's Construction Industry and the Birth of ABAD:

• Zulfikar Ali Bhutto's era made three previously coveted, inaccessible commodities available to all Pakistanis: the passport, the driver's license and the telephone line. These in addition to his Middle East Policy sparked the housing boom in the 1970s—owing largely to the availability of cash within the *diaspora* working in various Gulf countries. These Pakistanis pooled together their advance salaries' money to return to Pakistan and buy land. At that time, for example, Gulshan-e-Iqbal was introduced as a housing scheme and KDA being the sole building regulation authority registered both construction companies and sellers in the area, whilst providing incentives for buyers. Resultantly, it rapidly developed. Nazimabad and North Karachi followed suit soon after, along the same pattern.

- At the time only those who were registered with the KDA got a package consisting of, subsidized land and bridge financing facilities in addition to patronage. All construction was time bound but builders usually got an extension, overbooking was an unheard of occurrence and business was fair, prosperous and guided by ethics. There were strong concepts of education and certification within the builders' community and everyone abided by the due process.

- It was around this time that the educated elite entered the profession— in sharp contrast to today's contractor phenomenon—and as similar people came together, ABAD was founded. In the times when there was a shortage of cement. ABAD was allocated a quota for further distribution amongst its members. Meanwhile, HBFCL used to provide bridge financing to the company and its own criteria had fewer restrictions. ABAD had a very good reputation, known to meticulously follow laws and regulations, until the tenure of Nizami Saheb in the 1980s.

- It was the result of four buildings including Mashadi Square, Rimpla Plaza and one block of the Mimar building falling that caused the government to institute the Sindh Building Control Authority (SBCA). For a while, the SBCA provided the moral standard for Karachi's construction industry. However, following consecutive cases of buildings falling, KDA passed a law whereby 5% of the total cost of construction was to be submitted as a security deposit in cases of maintenance and/or accident. ABAD managed to get this charge excused for its members.

Corruption: Past and Present

- In the 1950s, friends of Mr Nuruddin who worked in customs were actually embarrassed because they owned automobiles, so they parked their cars at a distance and came to meet him by bus. Although as early as the 1960s and 1970s the ministry of industry was notorious for ill practices, no one took pride in corruption.

- Up till the 1970s the closest one got to corruption was the concept of *bakhsheesh*, where one party would pay another a mere fraction in good will– usually called *chaai paani*—literally translated as tea and water.

- Corruption was at the individual and not the institutional level.

- Over the last two to three decades, however, the situation has undergone a paradigm change. A lot of people from other backgrounds came into this lucrative business and with them came the practice of overbooking, post-dated cheques and overheads' charging.

- There were a number of examples Mr Nuruddin highlighted:

  → Husseyn Bhai of Husseyn Electric who built the landmark *Do Talwaar* roundabout in Clifton is a glaring case in point. Although a very intelligent man, he was not known for following rules and regulation or even the plans that he got approved by the KDA.

→  The commercialization of Khalid bin Waleed Road is an example where builders and developers made deals under the table with the controlling authority personnel and legalized all illicit actions, at least on paper.

→  Jam Sadiq Ali increased the cost of land from Rs. 20 to Rs. 80 per square foot and made predated allotments and requisites. The difference of Rs. 60 was supposed to be distributed in three equal shares: Rs. 20 for party fund, Rs. 20 for Jam Sadiq Ali and Rs. 20 for builders. ABAD after discussion decided it could not afford the same and the company's worst fears that these measures would be construed as corruption came true when after 1977 Martial Law investigations were initiated against such practices.

→  In 1983, ABAD negotiated with the Steel Mill for the construction of 15,000 houses. Mimar was the chief negotiator and construction was to be completed in 3 phases. 19 ABAD member companies were involved. In phase one, 7,500 houses were completed but when the government changed this three year project became a 13 year project and once phase two was completed the remaining plots were sold off.

→  Chawla and Company started in the sewing machine business and ended up being the builders of Seaview. They were the first company to be thrown out of ABAD.

→  Rufi Builders' were originally car dealers. They got a showroom situated across from Dawood College. Here people used to come to invest in the cars they sold and in return they made easy money on commissions without investing in anything, simply acting as middlemen.

→  Al-Azam, Mr Nuruddin says, was the leader in corruption in the 1980s—soon after, the rest followed.

•  With respect to corruption and quality, the greatest blow to Karachi's construction industry was the advent of the cloth market traders. These people had made a lot of money fromlending huge amounts to people at exorbitant rates sans collateral. They knew how to conduct business and optimally manipulate finances, but they had no idea and nor were they interested to learn of the technical know-how required in the construction business.

Their mode of operation was to get the most amount of work done in the least amount of time, allowing for all sorts of shortcuts leading to quick results. Bills of quantities and costing per square foot were decided prior to the design or construction of any project, where the cloth market traders calculated and controlled the *reti bajri* allowance. They also propagated the heightened status of the middleman since all relevant architectural engineering, the same person did police and legal work—they considered that less people involved was equivalent to fewer overheads. Subsequently, the calculations of strength and durability were disregarded whilst monetary advantage was continually accrued by removing what was perceived as overheads—all at the cost of greater risks to the inhabitants of the buildings. Incidentally, a close relationship simultaneously grew between the cloth market traders and the KBCA, and the duo eventually knocked out all other competition.

This process of simplification consumed by lack of occupational expertise gave rise to the contractors' phenomenon that the Pakistani architectural and construction industries have largely succumbed to today. In conclusion, their methods ended up changing the system altogether.

- Another major and probably connected reason for the meteoric rise in corruption was the Afghan War of the 1980s, within which General Zia ul-Haq had deeply involved Pakistan. Enormous amounts of money filtered into the economy through smuggling and trafficking of heroin and other drugs' as well as arms and ammunition.
- This money spurred the construction trade since—especially for the cloth market traders and these contraband traffickers—construction was the best source to whiten all their black money.
- It's a good question when one asks 'Why was the corruption not controlled in time?' The answer remains, when someone is in such a position where he has one of two choices, i.e., send the corrupt individual to jail or partake himself in what there is on offer; more often than not, it was the second choice that person opted for, thus linking one perpetrator to another, which today completes a (gargantuan) chain of corruption.

Consequences and Rectifications:

- Discretionary powers are destroying people.
- Today the demand for land is increasing and the only land available is in DHA, where construction is only allowed up to the first floor and which limits the scope of developers in the city. *Also, since land within the city is unavailable, the illegal conversion of amenity plots is rampant.* None of the infrastructure agencies can provide connections and services without approval of the registrar and thus all parties have their due share in corruption. ABAD too, is highly corrupt, but one cannot blame the members, as they are business people for whom business interests and concerns overshadow all other obligations.
- To clean the mess, professionals should get more involved. Today there are 12,000 members in ABAD and the organization is trying to put impersonal systems in place as personalized interactions breed corruption. ABAD is of the opinion that self-cleansing is required for which honest people are needed. Technology should also be taken advantage of in communicating the honest lobby, which will be generated, by honest voices and correct information about the systems in place.

Further Discussion:

1. Players with extra cash in hand used to came into the construction business as land was available and for other reasons. Now with land shrinking in Karachi city two questions arise: One, where they will invest that amount in future? Two, in the current economic setup who are the new money holders who have that kind of money available with them?

2. Can we conclude from the above that ABAD has actually developed a closed liaison with drug pushers or drug smugglers have taken over ABAD? If yes, than how can IEP improve the 'systems'?

3. Can we also conclude that conversion of amenity plots in the city will go unabated? In the scheme of things what is the role of judiciary and court rulings?

4. How far can civil society organizations (such as Shehri) fight this war, as hefty amounts of various players are at stake? Or they will civil society organizations be reduced to just whistle blowers?

## INTERVIEW—03: RAO MUHAMMAD MAZAHAR (DEVELOPER)

Rao Mega City, Karachi. Interviewed on 6 October 2011.

- We belong to Galantra Village in District Karnal, pre-Partition India. My parents settled in Vehari: my paternal side is from Bhorewala and maternal side from Okara. My mother died during my childhood. We belong to a Rajput family and as you may know Rajputs are very egoistic. My father had differences with his brothers, which led him to move to Karachi. He got a job at MCL with Zaidi Sahib, who built the Natha Khan Bridge, and that's how we made Karachi our permanent abode.

- Since we had no woman in the house, my father arranged my marriage at a very young age, which proved to be the biggest impediment in my education: I had to leave college whilst I was at the intermediate level.

- Earlier, we used to live in Manzoor Colony, now our house is in Al-Falah. You must know that Manzoor Colony is the biggest timber and furniture market—bigger than Chiniot—in Asia. 70% of the artisans are Seraikis and the rest are of varying ethnicities.

- It was a very well thought out decision that I would start my own business as opposed to seeking to get a job. I experimented with a lot of ventures. Just to give you an idea: I started as a salesman of *daal* (lentils/pulses) and rice, a project that grew into a full-fledged company called Nayab Foods. Nayab met its fate in the days of Musharraf, as one of my partners and close associates fell prey to his political aspirations.

- I have a simple business philosophy: Start small with little money of your own and gradually develop the venture into a big one.

- I have been in land development since the year 2000. Previously I was associated with Haji Rauf and Haji Saleem, who sold plots of 64 and 84 sq. yards, with single storey bungalows in the Defence area close to Korangi. *Yeh jo kaam hae iskey pardey haen. Yeh field bharam kee field hai* (This field, it has its veils. This field is a field of attitude).

- Later, Chaudhary Saleem was murdered. I was employed in the capacity of his assistant. He worked as a middleman and sold other people's land for them. Middlemen tend to run 60% of this business.

- The business *operandi* is interesting and I would like to explain it to you (*Tasweer camera ke peechay kuch aur hooti hay*: the picture that can be seen behind the camera is very different from what it actually is). Let's assume you have 50 acres of land and you want to sell it for Rs. 2.5 million. I will pay you Rs. 500,000 as *bayana* (security deposit) and then begin my search for an interested party who might perhaps cut the deal in Rs. 4 million. You don't know him and I will photocopy of documents from you for the client. He will verify the documents and it's only at the time of registry that you will be there otherwise he completely unknown to you, in the same manner as the mentioned buyer is least concerned with you. Two cheques/pay orders will be made: one for the owner and one for me.

- In our business it is least likely that a property owner takes the *bayana* and then goes back on his word. We have methods of dealing with such situations and can resort to pressure tactics if need be. If someone turns his back on the deal he has to pay double the *bayaana*. If he refuses to pay the penalty then a power struggle will begin and the one who has the *dum* (will power) will win the game. If I have the *dum* then he will forfeit the entire property to me. Anything is possible in this city. Or there might be a domino effect where whoever makes a loss will further cheat a potential buyer to recover the set back. Do you know that I can lodge an FIR against you, without even moving from my place –simply by making a single phone call? The SHO charges only Rs. 50,000 in such circumstances. Give me your ID card and I will demonstrate to you the veracity of my claims.

- All land ultimately belongs to the government of Pakistan. Land is allotted to the KDA, MDA, LDA, and DHA through the board of revenue. The provincial chief minister has discretionary powers and he or she can allocate land for mining or for poultry farms. The only catch is that these allocations are then viewed as political allotments and if and when the government changes, such land could be confiscated on one pretext or another—in most of the cases, the rates of land are made contentious.

- Similarly provincial governors and the president have discretionary powers and one can get cheated in the process in the very same way. In 50% of the cases you pay and you will end up with a false FIR against you, resulting in loss of your assets. Meanwhile the courts will take their own (usually long) time to decide the case.

- The official Gothabad scheme closed down some 15–20 years back after it reached a certain saturating point? Each subsequent government temporarily lifted the ban and in the process 5–6 *goths* (villages) were regularized. Records of board of revenue were burnt to cover up mishandling in the Gothabad schemes, e.g. the conversion of two acres of land to 200 acres of land. Spend some money, spare some time and come with me to Hyderabad, you will get to hear thousands of hair-raising stories.

- In the past three years, approximately 1 to 1.2 million plots have been carved out of land along the Northern Bypass. One can easily bribe the relevant agencies for necessary approvals.

- There are a lot of fake housing and residential apartment schemes in the city. The fraudsters set up an office, hire some staff but seldom come in themselves. They run advertisements for their proposed schemes through cable operators on movie channels such as Star Plus, Sony and Star One. They fleece money from potential clients and one fine morning the client discovers that the office is locked and there is nobody to get in touch with. To avoid such gimmickry, the first thing the buyer should inquire about from the developer is the newspaper ads and hoardings around the city.

- I am a member of ABAD. I have spent Rs. 10 million on advertising my scheme, this included newspaper ads, ads on Geo TV Channel and hoardings. I have clippings of the advertisements here in my file.

- My housing scheme is for investors and for contractors, meant to start development after 8 years; it could however even begin next year. The area is close to DHA Phase IX. We offer various plot sizes, between 80 sq. yards to 240 sq. yards, and instalments are paid within 5–6 years. 80% of the plots in our schemes are kept aside for our Aryan *baradari*, and the ownership of the rest open to all, irrespective of creed.

- To establish an *abadi* (settlement) you need to provide a school, a decent transport system, water, gas, electricity, a mosque and a dispensary. A gas cylinder can easily replace the need for a gas infrastructure.

- Residents of Karachi are worried about the increasing rent, and rightly so. The typical monthly income of a middle/lower middle class salaried person ranges between Rs. 8,000 to Rs. 12,000, whereas rent is a minimum of Rs. 3,000 to Rs. 6,000. How are they expected to survive and make both ends meet?

- Then there are advantages of living at the city periphery: No daily shopping by housewives, less socialization and hence fewer expenses. One can excuse oneself from late night weddings under the pretext of the law and order situation in the city. Also, people living on the edge can establish community transport system, as a lot of people and housing societies are considering and/or have already relocated there. One also gets rid of the psychological competition within children and womenfolk living centrally that arise from easy access to markets. One tends to keep better health as well, as the environment is cleaner as compared to city centres.

- The market is slow these days, and as the sale of plots is not very high, people are not buying land in my scheme.

- I can clearly state: If I didn't have to bribe the line departments, the price of the plot would be up to 25% cheaper. For example, the official price for Form 7 is Rs. 2, but we have to offer bribe first to the *patwari*, and then again at the time of registry.

- Increase in publicity equals increase in sales; the more you invest in advertising, the greater the response you receive—and the public will eventually pay back the price of the advertisement.

- Development charges are additional to the cost of the land. We can act as facilitators but it is not our ultimate responsibility.

- HBFC is generally free of bribery. It may be a norm at the lower levels but correct documentation holds prime importance in the process. We can arrange for a loan from the HBFC but the buyer will be the party directly concerned, we will only act as the go-between.

- There is local intervention of relevant political parties at the lower level and they intercede for money.

*Jab shahar upper level ka ho jaey to ghareeb admi shehar maein naheen reh sakta. Woh nafseeati ho jata hae.*

## INTERVIEW—04: MANSOOR HUSSAIN (ESTATE AGENT)

Pak Estate Agency, North Nazimabad Karachi. Interviewed in his office on 22 June 2011.

1. The market value of a plot is usually 200 to 300 times the value estimated by the land authorities. In line with specific written agreements, builders purchase land at a certain price from the KBCA, and proceed to sell it to the buyer at an exorbitant rate. According to the law, the builder is subject to provide a copy of the agreement between buyer and seller to the KBCA—this law is never followed. Upon observation one may usually discover the contract to be illegible, owing to a deliberately minute script.

2. The process is simple: Builders identify an area, pay the price for it to the KBCA and obtain its lease. Subsequently, they carve out chunks of land and sell these to buyers on a sub-lease. The builders tend to charge the buyers 150% of the price of this land in development charges, which include sewerage secondary line charges, provision of electricity poles (not the meters) to the buyer, gas lines and an asphalt road. All related departments are ridden with corruption and a lot of invisible money is involved in the process. For example for the No Objection Certificate requisite for any building venture, the builders usually submit a fake certificate.

3. The list of documents outlining the sale-purchase of land between builder and buyer are

   a. Payment receipt
   b. Allotment title upon 50% of the payment
   c. Possession order on full payment
   d. Acknowledgement of possession
   e. Site Plan
   f. Lease/Sub lease (if further sale/purchase is made before the lease, it will be through a Transfer Order; if made after the lease, it will be through a Sales' Deed)

4. If the purchaser opts for a loan to finance construction then:

   g. The city government's permission to mortgage via Form No. 6 (costing Rs. 700) is required.
   h. The complete file is submitted to HBFC, after which the original is returned and photocopies kept.
   i. A simultaneous move is made for the approvals of map/building plan.
   j. HBFC determine the buyer's repayment capacity and once the loan is approved it is released in three tranches, before the plinth construction, when the structure is laid and at the finishing stage.
   k. The loan usually gets cleared in 15 years repaid or approved.
   l. HBFC issues a redemption deed and a closing letter.
   m. The owner is now free to make further sale/purchase. Before acquisition of the redemption deed, the purchase can be accomplished through Power of Attorney.

5. Outlined above is a standard procedure, each step of which is infested with corruption and thereby has many variations.

6. Builders in Karachi are definitely in partnership with the city's political leadership. It is in fact more than a simple business partnership: Earlier, these builders used to hire retired army officers to tackle the land regulating authority and utility service providers, using clout, connections and money to get what they wanted. Today, however, it is only the language of money that is understood, no need for clout or connections.

Partnering with political leaders has an added advantage: Party workers may be freely employed to curb dissention by neighbours or any individuals, and take care of the matter in any way as along as the court is not moved against a particular project. Also, together they connive for the conversion of amenity and residential plots into commercial plots.

7. It is important to note that KBCA's approval is made strictly by the book. Deviations from which occur in the construction and sale/purchase phases. Government agencies must be willing and available to monitor all activity.

8. *Mistri Hoshiar Baash* is the key phrase in sale/purchase: the buyer is considered a big time loser in the case of any discrepancy in the process.

9. To avoid cheating, the buyer must make complete inquiries from all relevant departments. The increasing dishonesty in people today is constantly adding unnecessary risk to the sale/purchase process—very different from what the situation was 25–30 years back.

## INTERVIEW—05: SOHAIL (ESTATE AGENT)

Bismillah Estate, Taiser Town, Scheme—45. Interviewed on 21 July 2011.

*Taiser Town Scheme-45 is a neighbourhood of Malir Town in Karachi. The Malir Development Authority developed Taiser Town to resettle the people displaced by the construction of the Lyari Expressway along the Lyari River. It is located near the Gulshan-e-Maymar toll plaza. There are several ethnic groups in Taiser Town including Muhajirs, Punjabis, Sindhis, Kashmiris, Seraikis, Pakhtuns, Balochis, Memons, Bohras, Ismailis, etc. Over 99% of the population is Muslim. The population of Malir Town is estimated to be nearly one million.*

1. Investors in Taiser Town purchase land from the villagers.

2. According to hearsay, initially Yusuf Haider Gill purchased land from Speen Khan and proceeded to divide it into plots measuring 120, 100 and 80 sq. yards.

3. However, apparently there is a twist in the narration of the development of this estate since subsequently it was mentioned that the Bismillah Estate functions as a clearing house/front desk for Speen Khan, since Yousuf Haider Gill never paid him the full amount for the land.

4. Bismillah Estate has been in business for the last 4 years, prior to which Yousuf Haider Gill was a male nurse at the Baqai Hospital.

5. A discount of 10%–15% is offered in the case of a total (full) payment made at the beginning whereby a plot worth Rs. 140,000 may be acquired at Rs. 120,000.

6. The lease title of the plot is valid for 99 years.

7. It is claimed that the scheme is approved by the Malir Development Authority.

8. Phase I has 950 plots, Phase II has 500 plots and Phase III has 410 plots.

9. In Phase I, 200 plots were purchased by the Hindu community.

10. This is the third project or Phase III of Joshua Gardens. In Phase III special discounts are available for pastors, priests and widows. An advance payment of Rs. 30,000 allows the land title to be changed in favor of the buyer. As set by Yusuf Haider Gill the sale value per plot is fixed at Rs. 200,000. The plan includes provision for a Church: Soheil was of the opinion that the prices of the plots will increase once the church is constructed. Bismillah Estate will also provide electricity and water to the residents of the scheme.

11. The prices of the plots measuring 120 sq. yards in Phase—II were significantly lower than those of the same sized plots in Phase—III: being Rs. 170,000 and Rs. 200,000 respectively.

12. In another twist in the narrative it was mentioned that Speen Khan purchased land from the MDA and not from the Sindhi locals.

13. The scheme offer couplets: a combination of two 120 sq. yards plots, as well.

14. It was highlighted that there is no water shortage in the area.

Apparently:

1. There is Barelvi and Deobandi religious influence in the area in the form of religious establishments and graffiti and there is also a general feeling of insecurity, so much so that at one point our researchers were questioned for taking photographs by the people sitting in front of shops; despite that it seems that minority communities feel confident to invest in the area; why?

2. What is the interplay of various actors under the ambit of the Gothabad Scheme?

3. Where do the original inhabitants relocate to after selling off their land, and what are the means of livelihood?

### INTERVIEW—06: MR FARID AND MR RANA SADIQ (ESTATE AGENTS)

Omer Colony No. 1, P.E.C.H.S. Karachi. Interviewed on 8 September 2011.

*Omer Colony 1 is located in Jamshed Town along a portion of the railway tracks, adjacent to Baloch Flyover on Shahrah-e-Faisal, in the southern part of Karachi. The settlement comprises of 1,148 houses spread over 12.75 acres and dates back to 1956. At the time the land was part of a natural rainwater drainage channel and a 60 sq. yard plot cost Rs. 100. Today, a house on the same plot costs around Rs. 700,000. The area is home to various ethnicities: 60% are Kashmiris, Punjabis and Pathans and the rest are Hazaraywaal, Mohajir, Sindhi, and Baloch. 62% of the houses have a cement/tin sheet roofing system, the rest employ the tile/beam system and RCC in their roofs. The streets are in bad shape owing to the use of substandard carpeting materials. Provision of water is through 30 wells dug on site, a connection to the main line was built in 1980. The government also built sewerage lines which proved to be insufficient, thus with the help of the OPP self-help mechanism, a functional system was put in place. KESC began supplying electricity to the area in 1976 and*

*SSGC introduced gas to the area in 1985. Most of the population, including women, work as domestic help in the nearby affluent areas; others are formal and informal vendors. With a literacy rate of 2% in the area, there are no public schools: there is albeit one large private school and a vocational training centre for women. The colony has a disputed position in the Katchi Abadi Regularization process, as the land is situated within the parameters of Pakistan Railways' land.* (Taken from URC Case Study 2009).

1.  Thirty years ago when I was 6 years old, I moved from Thandiani in Abottabad to Karachi. My father and grandfather were hawkers. I attended school till grade 5 and then started my career as a domestic servant.

2.  Eventually, I joined an estate agent as an apprentice. He was an Indian migrant of 1947's Partition period, who dealt with the sale/purchase of property in both *katchi* and *pakki abadis* (informal and formal settlements, respectively). I continued to work with him for 12 years and learnt from him the tricks of the trade. Later I started my own realty business and it's now been 18 years since I've been involved in this field.

3.  The change in real estate value is subject to the variation in law and order situation of the city.

4.  The Pakistan Railways' staff is involved in the illegal sale of land and we have to give them a requisite share of the booty. I cannot comment on the specific amount of the *bhatta* (informal tax) to the police, but most of the time they are unaware of the deals. Construction on the said land is carried out at night.

5.  Today, Umer Colony is saturated and plots are not available in the area. Legally only 90' of land along the periphery of the Railway Line has been leased—the rest has not. The leasing rights were granted after the year 2000, following which there was an increase in price of the property. The grant inadvertently signalled an increase in the prices of the non-leased property. The cost of land for this hotel is about Rs. 6.8 million whereas had it not been leased the price would have practically been reduced to half.

6.  The maximum plot size is 160 sq. yards, roughly 200 sq. yards and there is only a nominal price difference between residential and commercial plots.

7.  The construction on the plot influences price estimations and usually one room, one bathroom and one kitchen are constructed per plot. I work on 2% commission from each party—this percentage may vary from party to party. On an average I succeed in sale/purchase of 12 houses in a year. The commission rate varies: 2% on less than Rs. 5 million and 1% on houses worth Rs. 5 million and above.

8.  Even 18 years ago the price of property here was in lacs (hundreds of thousands) and not thousands. I bought my piece of land, measuring 43 sq. yards, for Rs. 230,000; it has two rooms, one bathroom and one kitchen. A shop measuring 12' x 14' was recently sold for Rs. 1.1 million.

9.  75% of the dwellers are owners and 25% are on rent. Most of the sale/purchase of land is dealt with by people dwelling within the *basti*, but owing to the law and order situation in the rest of the city, the demand from external buyers is increasing. Residents do not want to leave the colony since a number of facilities

are readily available: water, transport and above all security. I don't think that the business of sale/purchase will come to an end in this *basti*. It will continue lifelong.

Chances are rare that big developers will succeed in convincing people to abandon their places by offering them hefty amounts of money.

10. This area has always remained trouble free. In order of majority the ethnicities of the residents are Punjabis, Kashmiris and Muhajirs. They rely on jobs for livelihoods and are employed in banks, homes and private companies. The womenfolk seek employment in bungalows. There are some who are employed in the Gulf States as well. Intercommunity *(baradari)* marriages are in vogue. There are two schools in the *basti*: Shah Public and Mariam Academy. However, most of the children attend school outside the *basti*.

11. Density is increasing due to the property owners' desire to earn more money from tenants. Homes are usually rented out to acquaintances and not to non-NIC holders. The rent for a *katcha* house of one room with a kitchen and a bathroom is Rs. 3,000/month and for a *pacca* house of the same size, its Rs. 4,000/month.

The increases in family size, as well as children and siblings' marriages also contribute to the rise in construction activity.

12. For non-acquaintances, an agreement that is otherwise verbal is drawn up—the tenure of which is 11 months and therein is a one-month vacation period clause, valid for both the landlord and the tenants. There is seldom any breach of the agreement.

13. There are no moneylenders in the *basti*. *Bisi* committees are functional and allow people to save enough money for their construction purposes. Earlier, moneylenders living near *Kala Pul* used to lend out meagre amounts of money: Rs. 10,000 or 20,000.

14. I haven't observed any guesthouses in the vicinity of Omer Colony.

15. Fortunately there is no *bhatta* mafia here, although at the Civic Centre I have to offer money to the officials. A recent example: I had to pay Rs. 14,000 against an official slip of Rs. 480 for a transfer order.

16. Apart from immense tension, I face no issues in my business—but by virtue of responsibility I would never include my siblings in it.

Further Discussion:

1. What is the interest of Railways to remain as a silent spectator and see its lands going to grabbers?

2. Why it is easy to grab the land of Pakistan Railways?

3. People used the methods of asset selling, remittances, loans, *bisis*, graduating sale/purchase of land and by broadening their investments portfolio, to obtain house for themselves. What are the advantages/disadvantages of each method from people's perspective?

## INTERVIEW—07: NASER KHAN AND OTHER ESTATE AGENTS

Real estate agents at Maula Madad Bus Stop, Lyari. Interviewed on 8 October 2011.

*Lyari Town is one of Karachi's eighteen constituent towns and in comparison to the rest, has the smallest spread of area and the highest population density. It is bordered by SITE Town to the north across the Lyari River, Jamshed and Saddar Towns to the east, and Keamari to the west across the main harbour of Karachi. Lyari is one of the oldest places in Karachi but somehow has few schools, substandard hospitals, a poor water supply and drainage system, limited infrastructure and broken roads. Lyari is also the centre of Karachi's Sheedi community of Afro-Arab and Black African descent. It is a stronghold of the Pakistan People's Party (PPP).*

- Before the advent of the British, a majority of Baloch migrated from Iran to Lyari—the oldest of them were the Karamati Baloch.

- My forefathers were from Iran but we don't have any connections with Iran now.

- Before coming back to Karachi, I spent 22 years in the UAE where I ran a shop by the name of Balochistan Tailors. Afterwards Rasheed Rehmani called me up for this business.

- Prior to working at the Rehmani Estate Agency, I was employed at another agency on Omar Lane in the same capacity. This has been my occupation for the last 12 years. Here I am neither an investor nor a developer- I purely act as an interlocutor for other peoples' investments.

- Lyari used to be a Sindhi settlement where *kumbhars* (potters) used clay from the Lyari River to make their wares. A herding tribe of *Wachanis* used to own land and rear livestock here. They later moved to *Mawach* on *azaad zameen* (open land). Also, the majority of Lyari's residents used to be the Baloch; nowadays there is an obvious ethnic mix of Punjabis, Sindhis, Pathans, and Muhajirs.

- Traditionally, the decision-making was done by the elders/*sardars/mautabars* of the area. Now it is carried out by *nazims* and councillors now; a new breed of *sardars* has emerged.

- The process of leasing began in 1972 under the tenure of Z. A. Bhutto. Leased plots tend to have greater value: A leased house measuring 50 sq. yards costs Rs. 800,000. There are still a lot of places that are not on lease: old maps show a lot of amenity plots.

- These days it is conventional practice for investors to stake money in a 120 sq. yard plot belonging to a seller, construct three floors of a building, offer the owner a floor and sell the remaining two floors independently. The seller thereby receives the cost of his land as well as a place to live in. It was the *katchi* (informal) community that initiated this process, but now the Baloch, Memons, and Sindhis are all part of the business: all investors are local.

- In 1972 most of the houses were single story buildings; today they are double and triple storey houses.

- To lend a two room house on *pagri* (security deposit) is very common. *Pagri* rates vary between Rs. 700,000—Rs. 750,000, in which case the monthly rent is Rs. 200, without the payment of *pagri* a two-room apartment would cost around Rs. 3,000 month.

- There is lower occupancy and less demand for flats owing to a lack of civic facilities; there is also a slump in the real estate business. Before I used to sell 4–5 flats in a month, now I manage to sell one flat in 4–5 months. Commission for rentals is one rent.

- There is a 2 % commission on sales. But we never receive full commission because of *baradari* (community) connections and the economic condition of our people. At times, buyers bypass us and establish a connection directly with the seller.

- There are no parks or open spaces left in Lyari: *Aab yahan koel kee awaz naheen aatee.* (One cannot hear the song of the koel bird here anymore).

- 90% of the community based organizations and street schools in Lyari have closed because of gang wars.

- Influential people in Lyari are generally gun-toting individuals.

- Billions of rupees are buried underground in the form of sewerage and water lines in Lyari.

- The original owners of the godowns died with the passage of time whilst their siblings have developed luxurious lifestyles. The leases of lots for many godowns have lapsed and people are applying for extensions to the same. Godowns are generally converted into residential plots by the Memons. Approval is sought from the LDA for ground plus 3 and at times ground plus 6 floors. They are sold and apartments are constructed. Remittance money plays a key role in the phenomenon. With the remittance money people buy house or land. The Baloch psyche wants to live within their community and they, unlike the rest of the investors in the city, should not be termed as land grabbers.

- The government owns warehouses, but the legalities are hazy. Can you imagine a godown covering 2500 sq. yards costing Rs. 6 million anywhere else in Karachi?

- (*Another estate agent Jawaid joins in*) I have been in this business for the last 25 years. The apartment trend is on the rise. Property rates in Lyari are high as it is a relatively peaceful area.

- The apartment trend is converting the Baloch into a minority. High rises are a manifestation of capitalism and are insensitive towards the poor and diversity of culture.

- The price escalation of property is forcing people with fewer resources to migrate out of Lyari, whereas those with money are shifting to Askari IV, Gulshan-e-Iqbal, and Defence. 30%–40% of Lyarites have moved to *katchi abadis* (informal settlements), but we maintain our relationships with them. However, within Lyari people have control over their property, in stark contrast with the rest of the city.

- Hindus are moving to Lyari as they find it more secure. They occupy 90% of the Baghdadi flats.

- Except for Kalari Leather Works, other tanneries in the area are finishing. Large, well-known tanneries like Shafiq Tanneries that previously were situated in Lyari, have shifted to Korangi.

- It is common news that MI and ISI people used to meet with the gangsters here, as the establishment does not want stability in Lyari. They are intimidated by our cultural and political affinity with Balochistan. The shock of Nawab Sahib's (Nawab Akbar Bugti) murder was felt more strongly in Lyari than in Balochistan.

- MQM says that Karachi was more stable in the days of Musharraf; however 3–4 people were killed on a daily basis in the streets of Lyari at that time. The people here have no choice except PPP.

- It is ironic that the fisherfolk and boatmen are Baloch, but those that invest in the boats are not.

- The recent disturbances and gang wars are over: the prices have stabilized at the level of pre-disturbance period.

## INTERVIEW—08: MR SHAHID

(Manager, Khuda-ki-Basti—3 Site. Interviewed on 21 July 2011.

*Khuda-ki-Basti, a settlement spread over 40.8 acres/16.5 hectares, is located 25 kilometres from the city centre. It was planned according to KBCA's town planning regulations whilst the land was provided to the NGO Saibaan at subsidized rates. Saibaan had the settlement planned as a pilot scheme whereby only low-income families were eligible to purchase a plot, provided they inhabit the said plot immediately. Repayment for the plot is planned in affordable instalments with a remittance period of seven years.*

1. Earlier, owing to the inaccessibility of KDA, the process of purchasing plots was through the ballot process.

2. Today, under the Sindh government board of revenue's *Gothabad* Scheme, one can purchase a plot with the payment of meagre Rs. 15,000 as advance. The *Gothabad* authority is under provincial government and has little to do with city government

3. Claims stating that Malir Development Authority (MDA) approved a scheme are farcical: Developers make such claims because the MDA, after being paid a due amount, does not interfere in/comment on any such claims. The silence henceforth is perceived as approval although it is purely implied and there is no official confirmation.

4. The conventional procedure of the land grabbers follows initial payments of around Rs. 200,000 per acre to the village elders/owner—the village elder/owner being in possession of an identity card and the village generally being named after his clan—Rs. 200,000 to the Board of Revenue (BOR) and a further Rs. 200,000 to the MDA and *Gothabad* Authority for approval. In the process the land grabbers spend a total of Rs. 600,000 for a 1-acre plot, which ultimately has a market value of Rs. 1.1 million with a net profit of Rs. 500,000. The entire process remains out of bound of provincial exchequer, hence termed informal.

5. Every *patti* (strip of land) secured by the land grabbers has a share of plots for local police officials. It is understood that plots having the least competitive price are allotted as buyers don't usually trust police personnel in such dealings—these plots are also the ones that are sold first. *Pattis* may be sold as a singular stretch of land or in the form of plots spanning 120/100/80 sq. yards carved from it.

6.  An advance share is given to all participants so that the process of grabbing may carry on smoothly and without unnecessary delays.

7.  There are shifts in the land grabbing factors/paradigms: Ethnically, those investing in the land grabbing were predominantly *Pathaan*, now *Muhajirs* are increasingly found to be joining their ranks. Also earlier, people in possession of money and a locally renowned background grabbed land. Lately however, political activists have emerged as the new players in the game and *goths* (villages) with political patronage are considered safer to deal with.

8.  Usually three to four villages are purchased at a time and the villagers relocated in far off places. Owing to the abundance of plots in nearby areas prices of plots in Khuda-ki-Basti have dropped. I think that the number of such plots in the vicinity is between 4 to 5 million. Consequently after getting its share, the police do not disturb the developers or the entire process.

9.  Despite all the unfair play, it appears that this is the only method through which the poor can own a piece of land—no other option is available to them.

10. Before starting construction the owner of each plot pays the SHO Rs. 5,000 to guarantee *de facto* security.

11. Land grabbing has set a new morality along the lines of *jo dareh woh reh jae* (he who gets scared, will be left behind)

Further Discussion:

1.  What is the *Gothabad* scheme?

2.  How is a piece of land identified for grabbing? What are the parameters?

3.  How much time is taken in the process? Right from identification of the land to be taken over to the final selling of the plots?

4.  What are the deviations in the process? Under what conditions does a deal fall through creating animosity?

5.  How do the political players view the process? How does this process affect the city?

6.  How far will this process go? Is there an end to it?

## INTERVIEW—09: SHEIKH MOINUDDIN

Developer and Civil Lawyer. Interviewed on 22 November 2011.

*   I can tell you the story of the recently launched Naya Nazimabad housing project. This land belonged to Valika Estates, comprising of Valika Cement, Valika Chemicals and Valika Wine Factory, covering around 1,000 acres of which factories took up 300 acres. The remaining 700 acres were mortgaged to various banks. During the process of nationalization, the owners were deprived of their property rights and filed cases against the seizure. It was at the time of the hearing of these cases in court that the sale of the aforementioned land was discovered. Al-Abbas and Arif Habib group had purchased approximately 250 acres of Valika Estates from the government. There are 15–20 further claimants of the land which include

Sindhi families that have been living there for centuries. The labour colony was paid to vacate and there are no clues as to where they may have relocated.

- The occupation of land owned by the government is not possible without the help of the *mukhtiarkar* (middle level revenue officer). I have also filed a case, on behalf of a Brohi client of mine for him to reclaim his land from occupiers who worked in connivance with the *mukhtiarkar*. The *gothabads* (villages) and *katchi abadis* (informal settlements) are the main victims of land grabbing. Most of the revenue cases are linked with forceful occupation.

- Yes, I have faced threats and once had a very narrow escape. It was during the second of a series of land surveys for a housing scheme in Deh Thumi. My attackers had precise information about me: They knew that I used to have a cup of tea with my guards on site; it was there they came on a motorbike and opened fire. On that particular day I had left a little early as I had a phone call to attend but they injured both my guards.

- Most of my clients are old Sindhi tribes such as the Gabols, Jokhios, Samoos, and Brohis. The accused is usually the revenue department, as it's the main culprit behind the chicanery.

- Most of the time trouble takes place after the death of a father or legal heir. The property title needs to be replaced with the title of the next heir, within 45 days in a *Foutgi Khata* (land transfer after death). In the process of conducting their annual/bi-annual surveys, *patwaris* (revenue collectors) can easily discover the news of the owner's death and proceed to play around with the title of the documents.

- The land mafia includes both political and nationalist parties.

- Pathans have greater liquid assets because of their connection with black money, thereby they tend to invest a lot of their resources in land. They generally have three major sources of income 1) From NATO supply trips, where each trip gives them a profit of Rs. 80,000; 2) From Afghan Transit Trade and 3) Drug money: *Garda* (a combination of marijuana and heroin) is becoming increasingly popular nowadays.

- Usman Shah, grandson of Pir Pagara, is one of the land mafia's kingpins. He was disowned by Pir Pagara since his mother (daughter of Pir Pagara) had married a Pathan. They fell in love with each other and got married, only to be killed by the powerful tribe.

- 60% of the land in Scheme—33 is occupied by the land mafia and relevant cases are pending in court. In cases where decisions have been taken, the million dollar question remains as to who will implement these decisions? The Supreme Court had ordered the evacuation of Shirin Jinnah Colony Terminal almost nine months ago, but at the site one can plainly observe business going on as usual.

- Earlier, Pathans were not the *aarthis* (middleman in the sale process) of rice or in fact of any other commodity. In terms of return on investment, *aarth* is time consuming and Pathans usually tend to take part in prolonged transactions. I visited a friend who is a small landlord and he appeared quite happy to have sold his rice harvest in entirety to a Pathan *aarthi*. He claimed the *aarthi* paid him the sum total of the estimated money in advance and that too at higher rates: Rs. 15/

kg. This is contradictory to the conventional methods of payment to landlords for the sale of their final produce. The Pathans are able to do this because they have enough money to take risks.

- I started a housing scheme in Manghopir by the name of Mir Mohammed Housing Scheme. Mir Mohammed was my business partner and he was also the *Sajjada Nasheen* (spiritual heir) of the Manghopir's shrine. The first phase of our scheme was successful, but the second phase failed as the land mafia occupied the area. We fought the case for eight years and ultimately won but by that time development costs ran so high that the scheme didn't seem profitable anymore.

- Once a friend's friend in North Waziristan showed him bags full of US Dollars and Pak Rupees in his cellar. He claimed to have earned this money from the Afghan War and wanted to invest this in a business venture. My friend advised him to build an industry but he refused on the pretext of lack of quick returns.

- Judicial cases pertaining to land take a long time to decide. Courts are bound by the obligation of evidences and it takes a really long time, so people tend to lose hope and money during the process.

- Once the Memons became interested in the land alongside Sakro and purchased some farmhouses there. They settled the local Sindhis there to take care of the farmhouses. After some time, a series of kidnappings of Memon farm owners intimidated them and soon after they abandoned the land in favor of settlers.

- The land grabbing began in 1989, right after Benazir Bhutto came into power. The reasons were a) The land prices shot up, b) There is no time lag in return on investment, and c) Political representatives became more powerful than the bureaucracy.

- Earlier, the district management group (DMG) comprised elitist bureaucrats who religiously followed rules and policies. They were notorious for their by-the-book attitude. In those times if you submitted an application to the SDM and DC, action was definitely taken. Bhutto bulldozed that concept and everybody could become a bureaucrat. Later political groups planted their blue-eyed boys in bureaucracy and thus ruined the system.

- Karachi is in the grip of a land mafia and if you have a plot in Scheme—33, believe me, it will be occupied. There will be a boundary wall on the plot and a family with three kids –one or two women and a male member cooking food with wood as fuel for fire, over there. These are the typical signs of occupation. They have the power to buy a good lawyer and in the lower courts, the clout of the lawyer counts. The not-so-knowledgeable judges of the lower courts can usually be overheard asking the lawyer 'Sir, aap iss keh barey mein hamen kuch batayen' (Sir, tell us something about this …).

- Entire families are actually available for occupation on a rental basis. Rs, 15,000/month is the prevalent rate of renting a family without meals. Usually the families of *Bhagaries* and *Seraikis* render these services.

- I once tried this: I had developed a housing scheme that became controversial and the case went to court. I applied the same technique: It was when the case was in court that I sold the land to 100 different allotters, received payment from them and used some of the amount to settle 15 such families on the fringes and at some distance to the land. The land seemed occupied and I began constructing boundary walls within that circle of occupation. Ultimately I had the full payments from the allotters in hand and paid the police SHO Rs. 50,000 for his cooperation.

- Builders are obliged to pay *bhatta* (informal, usually illegal tax) to two to three parties. Although I took care of security issues in my Sea World Project by posting private guards there, the KKF jumped in and I had to oblige them as well. I didn't rely too much on the local police for security.

- In certain areas of Karachi, notorious gangsters fix the rate of *bhatta* and they have to be paid on the side for any property transaction. For example the rate of a 240 sq. yard plot varies from Rs. 15,000 to Rs. 20,000 and if there is a delay in the payment of *bhatta* there are additional charges to be paid as 'delayed payment'. The hot spots for such transactions are Korangi, Orangi and some parts of Gulistan-e-Jauhar, largely because resourceful people do not reside there.

- Saleem Zaki is the owner of Saima Builders. He named the agency after his elder daughter, Saima. I've heard that Chotta Shakeel and Babar Ghori are his business partners. He learnt the tricks of the trade and is now one of the big players.

- The Afghan War is responsible for all this mess as it gave birth to the culture of coercion. The heroin trade financed the Afghan War and the weapons let all hell loose in society.

Questions to be answered:

1.  Has the demand for land made people dishonest or vice-versa is true?

2.  In the symbiotic relationship of builders with political parties, who rules the power equation?

3.  Why is there such a huge demand for flats? The issues connecting the demand for flats to the nucleus unit family concept; increased consumption; emerging middle class/gender *glasnost* and the aspirations of today's youth need to be considered in this regard.

4.  Why is this particular belt of the Power House area in Karachi New Town ridden with flats?

5.  What are the terms and conditions for buyers? Are they open and transparent or hidden for future manoeuvring? None of the builders shared any substantial information concerning terms and conditions with the researchers.

6.  What makes people trust some builders?

7.  Money is the connecting chord amongst all players; the question is how much for whom in terms of a rough percentage? Is it possible to make a pie chart of these findings?

8.  What are the dynamics of loan approval from HBFC? Why does it vary from case to case and on what criteria?

9.  Builders are shifting from relatively affluent areas and city centres to the periphery of the city, why? Is there is a dearth of land, an economic recession, lowering of investment ceiling by the future wary middle class investors or is it the impact

of Karachi 2020 project that proposes to shift the commercial centres along the Northern Bypass?

10. The areas in Taiser Town exhibits Barelvi and Deobandi religious influence in the form of religious establishments and graffiti and a general feeling of insecurity, so much so that at one point our researchers were questioned for taking photographs by the people sitting in front of shops; despite that it seems that minority communities feel confident to invest in the area; why?

11. Under the ambit of Gothabad Scheme, what is the interplay of various actors?

12. After selling their native land, where do the original inhabitants move and what are the means of their livelihoods?

13. Why does the construction of a place of worship increase the prices of real estate?

14. What is the Gothabad scheme?

15. How is a piece of land identified by grabbers? What are the parameters?

16. How much time is taken in the process; right from identification of the land to be taken over to the final selling of the plots?

17. What are the deviations of the process? Under what conditions does a deal fall through creating animosity?

18. How do the political players view the process? How does this process affect the city?

19. How far will this process go. Is there an end to it?

20. Flat owners are in search of gentry and have an affinity towards spacious houses. How do house owners perceive the mushrooming of flats in their area?

21. Is there any institutional support (civic institutions) for such increased density of living quarters and the resultant demand on public utility facilities?

22. Why is the underworld interested in the construction business? Why not in the film industry, as happened in Bombay?

23. What is average profit from the sale of a flat?

24. Players with extra cash in hand used to came into the construction business as land was available and also for other reasons. Now with land shrinking in Karachi city: One, where will they invest in future; Two, in the current economic setup who are the new money holders with that kind of capital.

25. Can we conclude from the above that ABAD has actually developed a close liaison with drug pushers or that drug smugglers have taken over ABAD. If yes, than how can IEP improve the 'systems'?

26. Can we also conclude that conversion of amenity plots in the city will go unabated? In the scheme of things what is the role of judiciary and court rulings?

27. How far can civil society organizations (as Shehri) fight this war as hefty amounts of various players are at stake? Or they will just be reduced to whistle-blowers?

28. What is the interest of the railways to remain a silent spectator and see its lands going to grabbers?

29. Why it is easy to grab the land of Pakistan Railways?

30. People used the methods of asset selling, remittances, loans, *bisis*, graduating sale/purchase of land and by broadening their investments portfolio, to obtain houses for themselves. What are the advantages/disadvantages of each method from the people's perspective?

31. Why are moneylenders from outside Umer Colony?

32. Why are Baloch investors investing money in land ventures and not in other businesses?

## INTERVIEW—10: FAKHR-E-ALAM ZAIDI

Private party and seller of property in Federal 'B' Area, Block 10. Interview on 6 July 2011.

Owing to several setbacks Fakhr-e-Alam Zaidi became financially unstable and recently had to sell his property that had been passed on to him by his parents and that he had owned for 40 years.

He had moved out of his house in 2004 and gave it on rent to a renowned school on a three year contract. They stayed there for six years, but when the rent increased and the contract was to be renewed for the second time they backed off, saying that they would soon be shifting the school to another location. However, after a month they again showed interest in renewing the contract. In clear violation of rental ethics they stayed on in the house for four more months, keeping Zaidi unclear as to what rental he should charge them. It was after they had left that he discovered the shockingly dilapidated condition of the house. The repair works were estimated at Rs. 100,000. He made continuous pleas to them to pay for the damage they had done to the house but these were ignored and he received no compensation in this regard.

Thereafter he began searching for new tenants. A number of parties came to visit the house but owing to its dilapidated condition they offered insufficient rent. According to Zaidi the rent was not substantial enough to run his household, nor did he have enough money to repair the house. He said, 'If I had the money, I would certainly have opted to renovate the house since it had been bequeathed to me by my parents; I wanted to keep their home intact and well taken care of.'

During the search he came across the owner of another school, a man known to have amassed a huge amount of property in the area, second only to the owner of Mehfooz Sheermal. 'I don't believe in owning properties which are partially mine and partially yours, if you're willing to sell the house I'll be more than happy to buy it,' he said. Again the price he quoted was less than Zaidi's estimation, but the party mockingly told him that he wouldn't be able to sell the house for more than what he had offered. 'I take more time selecting and purchasing fruit than properties,' said the school owner to show how well he could estimate the value of properties.

Upon inquiry, Zaidi complained that the estate agents involved in the deal had played an unsatisfactory role. 'I had to change one agent after another and it seemed like they all were trying to take advantage of my predicament,' he said. He further said that he already had little trust in these agents because of a previous experience when an agent had turned out to be an accomplice of the buyers and had pressurized him to sell the house at a throw away price. The matter was taken to higher officials who helped him get rid of the party. This time he made sure he kept a strict check on the agent as well as the party.

Ultimately, he found an estate agent interested in buying the house but initially he was not willing to state his intentions; he had come through a third party. The purchasing/ selling amount was settled after negotiations and the deal was confirmed. He was given 15% advance money in token.

Even though there were no legal problems and the property documents were almost up to date, Zaidi still had to pay Rs. 50,000 to the authorities. 'It was my right to get it done without greasing their palm, but still I had to do that.'.

A lot of dubious personalities came to take a look at the house during the time that it lay vacant. They were interested in the house but did not give any straightforward answers the questions he asked. There was even an incident in which someone jumped over the wall and tried to break into the house, but thanks to a timely warning about the break in given to him by one of the neighbours, Zaidi immediately went to his house and was able to thwart the intruder.

## INTERVIEW—11: ALI RAZA ABBAS JAFFERY

Buyer of flat in Al-Ghafoor Residency. Interviewed on 26 July 2011.

1. Even before I got married, a friend of mine advised me to save some money and invest in a flat. Then some years ago I began my search for an apartment in a peaceful, secure area inhabited by an educated class of people. I first went to Ali Residency, but they cost Rs. 4.4 million per flat, which turned out to be too expensive. For a while I considered buying a flat in another scheme called Hammad Residency, but found it had parking problems.

2. Another reason for selecting this area is that my brother-in-law lives in Sector 11-A. The houses are good, spacious (of 240 sq. yards) and the area is peaceful. However, beyond the sector there starts a settlement with 80 sq. yard houses and then a *katchi abadi*, which I don't like.

3. I saw the advertisement for Al-Ghafoor Residency posted at a doctors' clinic. I went to visit one of Al-Ghafoor's on-going projects and spoke with the contractor onsite. He told me that Al-Ghafoor uses better quality materials, as compared to other developers. I eventually chose Al-Ghafoor because it had a proper boundary wall, adequate parking space and good construction references from past projects. To confirm my decision, I conducted an *istikhara* (religious method of divination) and received affirmative response.

4. I started talking with the builders, and although it took some time to negotiate with them for the final price, the schedule of payment was made according to my convenience.

5. I have not applied for a loan from HBFCL, for which I was made to understand that the process would start when the project nears completion and repayment would begin 11 months after the approval of the loan. The builder affirmed his full support to me to secure the loan from HBFCL and he is quite optimistic about acquiring the full amount. Interestingly, the builders offered me a loan of the same value sans interest, with a repayment period of 2 years and a monthly instalment amounting to Rs. 33,333. After the completion of the project, they tend to stay around for 2–3 years.

6. Developers such as these tend to have conniving marketing techniques, for which I can quote an example from my experience. In the early days of my negotiations, the principal salesman said that he had waived all extra charges for the flat I had specified: a corner flat with rooftop access, open to the west and facing the road. In the later stages of the project, however, he stated that only some, not all of the charges had been waived and simultaneously offered me a cumulative discount of Rs. 1,60,000. Consequently, with the loan (offered by the developer) the flat cost me Rs. 21,70,000: Rs. 13,70,000 paid in cash and Rs. 800,000 loan. Now after 3 years, the builders state that there is no documentation of the waiver and I have to pay Rs. 100,000 for the roof top access. In the hope of making them realize their unfair dealing, I haven't paid the last instalment as yet. I think I can manage to lower their last demand down to Rs. 50,000.

7. Another trick usually played by the builders is the foremost sale of flats on the upper/top floors. They try to hold on to the flats on the ground and first floors till the project is completed and for which purpose they use the pretext that they are already sold. Once the project enters its finishing stages, these lower floor flats are sold at premium prices, thus maximizing profits.

8. I paid an advance of Rs. 50,000 and the rest in monthly instalments. I have to pay an additional Rs. 200,000 for documentation charges, gas, electricity and water and sewerage utilities.

9. If the monthly instalments are not paid in time, the tone and attitude of the reminder calls becomes rude, demonstrating blatant insensitivity to any financial constraints the buyer might be facing, whilst threats of cancellation become routine. I was threatened a couple of times that my booking would be cancelled and the amount that I had paid so far would be returned with a 10% deduction and further that the refund would be subject to the sale of my booked apartment to another buyer and will be paid in instalments.

10. In stark contrast there is no penalty for late delivery on the builders' part. At the start it was announced that this was to be a three-year project: I made my first payment in June 2008 and now in June 2011, I've been informed that the flat will be handed over to me in December 2011. This is the most crucial phase for the entire venture and for me it's like a sword hanging over my head. Most of the developers run away in this, the finishing phase; I just pray for a quick hand over and possession.

11. Competition and market pressures compel builders to opt for deceptive techniques. For example initially Al-Ghafoor made no mention of the sale of studio apartments. When construction of relatively cheaper schemes were announced in the vicinity, the builders divided each flat on the 6th floor of Al-Ghafoor Residency into two portions, selling each portion as an independent unit.

12. Saima Builders are considered to be the most reputable builders, however paradoxically this acclaim stems from the popular theory that they possess plenty of black/underworld money and thus they don't have to wait for funds from advance booking and monthly instalment payments and their projects are completed on time. Therefore, one may observe that M/s Saima's projects get fully booked within a month. The builders are also known for their regular illegal acquisition of land for projects. The Saima Bridge View Luxury Apartments project

in Nazimabad is in its completion stages, regardless of it being a disputed project. The irony remains that despite being disputed, an apartment originally booked for Rs. 4.5 million now costs Rs. 8 million. Similar is the case of Saima Royal Residency along the Lyari Expressway (near Moti Mahal, Gulshan-e-Iqbal), the construction of which, I believe, is also illegal.

Further Discussion:

1. Flat owners are in search of gentry and have an affinity towards spacious houses. How do house owners perceive the mushrooming of flats in their area?

2. Is there any institutional support (civic institutions) for the increased density and subsequent demand in public utilities?

3. Why is the underworld interested in the construction business? Why not in the film industry, as in the case of Bombay?

4. What is the average profit from the sale of a flat?

## INTERVIEW—12: JANTI

Office Boy and messenger in a foreign mission, Interviewed on 21 October 2011.

1. I was born near the slaughterhouse at Lyari. My father was employed in the KMC, where he was allotted a government quarter. He was also born in the same quarter. After his retirement the KMC administration took away the quarter and from there began the long saga of our displacement.

2. My father then started work at the K2 (cigarette) Company, but later when the company closed down, he was deprived of his dues.

3. 17–18 years ago, we moved to Lyari where we rented a house at Rs. 2,000 per month. The house comprised of one room, one veranda, one kitchen and one bath room-cum-toilet. All six members of my family lived in that one room house.

4. 10 years ago, however, theft and dacoity increased in Lyari to the extent that it became impossible to continue living in the area since the male members of the family, who had to spend a substantial time of the day away from the house, were constantly worried about the female members at home.

5. It was around this time that after I passed my matriculation exam from the Okhai Memon School, I had to leave my studies and search for a job market, in order to make both ends meet. I still dream of pursuing my studies but cannot, owing to the ever rising cost of living.

6. We shifted to the Lines Area (near Numaish Chowrangi) soon after that (10 years ago), where we took a house with two rooms and a veranda. The landlord demanded rent of Rs. 3,500 per month, but we concluded the agreement at Rs. 2,500 per month. Unlike Lyari, here we had to deposit Rs. 10,000 as security. In Lyari, there was no system of deposit or advance, but the landlord could ask us to leave without any notice. Here, a month's notice was our right as per the legal contract we signed with the landlord.

7. We spent four or five years in the Lines Area until one fine morning we were informed that the entire building was sold to an investor. He gave us one month's notice and that too, through the estate agent who had initially helped us get the house. As we hadn't paid rent, the landlord deducted Rs. 5,000 from our security deposit.

8. We moved in to a house at Punjab Colony and made an advance payment of Rs. 30,000 after which we signed the contract. The two-room house cost us Rs. 4,500 per month and potable piped water was available. The landlord was a Muhajir (migrant from India after Partition). I preferred living in Punjab Colony owing to the relative security and peace, unlike Lines Area where the threat of violence was increasing. We also had a paternal relative residing in the area.

9. The tale of displacement didn't end there: One day the landlord gave us a week's notice on the pretext that he wanted to construct a building where our house stood. I mentioned the clause of a one-month notice in the agreement but he refused to acknowledge it and referred me back to the same estate agent through which we had first gotten the house. It was an exercise in futility for me to insist on my demand.

10. I now live in Chandio Village where I have paid an advance of Rs. 30,000 and the rent is Rs. 6,000 per month. I hope that when I leave the house I will get my money back. I want to own a house in my lifetime, although with my limited income I cannot manage to save enough money. I do subscribe to the *bisi* system for savings.

11. My elder sister is married but my younger sister's engagement did not last long, because I was unable to meet the demands of the groom-to-be *(here Janti broke into tears leaving the interviewers speechless. He continued with a trembling voice and tears rolling down his cheeks).* My wife cannot work since she had an operation and the doctor prohibited her from doing intensive physical labour. I earn a total of Rs. 20,000 per month of which I pay Rs. 6,000 in rent and Rs. 3,000 as motorbike expenditure. I have a car but its dilapidated condition is a hindrance in selling it off.

12. My community of Jain Hindus is largely based in Soldier Bazar and the Ranchore Lines but I cannot afford the rents there: the *pagri* (security deposit) is Rs. 100,000 albeit the monthly rent is Rs. 1,500. In Punjab Colony, if I had paid Rs. 200,000 as *pagri* and my monthly rent would've been renegotiated at Rs. 3,000.

13. There is an increasing trend in Punjab Colony, of investors purchasing properties, converting them into multistorey buildings and then selling each floor separately. One floor is also sold to the original owner who thus gets money for selling his property as well as his own place to live.

## INTERVIEW—13: BILQEES (A CASE OF POLITICAL PATRONAGE)

Interviewed on 22 October 2011.

1. I was born to peasant labourers in Multan and belong to the *Bhatti* clan (although not all the *Bhattis* of my clan have migrated). Most marriages in our area take place within the community and I too wed a distant relative of mine. My husband was a donkey cart driver in Multan employed by a *bhatta* (brick kiln) owner, but the

income proved too meagre to make ends meet. He was also heavily in debt. We moved to Karachi two months after our wedding, owing to lack of work in Multan.

2.  My *phuppi* (paternal aunt) was our contact in Karachi as she had been living here a long time and we initially moved to her place in Gulshan-e-Iqbal, near NIPA.

3.  Over the years we saved enough money to buy a plot in Adam Goth, near the NIPA intersection and construct one room, a kitchen, a bathroom and a veranda. Seven to eight years back when we lived there the amenities of potable water and sewerage lines were available there. The only problem was lack of gas supply.

4.  Unfortunately after only a few years our house was demolished. We received no compensation except for a plot along the Lyari Expressway. We moved to our allotted plot but it was too far away: I spent four hours commuting to and from Clifton. So subsequently I gave that place to my two brothers and shifted to the nearby *jhuggis* (informal makeshift houses). The current value of my house on Lyari Expressway is Rs. 500,000.

5.  I have four children: three boys and one girl. My husband is unemployed and stays at home all day whereas I earn approximately Rs. 10,000 per month for my work as domestic help.

6.  We were living in Gulshan-e-Iqbal at Adam Goth when Benazir Bhutto asked us to move closer to her residence. My mother used to provide massage services to Benazir and in return she gave her this place (near Shireen Jinnah Colony) where we have constructed a *jhuggi*. Somebody we don't know owns the plot and whenever construction starts here we will have to move out.

7.  People like us get jobs only through word of mouth. If I lose my present job, I will move to some rented place or go back to the village. We have a house back in our village, allotted to my father-in-law under Bhutto's (Zulfikar Ali Bhutto) 5-Marla scheme. Since my father-in-law's death the house has been empty. I know little about rents but I hear that it can fetch Rs. 2,500 per month rental. The problem with moving back to the village is the dire lack of job opportunities there. Moreover, my children don't want to go back.

8.  One of my children is studying and I cannot afford to admit the others in school. If ever I have enough money, I would purchase a plot in Shireen Jinnah Colony. Also if offered, I would accept the option of a flat at a monthly instalment rate of Rs. 5,000 per month for 15 years (but not at Rs. 7,000 per month).

# Appendix 6

## Localities where Consumer Surveys were held and Changes in Property Values

1. Apartments:

2. The apartments surveyed are: i) Civic View Apartments near Hasan Square, Gulshan-e-Iqbal; ii) Ali Plaza, Federal 'B' Area near Aisha Manzal; and iii) Karim Plaza near Aisha Manzal. All three are located in areas where the majority of the lower middle-income population of Karachi lives. The survey was conducted between 30 September and 5 October 2011.

The appreciation/depreciation of the 25 apartments as gathered from the information collected is given as follows:

| | Year of Purchase | Book Value | Survey Year | Market Value | Difference in Years | Increase/Decrease in Value | |
|---|---|---|---|---|---|---|---|
| | | | | | | Amount | Percent |
| 1 | 1999 | 900,000 | 2011 | 3,200,000 | 12 | 2,300,000 | 255.56% |
| 2 | 2006 | 3,800,000 | 2011 | 9,500,000 | 5 | 5,700,000 | 150.00% |
| 3 | 2001 | 1,200,000 | 2011 | 3,200,000 | 10 | 2,000,000 | 166.67% |
| 4 | 2003 | 1,200,000 | 2011 | 3,200,000 | 8 | 2,000,000 | 166.67% |
| 5 | 2000 | 1,100,000 | 2011 | 3,000,000 | 11 | 1,900,000 | 172.73% |
| 6 | 1999 | . | 2011 | 3,200,000 | 12 | NA | NA |
| 7 | 2004 | 1,950,000 | 2011 | 4,000,000 | 7 | 2,050,000 | 105.13% |
| 8 | 2004 | 1,800,000 | 2011 | 5,000,000 | 7 | 3,200,000 | 177.78% |
| 9 | 2001 | . | 2011 | . | 10 | NA | NA |
| 10 | . | . | 2011 | . | NA | NA | NA |
| 11 | 1997 | 1,535,000 | 2011 | 4,500,000 | 14 | 2,965,000 | 193.16% |
| 12 | 2003 | 1,200,000 | 2011 | 2,800,000 | 8 | 1,600,000 | 133.33% |

| | Year of Purchase | Book Value | Survey Year | Market Value | Difference in Years | Increase/Decrease in Value | |
|---|---|---|---|---|---|---|---|
| 13 | . | 1,800,000 | 2011 | 4,000,000 | NA | 2,200,000 | 122.22% |
| 14 | 2006 | 800,000 | 2011 | 4,000,000 | 5 | 3,200,000 | 400.00% |
| 15 | 2009 | 1,500,000 | 2011 | 1,900,000 | 2 | 400,000 | 26.67% |
| 16 | . | . | 2011 | . | NA | NA | NA |
| 17 | 2003 | 800,000 | 2011 | 1,700,000 | 8 | 900,000 | 112.50% |
| 18 | 2005 | 1,200,000 | 2011 | 6,500,000 | 6 | 5,300,000 | 441.67% |
| 19 | 2003 | 800,000 | 2011 | 3,000,000 | 8 | 2,200,000 | 275.00% |
| 20 | 2004 | 1,200,000 | 2011 | 4,000,000 | 7 | 2,800,000 | 233.33% |
| 21 | 2009 | 4,400,000 | 2011 | 3,800,000 | 2 | -600,000 | -13.64% |
| 22 | 2007 | 2,800,000 | 2011 | 2,000,000 | 4 | -800,000 | -28.57% |
| 23 | 2000 | 500,000 | 2011 | 1,600,000 | 11 | 1,100,000 | 220.00% |
| 24 | 2010 | 2,500,000 | 2011 | 1,900,000 | 1 | -600,000 | -24.00% |
| 25 | 2010 | 2,800,000 | 2011 | 3,000,000 | 1 | 200,000 | 7.14% |

2.  Developer's Built Housing:

The survey was conducted at Shaz Bungalows, Rufi Petals, Rufi Spring Flower, Gulshan-e-Shamim Bungalows, and White House all in Scheme-33, where most of Karachi's development built housing for low and lower middle income groups is taking place. In 1980, land along the Super Highway was parceled to various developers and housing societies. It became a subject of considerable controversy due to which further development was delayed. Even now the scheme is partially underdeveloped. The survey was carried out between 10 October 2011 to 18 October 2011. Most of the houses belong to lower-income groups.

The property appreciation/depreciation, as gathered from the data collected of 25 housing units is given in the following table:

| | Year of Purchase | Book Value | Survey Year | Market Value | Difference in Years | Increase in Value | |
|---|---|---|---|---|---|---|---|
| | | | | | | Amount | Percent |
| 1 | 2001 | 850,000 | 2011 | 3,500,000 | 10 | 2,650,000 | 311.76% |
| 2 | 2004 | 1,500,000 | 2011 | 4,000,000 | 7 | 2,500,000 | 166.67% |
| 3 | NA | 1,000,000 | 2011 | 3,500,000 | NA | 2,500,000 | 250.00% |
| 4 | NA | 1,200,000 | 2011 | 4,500,000 | NA | 3,300,000 | 275.00% |
| 5 | NA | 1,400,000 | 2011 | 4,000,000 | NA | 2,600,000 | 185.71% |
| 6 | 2001 | 850,000 | 2011 | 3,500,000 | 10 | 2,650,000 | 311.76% |
| 7 | 2003 | 1,200,000 | 2011 | 3,600,000 | 8 | 2,400,000 | 200.00% |
| 8 | 2000 | 1,200,000 | 2011 | 3,500,000 | 11 | 2,300,000 | 191.67% |
| 9 | 2001 | 1,200,000 | 2011 | 4,500,000 | 10 | 3,300,000 | 275.00% |
| 10 | 2010 | 4,000,000 | 2011 | 4,200,000 | 1 | 200,000 | 5.00% |
| 11 | 2003 | 1,500,000 | 2011 | 4,500,000 | 8 | 3,000,000 | 200.00% |
| 12 | 2006 | 2,000,000 | 2011 | 3,500,000 | 5 | 1,500,000 | 75.00% |
| 13 | 2005 | 1,800,000 | 2011 | 3,600,000 | 6 | 1,800,000 | 100.00% |
| 14 | 2000 | 1,200,000 | 2011 | 5,000,000 | 11 | 3,800,000 | 316.67% |
| 15 | 2006 | 1,200,000 | 2011 | 4,000,000 | 5 | 2,800,000 | 233.33% |
| 16 | 2004 | 1,400,000 | 2011 | 3,200,000 | 7 | 1,800,000 | 128.57% |
| 17 | NA | 4,000,000 | 2011 | 4,500,000 | NA | 500,000 | 12.50% |
| 18 | 2005 | 1,500,000 | 2011 | 3,200,000 | 6 | 1,700,000 | 113.33% |
| 19 | 2001 | 1,000,000 | 2011 | 4,500,000 | 10 | 3,500,000 | 350.00% |
| 20 | 1996 | 1,000,000 | 2011 | 4,500,000 | 15 | 3,500,000 | 350.00% |
| 21 | 1999 | 1,500,000 | 2011 | 4,500,000 | 12 | 3,000,000 | 200.00% |
| 22 | 1990 | 100,000 | 2011 | 5,000,000 | 21 | 4,900,000 | 4900.00% |
| 23 | 2003 | 2,000,000 | 2011 | 3,500,000 | 8 | 1,500,000 | 75.00% |
| 24 | 2000 | 3,000,000 | 2011 | 10,000,000 | 11 | 7,000,000 | 233.33% |
| 25 | 1995 | 2,700,000 | 2011 | 10,000,000 | 16 | 7,300,000 | 270.37% |

APPENDIX 6

3.  Self-Built Housing:

The survey was conducted at Al-Muslim, Pioneer Foundation and Rizvia-II Cooperative Housing Societies, all located in Scheme-33. The members themselves purchased the land from Al-Muslim and further hired contractors to construct their houses. The survey was conducted between 10 September 2011 and 25 September 2011.

The perceived appreciation/depreciation in the property value, as gathered from data that was collected is given in the following table:

|  | Year of Purchase | Book Value | Survey Year | Market Value | Difference in Years | Increase/Decrease in Value | |
|---|---|---|---|---|---|---|---|
|  |  |  |  |  |  | Amount | Percent |
| 1 | 1985 | 7,000 | 2011 | 10,000,000 | 26 | 9,993,000 | 142757.14% |
| 2 | 2001 | . | 2011 | 10,000,000 | 10 | NA | NA |
| 3 | 2007 | 650,000 | 2011 | 30,000,000 | 4 | 29,350,000 | 4515.38% |
| 4 | 2000 | 1,500,000 | 2011 | 1,400,000 | 11 | -100,000 | -6.67% |
| 5 | 2003 | 2,500,000 | 2011 | 1,400,000 | 8 | -1,100,000 | -44.00% |
| 6 | 1996 | 100,000 | 2011 | 10,000,000 | 15 | 9,900,000 | 9900.00% |
| 7 | 2007 | 1,700,000 | 2011 | 8,000,000 | 4 | 6,300,000 | 370.59% |
| 8 | . | 500,000 | 2011 | 10,000,000 | NA | 9,500,000 | 1900.00% |
| 9 | 2006 | 6,000,000 | 2011 | 1,400,000 | 5 | -4,600,000 | -76.67% |
| 10 | 2001 | . | 2011 | . | 10 | NA | NA |
| 11 | 2005 | 700,000 | 2011 | 1,400,000 | 6 | 700,000 | 100.00% |
| 12 | 1997 | 600,000 | 2011 | 12,000,000 | 14 | 11,400,000 | 1900.00% |
| 13 | 2001 | 600,000 | 2011 | 10,000,000 | 10 | 9,400,000 | 1566.67% |
| 14 | 2008 | 4,200,000 | 2011 | 9,000,000 | 3 | 4,800,000 | 114.29% |
| 15 | 2001 | 5,000,000 | 2011 | 25,000,000 | 10 | 20,000,000 | 400.00% |
| 16 | . | . | 2011 | . | NA | NA | NA |
| 17 | . | 450,000 | 2011 | . | NA | NA | NA |
| 18 | . | 400,000 | 2011 | 4,000,000 | NA | 3,600,000 | 900.00% |
| 19 | . | 350,000 | 2011 | 5,000,000 | NA | NA | NA |
| 20 | . | 200,000 | 2011 | 5,000,000 | NA | NA | NA |
| 21 | . | 5,300,000 | 2011 | 7,800,000 | NA | 2,500,000 | 47.17% |
| 22 | . | 2,500,000 | 2011 | 5,000,000 | NA | NA | NA |
| 23 | . | 1,600,000 | 2011 | 7,000,000 | NA | 5,400,000 | 337.50% |
| 24 | . | . | 2011 | . | NA | NA | NA |
| 25 | 1992 | 1,100,000 | 2011 | 6,500,000 | 19 | 5,400,000 | 490.91% |

4. A Listed *Katchi Abadi*:

Located amidst the Khasa Hills that run between blocks P and Q, North Nazimabad to the north of Karachi, Pahaar Ganj is a haphazard development of around 1,000 houses spread over 7.5 acres. 60% of these are permanent concrete constructions. In 1975, when habitation of the area began, a 60 sq yards plot cost Rs. 2,000; today, a house on the same plot costs between Rs. 300,000 and Rs. 500,000. In the nearby formal settlement of North Nazimabad's Block P: a house on 120 sq yards costs between Rs. 2,000,000 and Rs. 2,500,000. 70% of the population of Pahar Ganj is Christian and 30% is Muslim—consisting of Pathans, Mohajirs and Punjabis. The main water connection was brought to the area in 1975. The OPP assisted the people in building connections to a vast majority of the houses in 1998. There is, however, still a shortage of water. Until 1979 the sewerage system was based on open drains and soak pits in 1998 the OPP-RTI self-help mechanism put gutter lines, toilet connections and connections to the main and secondary lines in place. KESC electrified the area between 1981 and 1985. Gas connections came in 1992. Owing to the multiple efforts to fix the road, which regularly breaks due to the usage of substandard road carpeting materials, the road level has risen above the level of the houses and flooding, as such, is a regular phenomenon. Residents work in CDGK and KWSB or as domestic staff in the private sector. Women work as teachers in the area or as nurses, beauticians or as domestic helpers in the middle income or rich areas of the city. Children usually receive education till the primary and/or secondary levels; only 20% attend college after their matriculation. There was controversy concerning the status of the land as it was originally meant for a hospital but eventually the hospital was built elsewhere and after some time Pahar Ganj was added to the list of Regularized *Katchi Abadis* in 1997. (Taken from URC Case Study 2007). Thus survey was conducted between 20 and 24 October 2011.

The appreciation/depreciation in property value, as gathered from the information collected is summarized in the following table:

|   | Year of Purchase | Book Value | Survey Year | Market Value | Difference in Years | Increase in Value | |
|---|---|---|---|---|---|---|---|
|   |   |   |   |   |   | Amount | Percent |
| 1 | 1970 | . | 2011 | 500,000 | 41 | NA | NA |
| 2 | 1965 | 1,000 | 2011 | . | 46 | NA | NA |
| 3 | 1970 | 1,000 | 2011 | 1,000,000 | 41 | 999,000 | 99900.00% |
| 4 | 1970 | 25,000 | 2011 | 800,000 | 41 | 775,000 | 3100.00% |
| 5 | 1956 | 50,000 | 2011 | 1,000,000 | 55 | 950,000 | 1900.00% |
| 6 | 1970 | 50,000 | 2011 | 1,000,000 | 41 | 950,000 | 1900.00% |
| 7 | 1960 | 40,000 | 2011 | 2,100,000 | 51 | 2,060,000 | 5150.00% |
| 8 | 1970 | 50,000 | 2011 | 900,000 | 41 | 850,000 | 1700.00% |
| 9 | 1966 | 200,000 | 2011 | 600,000 | 45 | 400,000 | 200.00% |
| 10 | 1985 | 150,000 | 2011 | 400,000 | 26 | 250,000 | 166.67% |
| 11 | 1975 | 5,000 | 2011 | 500,000 | 36 | 495,000 | 9900.00% |
| 12 | 1966 | 500 | 2011 | 1,400,000 | 45 | 1,399,500 | 279900.00% |

| | Year of Purchase | Book Value | Survey Year | Market Value | Difference in Years | Increase in Value | |
|---|---|---|---|---|---|---|---|
| 13 | 1960 | 500 | 2011 | 800,000 | 51 | 799,500 | 159900.00% |
| 14 | 1970 | 500 | 2011 | 500,000 | 41 | 499,500 | 99900.00% |
| 15 | 1990 | 100,000 | 2011 | 1,000,000 | 21 | 900,000 | 900.00% |
| 16 | 2009 | 675,000 | 2011 | 800,000 | 2 | 125,000 | 18.52% |
| 17 | 1960 | . | 2011 | 800,000 | 51 | NA | NA |
| 18 | 1970 | . | 2011 | 800,000 | 41 | NA | NA |
| 19 | 1960 | . | 2011 | 800,000 | 51 | NA | NA |
| 20 | 1975 | . | 2011 | 500,000 | 36 | NA | NA |
| 21 | 2003 | 400,000 | 2011 | 600,000 | 8 | 200,000 | 50.00% |
| 22 | 1965 | . | 2011 | 1,500,000 | 46 | NA | NA |
| 23 | 1980 | 3,000 | 2011 | 500,000 | 31 | 497,000 | 16566.67% |
| 24 | 1978 | . | 2011 | 350,000 | 33 | NA | NA |
| 25 | 1970 | . | 2011 | 400,000 | 41 | NA | NA |

5.    A Non-listed Informal Settlement in front of Karachi University:

The informal settlement, which is at least 40 years old, is located across the road from the University of Karachi. It has a linear configuration and is comprised entirely of *jhuggis* (informal, tent-like dwellings) set up in a haphazard manner, with religion and ethnicity being the only decisive zoning factor amongst them. Hindus, Muslims, Punjabis, Seraikis, and Sindhis therefore live in different areas of the settlement. There is slight, though visible hostility between members of differing religions. The land that was considered (by the URC) to be part of the University seems to belong to the Sui Southern Gas Company (SSGC). A watchman who is actually positioned on the site by the SSGC to stop encroachments and maintain security, advises the new settlers on where to set up house. Residents are migrants from the rural areas of Sindh and southern Punjab, who have come to the city to earn a better living. Here they don't need to spend on rent or bills, and the cost of living is low. This is probably why they regularly return to this place after the annual eviction conducted by the KMC. They are mostly vendors and hawkers. Potable water can be purchased from a seller on site at Rs. 10. Jerry can and electricity is available through a *kunda* (illegal, makeshift connection) that has apparently been 'legalized' by paying a bribe by a person who has come to some agreement with the KESC. There are a couple of tiny *mandirs* and an *imam bargah* on the site, with a mosque in close proximity to the settlement. The sick usually go to Jinnah or Civil Hospital. Transportation is also readily available owing to the road that runs adjacent to the settlement. The survey was conducted in November 2011.

# Appendix 7
# NGO/CBO Workshop Methodology and Profiles

The following three methods were used in order to obtain feedback from Community Based Organizations (CBOs) and Non-Government Organizations working in the land and housing sectors.

1. Interviews with relevant CBOs and NGOs in their respective survey area offices.

2. Interviews with city level NGOs in their offices.

3. A focus group discussion was held at DAP-NED on 1 December 2011. The following methodology was adopted for the discussion:

   3.1 Introduction to the study

   3.2 Group discussion on housing issues in Karachi with respect to each aspect of this study:

   - Plot owners in low-income areas and their perspective.
   - Tenants in low-income areas and their perspective.
   - Hawkers working and living in low-income areas and their perspective.
   - Informal businesses in low-income areas and their perspective.
   - Communities to be displaced and their perspective.
   - Already displaced communities and their perspective.

   3.3 The above-mentioned groups' accessibility to the following aspects was discussed

   - Land
   - Credit
   - Technical Support
   - Regularization
   - Amenities & Utilities
   - Views on,

     - Affordability
     - Employment
     - Location of housing
     - Commuting time (to work)
     - Plot development versus apartment living
     - Real estate prices in low income areas
     - Mega projects and evictions
     - Security of tenure and related issues

3.4   Focused interviews were held with each NGO and CBO regarding their work on housing and land provision in their area and the city.

4.   All proceedings were recorded and have been incorporated in the sections dealing with the profiles of NGOs and CBOs, area profiles, the role of the NGOs and CBOs in housing provision and the specific issues of plot owners, tenants, hawkers, informal businesses, evictions and affected communities.

The following is a detailed list of all the NGOs and CBOs interviewed for this study:

| Sr. No | Institution | Name of Person Interviewed | Designa-tion | Location of the NGO/ CBO | Area of Intervention | Scope of Work |
|---|---|---|---|---|---|---|
| Non-Government Organization (NGOs) | | | | | | |
| 1. | Orangi Pilot Project Research and Training Institute (OPP-RTI) | Mr Saleem Aleemuddin Mr Ashraf Sagar Ms Rana | Joint Director OPP-RTI Researcher Researcher | Orangi town, Karachi | Originally Orangi town. Replicated in various areas of Karachi and other cities of Pakistan | To provide social and technical guidance and credit for: Low cost sanitation, Clean water, Low cost housing, Micro enterprises, Health and Education |
| 2. | Aga Khan Planning and Building Services Pakistan (AKPBS,P) | Mr Asif Merchant | Chief Executive Officer (CEO) | Clifton, Karachi | Various areas of Karachi and of Pakistan | Work in rural and semi rural areas of Pakistan, finding technology and materials for low cost housing solutions. Also develop housing for the urban Agha Khani community. |
| 3. | Al Khidmat Welfare Organization, Sisters Wing | Mrs Munawar Ikhlas | Nazima | New Town, Karachi | Various areas of Karachi | Helps in funeral services, provide loans for housing. |
| 4. | SHEHRI—CBE | Mr Farhan Anwar | Researcher | P.E.C.H.S., Karachi | Various areas of Karachi | Acts as a pressure group against illegal encroachments, land grabbing of amenity spaces and others assets of the city through legal action. |

| Sr. No | Institution | Name of Person Interviewed | Designa-tion | Location of the NGO/ CBO | Area of Intervention | Scope of Work |
|---|---|---|---|---|---|---|
| 5. | CARITAS Karachi | Mr Mansha Noor | Programme coordinator | P.E.C.H.S., Karachi | Various areas of Karachi | Relief and development work in Microfinance, Disaster management, Livelihood programmes and development of low cost technology and materials. |
| Community Based Organization (CBOs) | | | | | | |
| 6. | Clifton Welfare Organization (CBO from a community of settled owners and tenants) | Mr Asif Ali Khan | Social Mobilizer | Clifton, Karachi | Shah Rasool and Neelum Colony, Clifton | Works for the general betterment of only people from its specific locality. Organizes loans, interface between community and government. |
| 7. | Musharaf Colony Welfare Ittehad (CBO working for one of the community already displaced) | Mr Malik Fazal | President | Hawksbay, Scheme 42, Karachi | Lyari Expressway* Resettlement Project (LERP), Hawks Bay, Scheme 42, Karachi | To solve problems and help the residents of Musharraf colony. Arrange funds for the needy through savings and charity. Try to and resolve area's civic issues. |
| | | Mr Baba Buksh | Member | | | |
| | | Mr Banaras Khan | Member | | | |
| | | Mr Iqbal Rajput | Member | | | |
| 8. | Korangi No. 6, Welfare Organization (CBO from a community of settled owners and tenants) | Mr Abdul Sattar Khan | Member | Korangi No. 6 | Korangi No. 6 | To improve literacy and consequently improve area conditions. To arrange funding for the poor via saving groups and arranging for guarantees for the loans. |
| | | Mr Akber Hussain | Member | | | |

| Sr. No | Institution | Name of Person Interviewed | Designa-tion | Location of the NGO/ CBO | Area of Intervention | Scope of Work |
|---|---|---|---|---|---|---|
| 9. | K.C.R Mutasareen Action Committee (CBO working within one of the community to be displaced) | Mr Rana. M. Sadiq | Member | Umer Colony Kashmir Mujahid Colony | Provide legal support and mobilization in all 28 settlements which are under threat of evictions due to the K.C.R* extension project | To work as a pressure group and provide legal support for the rights of communities under the threat of eviction. Work on housing rights/issues with the support of NGOs like OPP&URC. Residents work on a selfhelp basis to achieve physical development. |
| | | Mr Waqar Awan | Member | | | |
| | | Mr Mohammad Tariq | Member | | | |
| | | Mr Mohammad Saleem Khan | Member | | | |
| | | Mr MUNAWAR KHAN | Member | | | |
| 10. | Hasan Aulia Welfare Society (CBO working for a community under threat of eviction) | Mr Tariq Aziz Hout | President | SITE town, Karachi | Intervention in Hassan Aulia Village | Arranging guarantees for credit and loans. Guarantees' provision for tenants. Support in provision of services and infrastructure. |
| | | Mr M. Umer | Secretary | | | |
| | | Mr Jamal Nasir | Secretary | | | |
| | | Mr Abdul Basit | Secretary | | | |

## PROFILES OF THE NGOs AND CBOs

Orangi Pilot Project (OPP)
> Website: <www.oppinstitutions.org>
> Location: Orangi Town, Karachi.
> Resource Person: Mr Saleem Aleem-ud-Din (Joint Director)
> Category: NGO

Aga Khan Planning and Building Services
> Website: <www.akdn.org/akpbs_pakistan.asp?type=p>
> Location: Clifton, Karachi
> Resource Person: Mr Asif Merchant (CEO)
> Category: NGO

Al-Khidmat Welfare Society Sister's Wing
> Website: <www.pakistanherald.com/Profile/Al-Khidmat-Welfare-1142>
> Location: New Town, Karachi
> Resource Person: Mrs Munawar Ikhlas (Nazima)
> Category: NGO

SHEHRI-Citizens for a Better Environment (SHEHRI-CBE)
    Website: <*www.shehri.org*>
    Location: P.E.C.H. Society, Karachi
    Resource Person: Farhan Anwer (Member)
    Category: NGO

CARITAS
    Website:
    Location: P.E.C.H. Society, Karachi
    Resource Person: Mr Mansha Noor (Programme Coordinator)
    Category: NGO

Clifton Welfare Organization
    Location: Clifton, Karachi.
    Resource Person: Mr Asif Ali Khan (Social Mobilizer).
    Category: CBO from a community of settled owners and tenants

The Clifton Welfare Organization has been working in the Shah Rasool Colony and Neelam Colony since 1980s, where the elders of both colonies are directly responsible for informing the organization about the needs of their respective *mohallas*. The organization assists in providing legal support for development work by assembling communities, writing letters to the government, coordinating groups who meet and negotiate with the government and follow up. If advocacy proves ineffectual, they support the communities' self-help undertakings.

The organization is also involved in resolving their communities' social issues and provides financial and moral support in the case of marriages, accidents and/or death. In such situations, members of the organization exclusively divide all relevant responsibilities (funeral costs, hospital fees, etc.) among themselves, so that everything is taken care of and the distressed family is hassle-free. Similarly, they may be contacted in order to ascertain tenants' reputations and it is only via collective permission that one may rent a house in their localities.

For social amenities, the Clifton Welfare Organization works in tandem with Health, Education and Literacy Pakistan (HELP), an NGO that currently delivers health and educational facilities to locals at a minimal cost. HELP has organized and subsidized the only dispensary (with a qualified doctor)in the area. It also runs a school that has two shifts with fifty students each: the fees for students attending the morning shift is PKR 200 and for those attending the evening shift PKR 150. Education is free for those unable to afford the fees. Uniforms are provided for and the parents are accorded facilities as incentive to keep their children in school. Additionally, HELP has trained education counselors who convince parents to send their children to school.

Concurrently, Mr Asif Ali Khan of the Clifton Welfare Organization arranges extra evening tuitions for the children free of cost. He also runs a nightly adult literacy program, where the youth is encouraged to join and improve their educational qualification and thereby their chances of employment. This CBO/NGO team has made Shah Rasool Colony a better place to live in, with a secure environment.

Although the CBO does not provide direct financial support for housing, its members try to facilitate people in getting rental housing by providing personal guarantees. Similarly personal guarantees are also extended in facilitating loans to individuals as well. The CBO has organized a fund to operate as a loan for income support. It is organized and operated by a group of ten women of the area who provide interest free loans of Rs. 10,000 each with the facility of returning it in easy instalments of Rs. 500 per month. Another group provides loans of maximum Rs. 10,000 on 10 per cent interest basis.

Musharraf Colony Welfare Ittehad
    Location: Hawksbay, KDA Scheme—42, Karachi
    Resource Person: Malik Fazal (President)
    Category: CBO working for a community that has been displaced

The Musharraf Colony Welfare Ittehad was formed in 2005, by the affectees of the Lyari Expressway Resettlement Project once they were relocated to Hawksbay KDA Scheme-42. It is not a registered entity, rather it is a charity based organization with no political agenda. The Welfare receives no external support and is thus an entirely self-supported organization. It consists of 22 locals that primarily provide its funding; sometimes, however, donations are collected from other residents of the area.

    They rent out tents and crockery for weddings at a 25% subsidized rate and at funerals free of cost, whilst the deceased's family is provided with food. Subsequently, the money earned is utilized in maintenance of the crockery and tents. They have also established a solid waste disposal system by hiring local sweepers, which costs PKR 30 per family per home. Area residents also contact the Welfare in order to help settle disputes and other personal problems; in return the Welfare dutifully works towards helping the community and resolving their issues.

    They are in need of technical advice to organize their work and efforts.

Korangi No. 6 Welfare Organization
    Location: Korangi No. 6
    Resource Persons: Abdul Sattar and Akber Hussain (Members)
    Category: CBO from a community of settled owners and tenants

Korangi No. 6 Welfare Organization was established by a group of residents primarily concerned with the level of education in their locality. Mr Javed, an industrial employee at the time, was so appalled by the rate of illiteracy in his area that he quit his job to start a small school. Today, the school has a student population of 750, and holds classes ranging from Pre-Nursery to Grade 10. Local children receive quality education at the nominal fee of PKR 300/month, whilst the school provides essentials such as stationery and uniforms for students whose parents are unemployed or unable to afford the fee. Most parents tend to avail this endorsement. In the case that a child is pulled out of school sans reason, Mr Javed personally looks into the matter and tries to persuade the parents not to do so.

    The organization is involved in resolving local issues and promotes the communities' self-help undertakings, such as savings groups and providing guarantees for persons seeking loans from HBFC/micro-credit organizations. They help in arranging social events, petitions addressed to the government and follow up on development issues. These activities, however, are all on a small scale.

Karachi Circular Railway Mutasirin Action Committee:
    Location: Umer Colony and Kahmir Mujahid Colony
    Resource Person: Rana Muhammad Sadiq (Member)
    Category: CBO working within one of the communities to be displaced (by the KCR extension)

The Karachi Circular Railway (KCR) Mutasirin Action Committee is one of 28 organizations involved in protesting against the proposed evictions that have been planned as part of the KCR Extension. They organize the concerned communities (in this case, Umer Colony and Mujahid Colony) to obtain legal help, arrange protests and in negotiating with the government. They receive their social and technical support from the Urban Resource Centre.

Hassan Aulia Welfare Society (HAWS):
    Location: Hassan Aulia Village, SITE Town, Karachi.
    Resource Person: Mr Tariq Aziz Houti (President)
    Category: CBO working for a community under threat of eviction

The Hassan Aulia Welfare Organization was created in 2000, as a direct response to the proposed evictions caused by the Lyari Expressway project. Through its political connections, negotiations and protest, the organization managed to convince the government to alter its design of the expressway and successfully halted the eviction process. The Lyari Action Committee and the Urban Resource Centre are its prime social and technical support.

Apart from arranging legal support for above settlement, the organization focuses on doing charitable work within the community: it helps members arrange for marriages and funerals, settles disputes and provides guarantees for individuals seeking both formal and informal loans. HAWS further supports local communities in launching campaigns for development work by linking them with the relevant development agencies.

They also encourage saving groups and help in arranging loans for the individuals. Similarly, they also help their fellow community members to find appropriate house to take on rent.

# Appendix 8

## Issues Associated with Affordability and Location: Socio-economic Survey of Poor Settlements, Informal Businesses, and Hawkers

### QUESTIONNAIRE ANALYSIS: RENTALS

#### BASIC INFORMATION

Locality (Q-01):
A number of surveys with the sample size of 27 questionnaires/area, covering the lowincome settlements of north-eastern Karachi and both the formal and informal settlements to the south and southeastern Karachi, was covered to get a holistic view of the city's situation.

Number of House Members (Q-04):
The average number of household members ranged from five to seven members. This statistic corresponds to the city's population density. It is evident however, that the sample represents a medium density population.

Living in Karachi Since (Q-05):
The surveys show that most population comprises of people who have moved to Karachi in the recent past from other parts of the country in hopes of improving their livelihoods. In a majority of the cases—21 respondents out of 27—are living in Karachi for the last 22 years or less, whereas ten of 27 respondents have been residing in Karachi over the last five years or less.

Living in this Area Since (Q-06, 07, and 08):
Of the 27 respondents 13 have been residing in the area since 10 years or less. The rest have been here between 10 years to 35 years. Of the 13 residing between 10 years or less, nine have been here for one year or less. That habitation is predominantly recent is testified by the fact that infrastructure development and construction is relatively new and still in the process of being built. Smaller plots represent the area's attraction for low income tenants and the rent is quite flexible: 5 out of 27 of the surveyed houses pay rent below Rs 2,000, whilst 9 of 27 households earned an income below Rs 7,000.

## EMPLOYMENT DATA

Tables 7 to 11: Employment Data (Q-9 to Q-13):
The nature of work of those surveyed represent the typical low income population of Karachi, with a majority employed as skilled and unskilled labour: 16 responses were unskilled whereas 11 were skilled labour. The areas also attract hawkers and people working in the surrounding houses as servants. 18 of 27 household shave a single working member, whilst nine of the remaining have more than one working member with five having more than two. Roughly half the respondents (13 of 27) work within their areas of residence and environs. It is thus feasible for the majority of respondents (15 of 27) to reach their workplace via walking and not spend much on commuting,

Work venue and affordability are main deciding factors in residents choosing locality.

## CONDITION OF PRESENT HOUSE

Tables 12 to 16 (Q-14 to Q-17):
80% of the plot sizes are less than 80 square yard in size and 10 of 27 sample plots are below 50 square yard, which corresponds well with the size of low income medium household sizes. However, a majority of the surveyed houses (20 of 27) consist of a single ground floor; of these 22 respondents live in two rooms. 19 of 27 are load-bearing structures with G.I./Asbestos sheet roofs. This also represents the medium density, low lying frail nature of the areas. The possibility of vertical development to accommodate future growth is quite high but the existing type of construction is bound to create limitations.

## FINANCIAL ASPECTS OF HOUSING

Tables 17 to 19 (Q-18 to Q-20):
63% of the respondents earn below Rs 15,000, whilst nine have an income below Rs 7,000. 19 of 27 respondents were found to be spending the equivalent of or less than Rs 4,000 on rent whilst a fifth of spent Rs 2,000 or less on rent. As a result, 17 of the 27 households surveyed had no finances left to save by the end of the month.
Tables 20 to 23 (Q-21 to Q-24):
As usual in the low income areas in Karachi, people tend to find their residences personally, that is, through their relatives, friends or by themselves. Estate agents are generally considered the last priority as few can afford the requisite commission. For various reasons, the people here are inclined to live near their relatives and friends.

5 out of 27 people were not ready to reveal their mode of acquisition: it is clear they have acquired their house through illegal means and procedures since many of the surveyed areas were informal settlements. There is a lack of formal contract between landlord and tenant where verbal contracts are considered enough for the landlords, who is often the person in charge of the informal development, and they are either the musclemen or are supported by one or the other political party. The presence of a political party is a quality sufficient to ensure that the tenant strictly abides by the verbal contract. 11 of 27 paid an advance/security deposit below Rs 5,000, whereas seven households received their house sans advance payment. The rent, however, is usually paid in advance, which in a way acts as a kind of security deposit for the month.

Tables 24 to 31 (Q-25 to Q-32):
17 out of 27 respondents revealed that they were unable to save any amount of money whatsoever by the end of the month. The fact that these people, living in rent houses with no savings at the end of the day is enough to prove that the majority does not have the capacity to purchase a house through conventional means. Some of the respondents (4 out of 27) did not want to share information regarding their savings, whilst another four stated that they could afford to spend below Rs 30,000 towards buying a house.

In this background the majority of respondents (20 out of 27) considered taking a loan as justifiable. Given the option of paying back the loaned amount in instalments, 11 claimed Rs 10,000 or below as a manageable amount for down payment; only 4 of the 27 respondents would be able to must earn amount between Rs 10,000–30,000. Six revealed that they would not be able to manage any currency for down payment at all. In the case that the down payment is pre-arranged, only 12 out of 27 respondents have the capacity to manage an amount Rs 2,000 or less per month as a payback instalment. Whereas three out of 27 respondents revealed that they would not be able to afford any instalment at all.

Within this framework, those surveyed agreed to having a preference towards relatives or the government, for loan acquisition. A few (2 out of 27) opted for informal moneylenders, whilst a sizeable number (8 out of 27) avoided the concept of taking loans altogether. It is important to note that a majority of the respondents (22 out of 27) do not have any assets to mortgage against the loan, making the formal possibilities of loan provision doubtful. However, 16 of 27 respondents are not expecting to receive any amount whatsoever, while eight are hoping to get some amount in the future through inheritance, savings or other means, which they can use for buying a house.

## OPINION

Tables 32 to 35 (Q-33 to Q-35):
It is obvious from the survey, as 20 out of 27 respondents stated, the people have very little hope of acquiring their own house under the given circumstances. When asked about what type of house they would rather own if given the choice, 12 out of 27 people opted for a singleunit house, whereas 10 of the 27 had not even thought about it. Regarding the choice of location, 5 out of 27 respondents showed interest in the same or surrounding areas, and four people wished for a place near their work place; the choice of location for a home is clearly governed by affordability and proximity to work and relatives.

Tables 36 to 37 (Q-36 to Q-38):
Interestingly, even when there is no hope for the formal acquisition of one's home, the majority of respondents (21 out of 27) showed little interest in illegal settlements; they would rather continue to live in their rented accommodation. However, a few of the respondents (6 out of 27) evidently chose the option of an unsanctioned abode, by either agreeing or not responding. The reason behind a majority of the respondents (16 out of 27) opting for tenancy is the utter lack of affordability for a house, while four of the 27 respondents chose tenancy since this option allows proximity to relatives, a beneficial resource. The same number of people chose to live on a rental basis owing to proximity of the workplace.

## ANALYSIS: OWNERS

### Basic Information

74 property owners were surveyed in the study to determine 'what the poor can afford'. They represented both the planned/formal and unplanned/informal areas. The survey focused on the south-eastern and south-western localities of Karachi. The number of persons per house is high, considering 43 of the 74 households surveyed supported six to ten family members, similarly 15 households had upwards of ten family members. This is a typical trend of any low income settlement in the city, the reason being larger family sizes (owing to the joint family system culture) and the economic realities bring people together to share resources.

### Residential History

The survey showed that a majority (52 out of 74) of the respondents have been living in Karachi for over two decades. Similarly, 57 of the 74 respondents stated that they had been living in the area over the past ten years. Only 13 respondents were found to be residing here for a time period less than a decade. The same pattern was also found in the category of home acquisition. 38 of the 74 respondents were previously living in other parts of the city and moved here after purchasing property in the area. A considerable number of respondents (17 out of 74) informed us that they had migrated here directly from other parts of the country/rural parts on the outskirts of the city. It is important to mention that 11 respondents revealed that they had been living in the same or surrounding areas prior to owning the respective property, which reflects the importance of these locations for the poor.

### Employment Data

Regarding the respondents' occupations, there were very few white-collared jobholders (9 out of 74) as compared to other formally planned areas, where residents tend to have a higher literacy level. Instead, 31 out of 74 respondents may be categorized as blue-collar workers, a mix of skilled and unskilled labourers of which eight were hawkers, rickshaw owners or drivers. With these low earning jobs and larger family sizes, it is understandable that half of the surveyed households (49 out of 74) would have more than one bread earner. 27 out of 74 respondents work in the same or surrounding areas, while 32 respondents had their workplaces in other parts of the city. This is another unique trend for a formally planned area: other surveys showed that in poorer (squatter) areas, the majority worked within or in the surrounding areas. This home-work relationship is also reflected in the majority (52 out of 74) of respondents' usage of public transport, who are spending a monthly sum of Rs 1,000 to 3,000 on commuting.

### Condition of Present House

It is interesting to note that townhouses are the most desired type of housing for the poor as well: 60 out of the 74 surveyed houses were found to be a town or a single unit house; there are very few (3 out of 27) apartment owners found here. Similarly, a majority of the surveyed houses (38 out of 74) had an area between 120 sq. yards–240 sq. yards: given the population's buying power versus property rates, this places them in the middle income bracket. A considerable number of surveyed people (16 out of 74) have plots with areas between 80 sq. yards and 120 sq. yards. Only 15 of respondents had plots measuring less than 80 sq. yards, which is typical of Karachi's squatter settlements.

Despite larger family sizes and plot areas, 42 of the 74 surveyed houses had a maximum of 3 to 4 rooms, which may be because more than half of the surveyed houses (50 out of 74) have only a ground floor, while only 24 were found to live in double or higher storeyed structures. The restriction in height is justifiable by observing the type of structures and the construction technology employed. A majority of the surveyed houses, 60 out of 74 to be exact, are supported by load bearing structures, and there is a preponderance (42 out of 74) of the G.I./asbestos sheet roofing system. 18 out of 74 houses were found to have girder/tile roofing systems. R.C.C. structures also exist, but in relatively smaller numbers.

## Reasons for Choosing This Area

Irrespective of the formal/informal and planned/unplanned nature of the settlements, the outstanding reason for living here, as per 63 respondents, is the proximity to relatives. It is clear that lower income groups prefer to live communally, a behavioural aspect relating to rural backgrounds. 52 of 74 people also mentioned affordability as the reason (amongst others) for being here; for the minorities, affordability may be the sole reason for choosing this area and considered a main point of attraction for new comers. This analysis can be backed by the fact that 44 out of 74 respondents got to know about this area through their relatives and friends, whereas only five out of 74 respondents found their property through an estate agent. This market mechanism is not a very common practice in the low income settlements of Karachi. The same phenomenon is observed in the buying and selling of property, as 38 out of 74 respondents had acquired plots directly from the owner, without the aid of middle men. Relatives and community members advised them in regard to buying property.

## Property Acquiring Details

Regarding details of property acquisition, it is important to note that more than half of the 74 respondents have legal documents in the form of contracts and agreements. This reflects the formal planned area in the survey, while only two respondents accepted a verbal pact, a typical occurrence in squatter settlements. 25 out of 74 respondents did not respond to this query, indicating that they wanted to hide the legal status of their property and thereby suggesting that a majority of these might be informal developments, and without any formal documents.

Irrespective of legal status, 59 out of 74 respondents claim to have planned and constructed their own houses, Four had consulted architects/engineers and others undertook the services of a contractor, displaying a typical low income group trend. Only 10 out of 74 respondents have professed to have taken permission from the concerned authorities for construction, while 39 did not take any such leave and 12 were unaware of these procedures or had occupied an area not on lease. Another important reason for not getting consent is that the majority (28 out of 74) of respondents were unaware of the necessity of following these procedures and they get away with making informal payments.

## Cost/Finances

The current value of the majority of properties here have a real estate value between Rs 1,000,000—10,000,000 as gauged by 60 out of 74 respondents. Only 7 out of 74 quoted the value as being less than Rs 0.1 million. Irrespective of these high prices, none of the properties were originally worth more than 0.1 million at the outset.

If Payment of Property was in Instalments, What was the Value:

Whilst analysing the financial aspects of the area's property, it is important to mention that the majority of them were bought over a decade ago. Thus the values reflect the trend of payments in instalments, and not the current situation.

61 out of 74 respondents bought their property in a single cash deal. Only 13 out of the 74 were at liberty to pay their dues in instalments; of these, five had to disburse a down payment less than Rs 10,000, whilst seven paid between Rs 50,000–100,000 to the effect. Furthermore, in nine out of the 13 cases, the cost of each instalment was greater than Rs 10,000, only in three cases did the instalment cost between Rs 1,000–10,000. In the majority (9 of 13) of these transactions, there were three instalments in total and the remaining 4 respondents had paid in one to two instalments.

Regarding the capital required for the purchase of property, 38 out of 74 respondents marked personal savings as their source of funding, whilst 19 had taken a loan and another 16 mentioned that they sold their assets to arrange the funds.

**If Loan was Taken**

19 out of 74 respondents had managed their resources by taking loan at any stage of the transaction: 12 of these 19 respondents had borrowed from relatives and/or friends and two had formally acquired a loan from the HBFCL. In the process, there was no need for informal payment towards loan acquisition. In all cases, the loaned amount was below Rs 100,000. 10 of the 19 borrowers had borrowed an amount between Rs 10,000–30,000. 14 of the 19 had a repayment period of over one year. Most importantly, in a majority of the cases the loan was procured sans any mortgage.

**Construction**

52 out of 74 respondents stated that the time it took for the construction of their house lasted between one to ten years' time. This suggests an incremental housing strategy, since the plot sizes are not so large as to require such a long period to complete. However, 15 of the 74 respondents had managed to complete the construction within one year. Although, a majority of the construction as probably carried out in phases, the respondents were unable to provide a clear answer, as there was no proper documentation of the process.

56 out of 74 respondents informed us that they had bought construction material from the neighbouring *thallawala*, of which 21 had obtained the material on credit.

## ANALYSIS: POPULATION TO BE DISPLACED

### BASIC INFORMATION

#### Location

The sample size for this survey was 57, targeting the population along the railway track, specifically on encroached areas along the Karachi Circular Railways' (KCR) right-of-way. The KCR is being replanned and reinstated after a period of two decades: its right-of-way is to be decidedly cleared. The areas that were surveyed belong to those earmarked for eviction and demolition by the government. These areas are therefore worthwhile in understanding the importance of location for the poor.

**Number of House Member**
18 of the 57 households surveyed support over ten members and 30 others have six to ten members. This is probably due to the culture of the extended family system commonly found in rural households, and simultaneously it is a result of the reality of the economic necessity that forces people to share their resources, however many members the house may have to sustain; as seen in a majority of the cases. Eight out of 57 households suggest the presence of bachelors in the form of single rooms and the subdivisions of plots rented out for income purposes.

**Living in Karachi Since**
Statistics shows that the majority of the population has been living in these areas, and in greater Karachi area, for over 25 years, as verified by 29 out of 57 respondents. Most inhabitants migrated here from rural areas of the country. 21 of 57 respondents directly moved to their current location and have been living here ever since, showing that the population is well woven in the city fabric, and resultantly, well connected with their own set of contacts, relations and businesses here.

**Employment Data**
Similar to other squatter settlements of rural immigrants in Karachi, there seems to be no specific trend in the residents' occupational capacities. As per usual, labourers, hawkers and skilled workers are present in the surveyed areas. Interestingly enough, however, 15 of 57 respondents are engaged in office jobs, this reflects the urbanized nature of the population despite their rural disposition, a phenomenon that can only occur after a substantial amount of time has lapsed. 22 of the 57 households had more than one bread earner, an understandable situation considering the average size and structure of the households. Nine out of 57 respondents are engaged in livelihood activities at home. It is interesting to note that a predominance (34 out of 57) of respondents work either within or close to their area. This is also demonstrated in their spending on commuting, which is considerably low, and highlights the importance of residential location—an aspect directly linked with the work place and eventually to the city.

**Condition of Present House**
7 of the 57 plots were found to be below 50 sq. yards in dimension and 28 of the 57 measured 50 sq. yards to 80 sq. yards, a distinct expression of a low income settlement. However, 16 other plots are 80 sq. yards to 120 sq. yards in size. The houses generally employed loadbearing construction technology, with 26 cases having tiled roofs, and the remaining 21 with roofs of galvanized iron. This technology has a definite bearing on the number of floors in the house, that is, 30 out of the 57 surveyed buildings had only a ground floor, while 20 were double storeyed. The restriction in height is also reflected in the number of rooms: 28 out of 57 houses had only two rooms, whilst 19 houses had a maximum of four rooms. Given the large family size, the plot size and the number of rooms seem insufficient. As far as services are concerned, since the areas are primarily squatter settlements with no legal status, the majority (32 out of 57) of respondents have illegal utility connections.

**Reasons for Choosing This Area**
Despite the lack of facilitation and standards, these people prefer to live here. 40 out of 57 respondents moved here (along with other reasons) because they wanted to live

closer to their relatives: they prefer living in a communal setting, typical of rural migrants. The illegal nature of the land also plays a role in this decision, as it is low in cost and thus affordable for the poor. At present, the respondents' link with their respective work places is strong and children can walk to their schools, both priorities were stated by 40 of the 57 surveyed.

### Land/House Acquisition Details

Although there was no response to whether respondents had squatted on the plot/house, almost half of the respondents (23 out of 57) had started off with an empty piece of land and constructed a house over it later on. This indicates old ownership and to some extent, encroachment as well. 30 out of 57 respondents had acquired property with the help of their relatives; this illustrates the encroachers' strategy to gain strength from the community in order to secure a better bargain. 39 out of 57 people, however, claimed to be in possession of the requisite documents (stamp papers or agreements). About a fifth of those surveyed (12 out of 57) had accepted verbal agreements, reflecting the illegal nature of the properties and the underlying power that makes sure all parties abide by these verbal deals.

### Cost/Finances

As per the majority of surveyed houses, the cost of property was below Rs 30,000 at the time of purchase. Today, the cost of the same property starts at Rs 500,000 and goes higher than Rs 1,000,000, as stated by 34 out of 57 cases. The property is now an asset for the people as well as a hope for the improvement of their living standards. The location is thereby precious to the people and it is clear they will not let it go.

### Opinion on Relocation and Resettlement

In the background of possible eviction, the majority (25 of 57) did not want to express their views on whether the KCR should be implemented or not. 19 out of 57 respondents were clear that it should not be implemented and that they will not vacate their land at any cost. 32 of the 57 do not want to avail any government schemes that offer peripheral relocation, however they do agree to a change of address in the case that the government compensates them according to the market value of their property. It is also evident from the statistics (34 out of 57), that residents of the area have plans to remain within or close to their current bearings, even after eviction, further reinstating the importance of the location for them.

## ANALYSIS: POPULATION ALREADY DISPLACED

### BASIC INFORMATION

#### Sample of Displaced Population

This group of people has either been displaced from their location in the past or rehabilitated out of city; they provide us with interesting aspects regarding the importance of location for the poor. 52 samples were taken from two different locations catering to the evicted population of the city. These people were shifted to the current location in the last ten years or so.

Household sizes are relatively high, as 38 out of 52 surveyed houses supported between six to ten members, and six out of 52 households were found to have more than ten household members: this is understandable considering these are low-income groups—rural migrants tend to live in extended family systems which additionally supports the household income.

## Physical Assets

Although eviction and subsequent rehabilitation destroy existing patterns of life developed over decades, it seems they also provide the rehabilitated person with legal ownership of his/her property and are brought into the tax-net through formalized services, etc. It is observed that all those who were surveyed previously occupied unleased properties, and are now in legal possession of their land, it does not matter to them who gives them the title of their property. Here again, the respondents' knowledge of the legalities and their concerned departments cannot be relied upon, as many have no valid knowledge of the same. Their information is often influenced by a number of other factors. 49 out of 52 respondents are the owners of the property and only five were tenants. However, the formal nature of the property adds to the inhabitants' budget expenses in the form of utility bills and taxes, whereas their previous (informal) locations gave them the liberty to resort to informal means, resultantly adding to savings on the individual scale.

## Condition of House

Previously, 32 out of 52 respondents had plots larger in area as compared to their current property of 80 sq. yards. Larger plot areas were only possible owing to their previous colonies being informal developments. Similarly, 38 out of 52 respondents currently have single storeyed homes with one to two rooms, whereas previously, 42 respondents had one to four rooms in their double storeyed abodes. There is no significant difference between the number of families and the types of roofing employed. A majority of the respondents were previously and also now are currently utilizing the tiled roofing system over load bearing walls.

Regarding the values assumed by the owners, the change in location has not affected any drastic change. Other queries regarding the cost of construction were either not correctly understood or dealt with a hesitancy to share numbers. Thus, a very low frequency of responses was achieved, on the basis of which it is very difficult to reach to any conclusion.

## Reason for Choosing This Area

Regarding their reasons for shifting here, respondents stated there was no other option, as the government was determined to demolish their previous houses. The only alternative left for the people was to shift to another place on rent or move in with nearby relatives. 28 out of 52 respondents opted for tenancy after the eviction since it was impossible to construct a new house given the time and monetary constraints. However, shifting the majority to this current location makes it clear that the option of rental housing was not financially feasible. There are many people who did not shift here and are thus not covered in this survey. It took almost five months for the residents to move here, and even so, their houses were not completed, since it takes longer than five months to fully construct an 80 square yard house.

## Impact of Transportation

The difference in transportation facilities has drastically impacted peoples' lives, especially since the day time availability of transportation routes has decreased. 47 out of 54 complained about the unavailability of transport, especially at night time and 25 to 30 respondents specified that the time and cost for commuting to jobs, educational institutes, health facilities, the market or even socializing with the relatives, has markedly increased and consequently impacted the lives of the people as far as transportation mode and facilities are concerned.

## Transport Condition in Previous Area (Mode of Transportation Used)

The comparison of transportation facilities between the previous and current locations of residence is quite clear: the use of public transport has drastically increased for all activities: including the market, schools, colleges and health facilities, as compared to their previous location, where people usually lived within walking distance of all of these. Now, around 30 to 45 (out of 52 respondents) people use public transport in order to reach their workplaces, whilst earlier only around 20 to 30 (out of 52 respondents) people were doing so. It is observed that walking to the activity place has declined to a considerable degree, clearly showing that distances have increased and consequently time and expenses and the frequency of social visits have also altered considerably.

## Facilities

Considering the overall situation and the hopes and opinion of the people, almost all (51 out of 52) of the respondents are sure they will continue to live here in the future. 45 out of the 52 respondents said they would not go back to their previous areas, even though they have not been facilitated properly in their new location and they have no hope that the government will fulfil its promises. This body of opinion was regardless of the fact that 22 respondents claimed that the change in location had definitely negatively impacted their living standards. Interestingly, 18 of the 54 respondents stated that the change in location had brought about no change in their standard of living.

With regard to the comparison of educational facilities in their current and previous locations, 46 out of 52 people say that primary schooling is available at the current location, as it was at the previous one, however, 23 respondents mentioned that secondary level education facilities have decreased and college facilities even more so. This reveals the area's weakened relationship with the city; this situation must surely be affecting the literacy level of the people, especially females.

In the context of a comparison of the availability of health facilities (clinics and dispensaries) at their current and prior locations, they find no considerable difference. However, 28 respondents said the accessibility and availability of hospitals for people has drastically decreased, since resettlement areas are too far away from the city.

Interestingly, 42 respondents stated that the number of playgrounds in the area has significantly increased, as compared to their previous location. This is a good case to study for the comparison between formal and informal areas.

## SOCIAL ASSETS

### Impact of this Location on Relation

The change in location has definitely made an impact on social relationships, as observed in the analysis of earlier focus areas: poor/informal areas are generally guided by ethnic groupings, an arrangement that usually falls apart after eviction, and gives rise to a mixed, relatively more neutral and accessible settlement. In the survey 30 out of 52 respondents identified a better relationship with the councillor, and the opposite with the town *nazims* and the musclemen of the area. Nevertheless, it is interesting to note that 16 respondents felt no change whatsoever in their relationships with relatives, whilst the same number of people claimed that they have no kinship left with their relatives (as they had compared to their previous location).

### Impact on Availability Of
47 out of 52 respondents complained that the change in location, along with other impacts, has created difficulties in finding new full-time or part-time jobs. Similarly, 31 out of the 52 bemoaned the difficulty in finding a school for their children and acquiring loans, amongst other things. This is because of the long distance between the locations of residences and job markets. This distance has adversely affected incomes and simultaneously increased expenditures.

Problems aside, the majority of respondents (41 out of 52) feel secure here and day by day, the pattern of living increasingly resembles their previous living patterns, especially since a majority of respondents live nearby. All the same, the peoples' understanding of their rights and how to avail them has not changed, and there is no affiliation with any particular association because of the lack of social interaction since the area is relatively new. The people hesitate to mention the presence of political parties.

The availability of provision of goods, especially items of daily usage, on credit, indicates an old relationship between buyer and seller. This fact was affirmed by 45 of 52 respondents. The reason being that although the area is not too old, people have been living here for a decade or so, and have managed to gain the shopkeepers' trust. As 38 out of 52 respondents complained of the unavailability of construction material on credit, it's clear that it will take a bit longer for the newcomers to gain the *thallawala*'s confidence.

### Financial Assets
The *bisi* system is an outcome of old, close social ties of mutual trust and reliability. 39 out of 52 respondents said it was obvious that there is abatement in the *bisi* option at the current location, as compared to that in the previous locality. People are quite hesitant to share their financial status and savings, which is obvious, given the law and order situation in the city.

Nineteen out of 20 respondents said there is no government facility to provide residents with jobs, and there is very little chance of obtaining a loan from the government. 40 out of 52 respondents have not opted for government issued loans.

## ANALYSIS: INFORMAL BUSINESSES

### Locality (Q-01)
The sample size comprised 30 questionnaires, covering the low income areas to the north-east, south and south-east of Karachi, within both formal and informal settlements.

### Business Detail

24 out of 30 respondents stated that they have been conducting business here for 10 to 15 years or less, whilst 13 of the 30 had been running their business elsewhere before moving to this area.

*The nature of work of the inhabitants responded to typical low income population, with the majority being skilled and unskilled labour.*

13 of the 30 businesses surveyed fell under the category of cottage industries, of which nine were engaged in manufacturing and four in packaging.

### Work-Home Relation

28 of 30 respondents live and work in the same (surveyed) vicinity, which accounts for most of them walking to their work place; the rest use public and private transport modes with fares ranging from Rs 300–1,000.

### Place of Business Details

*24 of the 30 surveyed shops have plots measuring less than 120 sq. yards;* 13 of these are on plots upto 60 sq. yards in size, to which the low-income medium shop sizes correspond well. A majority (22 out of 30) of the surveyed shops have permanent structures and are centrally located.

### Details of Place Acquisition

As is the case in Karachi's low income areas, *people find their place of business via personal contacts,* that is, through relatives, friends or by themselves. Only 2 out of 30 people found a place employing an estate agent. *Estate agents are the last priority in this regard as very few can afford the necessary commission, here too, people often rely on their relatives and friends.* Most of the people had acquired land through legal means and procedures, which is reflected in the response of 22 of the 30 surveyed being in possession of the stamp papers or other kinds of legal documents for their shops. 12 out of 30 businesses were found to be on owned land, while the remaining 18 were on rental premises. Regarding the advance or security deposit requisite for occupying rental premises, 10 out of 18 cases had paid less than Rs 5,000 or nothing at all. The rent, however, is usually taken in advance, which forms a kind of security deposit for the month.

### Cost/Finances

*Regarding tenancy, only 6 out of 30 respondents spent Rs 2,000 or less on rent. A majority of the population had nothing left to save by the end of the month.*

### Informal Payments

*They survey showed that the bhatta system is not very common in the area: 22 out of 30 respondents stated that they do not pay bhatta. A small number of people (2 of 30) who paid it, receive warnings in the case that they are unable to pay up on time.*

### Reason for Selecting the Area

*18 out of 30 respondents specified the reason for selecting this area to be the proximity to home and relatives;* this reason was supported by the affordable prices of land and running a business here. Furthermore the area fulfils all the major objectives when selecting an area such as security, transport, etc.

**Opinion**
The survey evinced that the business owners are satisfied with the amenities and services in the area, all except for water supply and electricity, which 10 out of 30 respondents deemed unsatisfactory.

## ANALYSIS: HAWKERS

### Basic Information
The average number of years for those starting at the same place where they are currently operating is 11.5. 80% of the hawkers are in the same area as where they began. On average, the permanent hawkers have been in their areas approximately four years longer than their temporary counterparts. Temporary hawkers in the Delhi Colony have been working there for 13.4 years. Hawkers that have moved from Ranchore Lines to Delhi Colony have on average stayed on for a longer time than those who were originally there. Furthermore, hawkers that moved from other areas to Delhi Colony have been there more than ten years ago on average.

66% of the hawkers that started out in Gulistan-e-Jauhar still work in the area. Recently, there have been migrations from other areas to Gulistan-e-Jauhar, the area has the lowest average of the number of years of the hawkers operating here. The hawkers currently operating in Saddar have been there from the outset and 60% are permanent. Saddar's permanent hawkers have, on an average, been working in the area for five years more than the temporary ones. Similarly, the hawkers in Lyari have been working there from the start, 60% are permanent. Finally in Liaquatabad, 80% of the hawkers are temporary and have been working in the area for an average of 7.75 years.

### Business Details
*14 out of 27 hawkers work as part of the markets, since this is where most customers come to purchase multiple goods under one roof.* Customers mostly come to the hawkers for fruit and clothes. Most customers belong to the local public. *Hawkers popularly employ a watchman as a safety measure, as 13 of 27 hawkers mentioned.* Due to general security concerns, 14 out of 27 surveyed hawkers use some sort of safety measure. 15 out of the 27 hawkers store their goods at the place of sale at night. The business places of the hawkers are evenly spread out in the various areas. *Almost all the temporary hawkers are found to be directly or indirectly connected with markets.* Owing to the congestion in the areas, the hawkers of Saddar and Delhi Colony areas are demanding a separate place for parking.

### Work and Living Area Location, Reason for Choosing this Area
*19 out of the 27 hawkers interviewed walk to their place of business,* since most of them live in the same vicinity. Owing to the convenience of saving time and money, 22 out of 27 hawkers preferred to have their work area close to their home or at least to relatives' homes. However, this preference often has its own disadvantages: they may suffer security problems; have to make *bhatta* payments and there may be lack of basic infrastructure, such as water. *Those hawkers not living in the same area spend a monthly average of Rs 4,000 on commuting. Public transport (7 out of 27) is the second most popular mode of transport because it is affordable.*

**Place Acquisition Details, Cost and Finance, Informal Payments**

Both the price and the rent of the spaces have increased significantly. *Almost all the hawkers in Gulistan-e-Jauhar are using illegal electrical connections/kunda.* Informal payment/*bhatta* is prevalent in almost all areas surveyed. *If a hawker from Gulistan-e-Jauhar is unable to pay his bhatta he is unable to operate in the area and may even be subjected to torture.* The efficiency of *bhatta* collection in this area is due to the fact that political workers are more active in accruing *bhatta* than criminal gangs or operators. *Political parties have a strong influence in certain areas and usually are a menace if their demands are not met.* Hence, by paying *bhatta*, the hawkers in Gulistan-e-Jauhar are primarily paying for peace and security in their area. In general, it is difficult for the hawkers to manage these illegal payments, since different bodies demand separate amounts from each hawker. The significant hike in costs of rent has further aggravated the financial situation. Normally, *if a place is bought through a certain party, that party is inevitably one of the bhatta extortionists.* Almost 13 out of 27 hawkers have been dislocated at some point in time, the reason being that they found difficulty in making *bhatta* payments.

# AREA PROFILES OF THE SURVEYED AREAS

The focus areas of the city were selected in relation to the five types of housing available to the poor. i) Home owners in regularized informal settlements; ii) home owners in settlements whose status is undefined; iii) tenants in different types of settlements; iv) families in relocation settlements; and v) settlements under threat of eviction.

The survey respondents included plot owners and residents of Neelum Colony, Shah Rasool Colony and Ghaziabad in Orangi, who are first generation migrants belonging to communities that migrated to Karachi between 1960–1970 as a result of the Green Revolution and the consequent industrialization and also the migration to West Pakistan after East Pakistan became Bangladesh. Initial migrants were either settled in these areas by the government or had squatted wherever land was available. Eventually they became the owners of these plots. By now, most of them have regularized legal status as per the Katchi Abadi Regularization Law passed in 1985.

The tenants are part of the second wave of migrants, who came to live in Karachi during the 1980s, a result of rural–urban migration and the Afghan War. These include the second generation of older residents and are found in all the localities surveyed and especially in Machhar Colony, Safoora Goth and Ittehad Town.

Then there are communities under the threat of eviction, as they do not have a regularized status on the land they occupy, such as General Abad and the already relocated communities of Taiser Town and Musharraf Colony, who are struggling in the resettlement process.

The survey is targeted towards understanding the following:

- The state's current role in: providing housing for the poor, its choice of locations for the same and the proposed resettlement schemes.
- The poor community's level of affordability and their choice of location. In the case of encroachments, their capacity to organize for regularization and development of their areas.

- The change of status of the old, poor settlements to possible housing schemes catering to the middle class, and their impending gentrification since these areas are mostly bordered by middle and upper income localities and consequently, have high real estate value.

- The second and third generation of poor who are upwardly mobile but opt to live in an extended family setup. They sometimes live in rented premises located in other poor areas close to their workplace, as opposed to buying new plots/flats on the periphery of the city.

- The conditions of the communities who are under threat of eviction by the state and/or develop proposed mega projects.

- The communities who have already been relocated and are currently tackling issues concerning the long commute to the city for work, education, health and other services.

- The choice of location and condition of informal businesses in the low-income areas of Karachi.

**Musharraf Colony**

Situated near Hawksbay in Keamari Town, Karachi, this is the Lyari Expressway's (see Box I) Resettlement Project (LREP), that was built in 2003 and is popularly known as Musharraf Colony. It is a plot-based development, where plots have been allotted to the affected of the displacement caused by the Lyari Expressway Project. They were moved here from old, settled areas near the city centre, such as Jahanabad, Shershah, Lasbela, and Mianwali Colony.

The colony was planned on LDA (Lyari Development Authority) land in 2000, where the layout included green belts, parks, amenities and utilities. Most plots measure 80 sq. yards in size and affected families were pledged an additional Rs 50,000 as compensation money, only half of which has been disbursed to date. The plot size per family has proven to be inadequate as these largely include extended family that is parents, grandparents, married sons and their families. The beneficiaries of the LERP were originally gainfully employed residents of the city centre. Their children attended the city's schools, colleges and universities, and were accustomed to services and amenities available there.

A site office was setup for the LERP with staff designated to look over the development and assist in the process of resettling the people. Initial blocks were developed as per the LERP plan, requests for electricity submitted, a girls' school was built and open spaces were developed. Once the area was settled by 2002, however, the LERP staff began to subdivide green belts and sell them as plots. Water tankers started to disappear; no teachers were arranged for the girls' school and open spaces apparently vanished. According to community residents, this was the doing of politically backed LERP employees who had turned into real estate agents, selling amenity plots and sharing the subsequent profit with others involved.

The situation worsened in 2005, as the LERP project came to a close, its site office was shut down and the projects' operations and maintenance handed over to the Lyari Development Authority (LDA). The LDA does not have a sense of ownership towards LERP: it is disinclined to listen to any complaints and following the earlier pattern of corrupt LERP officials, is busy with land subdivisions and the sale of subsequent plots in the open market. Currently, the resettlement area is riddled with development related issues, such as providing a sufficient water supply, an adequate sewerage system, transport facilities and the availability of social amenities. Water is acquired at Rs 700 per tanker; houses have pit latrines, and residents collect their own garbage through a system of sweepers hired on the Rs 22,000 community fund. Residents also organize the fund towards social issues, such as funerals, marriages, family disputes, and medical camps.

Both the LERP and the LDA portray the LERP as a successful project on paper and in the media, as this increases the real estate value of the land, and they can sell more illegal plots in the area. Residents were not given a lease on their land at the time of resettlement on the premise that they were not sanctioned to sell the plot for a period of five years: they were to apply for and obtain ownership documents after this prescribed time span. Since then despite the residents' pleas, plots are not being regularized as promised, this is causing insecurity among the allottees of yet another eviction.

The affected of the Lyari Expressway Project had opted for the LERP in hopes of access to a regularized plot of land where they could live, work and invest. Instead, the current non-regularized status of the settlement, the inability to operate businesses from homes, minimal amenities and services and the two-hour distance from the city has made life extremely difficult. This resettlement without tenure rights and development for these people is proving to be a very expensive housing option compared to their earlier location near the city centre, thus tempting residents to move back. Musharraf Colony is yet another example of a failed resettlement plan, leading to the country's massive housing backlog and wasted time and resources.

---

**BOX I: The Lyari Expressway Project**

The Lyari Expressway is a 16 km long, elevated expressway cutting through the city. Initiated by the Federal Government, this project was initially rejected by the city as it proposed the eviction, demolition and relocation of thousands of people, their properties and assets. Due to political pressure, however, the project was passed in 2000, leading to mass evictions.

---

### Mohammadi/Madni Colony (Machhar Colony)

Machhar Colony is currently known as Mohammadi Colony. It houses 700,000 people on a 4-km stretch of land and is a located along the railroad tracks on Maaripur Road in Karachi. The name is derived from both the large population of *machayr* (fishermen) residing here, as well as, from the abundance of *machar* (mosquitoes) found in the area at nigh time. Residents are currently dealing with issues regarding property rights with the Karachi Port Trust (KPT), the original owners of this land.

Many years ago the area was under water, till people started land reclamation by filling in stones at a depth of roughly 15ft. The area's *mohalla* committee, called the Pakistan Bengali Charitable Association, works for its development.

Although almost entirely Muslim, the community offers wide ranging ethnic diversity, as residents hail from three distinctive backgrounds: Afghanistan, Burma and Bangladesh. Bengalis, Burmese and Pathans have been living in segregated zones within the colony since 1971.

There is an 80% illiteracy rate in the area, whereby a majority of this percentage comprises of women and girls. Most locals are employed in the nearby fishing industries as shrimp peelers, fishermen, fish cleaners, or labourers in the ship breaking industry. The industry is exclusively dominated by the Bengalis, who are also a majority in the colony.

The Karachi Port Trust insists on relocation of the settlement, as it currently occupies KPT land. Although several proposals have been made to this effect, the communities insist on staying in the area, as this location is near their suitable employment centres, the city centre and the port. The impasse in the situation has resulted in Macchar Colony not having been regularized, and the lack of lease has affected real estate prices. Therefore there is a lack of interest among the inhabitants to invest in their property and this results in bad conditions of the locality.

### General Abad—Shireen Jinnah Colony

General Abad is situated near the new Ziauddin Hospital, 40 feet from the Karachi Circular Railway tracks. The area's proximity to a truck/oil tanker terminal and the port attracted Afghan immigrants during the 1980s. Here they could work as drivers, cleaners, and labourers. They were given patronage to settle by the then dictator General Zia ul-Haq, hence the name General Abad.

By the 1990s, the colony was popularly known as a pathan-dominated settlement, and many people migrated here from Mardan, Swat, and other tribal regions.

Salim Zia, a politician from the northern areas worked for its development. Initially, there was provision for electricity and water in the area, but no sewage facilities: a pit latrine system was used for sewage disposal. President Ghulam Ishaq Khan got electricity to be provided in General Abadand the residents, fulfilled the need for water on a self-help basis. Once fully serviced with utilities and amenities, the area was regularized and people have invested in construction since, resulting in multi storeyed structures available for rent and purchase for residence and businesses.

The area is currently under threat of eviction, owing to both the Karachi Circular Railway (KCR) project as well as impending gentrification, due to the high-income areas adjoining it. Development of the upscale Ziauddin Hospital has added to the land's real estate value.

The communities of General Abad are not willing to resettle elsewhere as they have invested in the area and it offers favourable opportunities for employment.

### Haji Ramzan Gabol Goth (Safoora Goth)

Haji Ramazan Goth is one of the settlements of Safoora, located at the tail end of University Road, falling under the jurisdiction of Union Council 13 of Gulshan-e-Iqbal Town. The population of Gulshan Town is estimated to be nearly one million.

The community boasts an ethnically diverse population consisting of Gabols, Jokhios, Muhajirs, and Punjabis. Over 99% of the population is Muslim.

Although the sewerage system was laid in the tenure of Prime Minister Nawaz Sharif, development conditions are not satisfactory.

People hear have invested in their houses over time and most of the residences comprise of ground floors plus 2 stories. The influential people of the area founded a *mohalla* committee, and named it Khaskhaili Welfare Association. The committee works for development within the area, and collects Rs 10 per household for a monthly fund, using the money towards funeral and wedding arrangements for the needy of the area. Abdul Ghani is the chairperson of this committee.

### Shah Rasool Colony

Shah Rasool Colony is a regularized settlement, set up in the 1960s and populated by rural migrants from various parts of the country, especially Khyber Pakhtunkhwa. It is bounded by the high-income areas of DHA and Clifton, areas that provide residents with multiple employment opportunities.

The colony faces a shortage of clean drinking water, a reliable sewerage system and owing to the narrow lanes, a lack of daylight within houses. There are additional ventilation and other environmental concerns too. Despite these issues, people prefer to live here as tenants rather than own a plot on the periphery of the city. 60–70% of the tenants pay up to Rs 2,500 for single room accommodation with a shared kitchen and toilet.

Being an old, legalized settlement, the area's real estate value has increased over time and resultantly, none of the owners want to move out.

Earlier, the city district government had proposed a revitalization scheme, converting all plot developments into high-rise flats, but the residents opposed the plan as they wanted to accommodate their extended families in vertical extensions of their plots.

The central, well-connected location ensures that these settlements are ideal for setting up businesses. A large number of middle level professionals reside here. People have invested in their housing and the area at large and they are upwardly mobile. These areas not only attract labourers and the working classes, but also the middle class who want to live near DHA or Clifton, as the area provides easy, low cost living and services in the form of rented rooms and illegal service connections. A large number of bachelors are also interested in the locale for the same reasons; however, with this influx come certain negative activities such as prostitution.

### Taiser Town

Taiser Town, Scheme-45 is a neighbourhood of Malir Town, Karachi. The Malir Development Authority (MDA) established Taiser Town in an effort to resettle people displaced by the construction of the Lyari Expressway, along the Lyari River. It is located near the Gulshan-e-Maymar toll plaza on the Super Highway.

24,419 families were displaced and allotted resettlement land in Sectors 6, 9 and 10 in Hawksbay Scheme-42, Sectors 35, 36, 36-A and 50 in Taiser Town, Scheme-45 and Sectors 21-B and 29 in Baldia Town. Besides, more land has been allocated in Taiser Town with the total area set aside for resettlement covering 998 acres.

There is a host of ethnic groups in Taiser Town, including Muhajirs, Punjabis, Sindhis, Kashmiris, Seraikis, Pakhtuns, Balochis, Memons, Bohras, Ismailis, etc. Over 99% of the population is Muslim.

There is a dire lack of efficient transport systems available to people here and locals have to walk several kilometres to access buses. Several deaths have occurred in this regard *en route* to the hospital in the city. The Chief Minister of Sindh, Dr Arbab Ghulam Rahim, has ordered an extension of the road coming from Ahsan Abad Industrial Area and Gulshan-i-Maymar, connecting Taiser Town site of LERP, and the adjoining Khuda-ki-Basti, so that residents of these areas may conveniently reach the industrial areas for employment. He also issued a directive for expediting work on a hospital to be set up in the area by the provincial health department; however, nothing has been implemented thus far.

At present 4,500 children are enrolled in the 11 primary and singular high school functioning in the town. Under the resettlement project, these students are provided books, uniform and shoes, free of cost. To meet the shortage of government teachers, local educated girls of the area are appointed as teachers and paid a monthly stipend.

### Ittehad Town

Ittehad Town is one of the neighbourhoods of Baldia Town in Karachi. There are several ethnic groups struggling to settle in Ittehad Town, including Muhajirs, Punjabis, Sindhis, Kashmiris, Seraikis, Pakhtuns, Balochis, Memons, Bohras and Ismailis. Over 99% of the population is Muslim.

The government of Sindh proposed a new scheme for the affected of the Lyari Expressway, called Hawksbay Scheme 42 in Ittehad Town. 80 sq. yards plots and an amount of Rs 50,000 for the construction of one room were distributed, but this amount proved insufficient and there were no other means of taking loans.

Ittehad Town is located a long way from the city, and the intermediate roads are consistently jammed with heavy traffic. The residents face a lot of problems, especially in this regard and more so in the case of an emergency. There have been a number of tragic incidents that illustrate this problem.

The population of Ittehad Town is around 65,550, with an overwhelming majority belonging to a low-income background.

### Ghazi Abad/Shamsu Mohalla

Ghazi Abadis part of Orangi Town, one of the largest formally planned low-income settlements in Karachi. Orangi's development started in the 1960s as a scheme of planned sites and services covering 1,300 acres of land. Since the pace of development of the formal area was slow, local communities began informally developing its adjoining areas.

The settlement at Ghaziabad started in the 1970s as migrants of the separation of East Pakistan came to Karachi. It has a mixed population of Biharis, Bengalis, Baloch, Muhajirs and Punjabis. The majority is Muslim and there are a few small Christian communities. In all the population is 300,000.

The development conditions are satisfactory: the sewerage system was laid on a self-help basis and roads were built during 2000–2005 by General Musharraf's government. Over time however, leakages have appeared in the sewerage and water lines, resulting in environmental and health concerns and damage to the foundation of houses.

Over time, people have invested in their houses and the housing stock is generally ground+2 stories high. Home industries make up 30% of the settlement, based on hand or power looms. These families are self-employed.

The lack of an efficient transport system has resulted in a drop in real estate value, whilst people have to walk several kilometres to access buses. For example the average cost of a 120 sq. yards house here is between Rs 1,500,000–1,800,000, whereas costs for plots of the same size in areas like Gulshan-e-Bihar which is closer to the highway, go up to Rs 2,500,000.

The disadvantage of the location is being borne by the communities as they have sufficient security and safety here. However, it is currently not an area attractive for rentals or businesses.

## Juma Khan Goth

Juma Khan Goth is a settlement in Gulshan Town, Karachi, started in 1983–84 when a man called Juma Khan gathered a group of people and occupied the area. His son, Amir Khan is the current chairman of the area committee; its president is Raza Khan. 10% of the residents are tenants, whilst the majority owns their land.

The minimum plot size is 30 sq. yards and maximum is 60 sq. yards yard. Most of the houses are temporary in nature, whilst some have improved on them over time, mainly on the ground floor.

---

**BOX II**

At the beginning, the Karachi Circular Railway was a success. In the 1980s it was performing at its peak: 104 trains catered to thousands of people on a daily basis. This state of affairs gradually declined due to a number of reasons: corruption, government negligence, interference of the road transport mafia and the security situation in the city at large. By 1994, the majority of trains were no longer operational and 1996–99 saw the complete closure of all KCR activities, resulting in pressure on the road infrastructure, longer travel times, extra cost of travel and pollution.

The mounting pressure of traffic, daily traffic jams and other factors have convinced the government to revive the KCR. As per the project, a 44 kilometre long dedicated dual track is to be laid down, serviced by 24 stations, 21 underpasses and overhead bridges. Electric trains are to operate at an approximate speed of 40 kilometres per hour, thus completing the entire circular railway loop in about an hour. Of the total route, roughly 22 kilometres will be elevated, 4 kilometres will run in tunnels, whilst the remaining 16 kilometres will ply at road level. A total of 246 trains are to travel the route, each with a capacity of 1,236 passengers, thus the KCR shall cater to 700,000 passengers per day.

After the closure of the KCR in the past, its tracks and many rights of ways were heavily encroached; the revival of the service will require the clearance of these. Over 4,650 families currently residing on the KCR route will be relocated. Pakistan Railways has agreed to provide approximately 300 acres near Jumma Goth (near Cattle Colony and Shah Latif Town) for the resettlement process. Each family shall be given an 80 sq. yards plot and PKR 50,000, to support single room construction.

---

There are several ethnic groups in Juma Goth including Muhajirs, Punjabis, Sindhis, Kashmiris, Seraikis, Pakhtuns and Balochis. The majority of the population is employed in the capacity of labourers.

The area began developing in terms of electricity, gas and other utilities after 1990. There are land ownership conflicts with the Karachi Circular Railway; currently, the government has notified the area.

## Korangi No. 6

Korangi No. 6 is another resettlement project dating back to the 1960s. Owing to the areas slow development, lack of employment and amenities, and the long commuting distance to the city people were initially unhappy with the area. However, once development picked up pace the community settled down and now, 50 years later, most of the land in Korangi No. 6 is developed. The area consists of plot sizes ranging from 60 sq. yards to 1000 sq. yards and is leased, except for the open spaces that have been encroached upon. New plots are acquired through estate agents and cost anywhere between Rs. 3 lacs and Rs. 1 crore.

At the outset, the government provided all facilities to the area, but as is the case in the rest of the city there is no operational maintenance: roads once made are never repainted, sewage lines are old and have leakages at several points thus destroying roads and pathways. Similarly, the new, informal housing development there is built on grabbed land and consumes illegal water and electricity, further burdening the infrastructure and worsening environmental conditions. The informal settlements, cabins and shops along the roads pay bribes to KESC for the illegal *kunda* system they employ.

HBFCL and other commercial banks do not sanction loans for construction in Korangi, unless the applicant owns a plot of 400 sq. yards and above. People who have taken house loans are struggling due to the high interest rates, inflation and recession. Learning from this example, people avoid banks and have started to try to build up their savings. Moneylenders charge high interest rates and harass people for recovery, using violent methods if required. There are also local loan sharks that people apply for in case of a severe need. Another form of loan facility in the area is the *thallawalas*, who provide building materials in loan, the cost of which is paid off within a particular time period.

Korangi's case illustrates the fact that a 1960s resettlement scheme, which has not been consistently supported by the state, needed about 20–40 years to consolidate. The initial hurdles of delayed development were taken care of by the informal transport sector, the communities' self-organization and the other developments in the city.

### Gulistan-e-Johar

Gulistan-e-Johar comes under the jurisdiction of Union Council 10, Pehlvaan Goth of Gulshan Town. It is bordered by Gulshan-e-Iqbal to the north and west, Faisal Cantonment to the south, Malir Cantonment to the east and Jinnah International Airport to the southeast.

The KDA developed Gulistan-e-Johar for the middle and upper middle-income groups of the city. It efficiently laid out the infrastructure, which led to the construction of residential-cum-commercial projects in the area. In most cases, the land was auctioned by the KDA and bought by private builders who then built these various projects for mixed use. Most of the apartments and shops were sold much before their construction was completed, owing to Gulistan-e-Johar's prime location.

There are several ethnic groups residing in the area, Mohajirs, Punjabis, Sindhis, Kashmiris, Seraikis, Pakhtuns, Baloch, Memons, Bohras and Ismailis. Over 97% of the population is Muslim.

In Gulistan-e-Johar, hawkers are organized along the service roads, especially on the main avenue 'Johar Chowk'. They have been coming to the area over the past four-five years, offering fruit, vegetables, juices, toys and other household items for sale. They usually live in the same vicinity and pay rent to the city government, hiring labour for work when required. Most hawkers hail from outside Karachi and have settled here to do business. When they return home to their villages, they hand their hawking spaces over to relatives. Many have bikes and Suzuki cars for commuting.

The hawkers who have been living and working in Gulistan-e-Johar for over four years have moved their families to Karachi. Their net income per day is between Rs 300–500. They pay more than Rs 100 in bribes to the union council employees, and sometimes to the police and rangers. The police aid them in finding a place and in return either take money or the stuff on sale, such as fruit or vegetables. The city government has recently formalized the hawkers and provided them with cabins, electricity connections and a solid waste disposal system, all at a monthly charge.

The informal businesses and hawkers in Gulistan-e-Johar do very well owing to the central location of the area and the connecting services of several bus routes. The surrounding upper middle and middle-income areas also makes a good clientele.

## Saddar

Saddar Town includes Saddar Bazaar (market) area. Jamshed Town and Clifton Cantonment border the town to the east, Keamari Town and the Arabian Sea to the south and Lyari Town to the west.

Saddar Bazaar is a major business district of Karachi. During the colonial era, Saddar Bazaar was considered the heart of Karachi, a status that it maintained between 1947 and the 1960s, when the federal government offices were based in Saddar. The offices of the provincial government of Sind have now replaced them. Many beautiful examples of colonial architecture can be found in the area, including the main building of Empress market. The largest informal bus terminal of the city and thousands of engendered informal businesses and hawkers can be found around the Empress market area.

Hawkers prove to be a major attraction for the bus commuters, the transit population and the shoppers who visit Saddar Bazaar. Amongst a huge variety of goods, they sell shoes, garments, watches, fruit, jewelry, and household items. The hawkers operate using an innovative variety of methods in their sales' areas, ranging from pushcarts and small collapsible shops, to a makeshift arrangement of spreading their wares on the footpath; also vendors use umbrellas and temporary boxes.

Umar Farooq market is known as the hawkers' market. Space is rented out at Rs 15,000–20,000 per month. Most hawkers are not originally from Karachi, and when they have to go back to their village, they pass their hawking place on to relatives. They store their valuables in the same space and collectively hire a watchman for the security of their wares.

The majority of hawkers live in the same vicinity, whilst others commute from Baldia, Banaras, Korangi, Orangi and SITE on public transport. Their daily net income is usually between Rs 300–500. They pay *bhatta* to the police and their respective political parties: Saddar Bazaar is a stronghold of the Awami National Party (ANP). The rate of *bhatta* is usually between Rs 20–100, depending upon the volume of the business. The hawkers face threats in case of non-payment of *bhatta*, and from the regular eviction drives carried out by the city government and the police. More often than not, the hawkers tend to reorganize as they are catering to the area's needs.

In the opinion of the hawkers the places they have occupied should be allotted to them on a rental basis, which can generate income for the city as well. They want peace and law and order so that they can improve their business. The small stalls and hawkers of Saddar Bazaar make a very profitable return as the area is connected to the main bus terminal and business centre of the city. Hundreds of thousands of people, mostly belonging to the lower income bracket, visit the area every day and shop from the hawkers. Even the people coming to the shopping malls and up-market shops in the area are attracted by the comparatively cheaper merchandise and specialties offered by the hawkers.

## Chakiwara, Lyari

Chakiwara is in the neighbourhood of Lyari Town. The area gets its name from the Chakee, a community of Gujarati Muslims. The term 'Gujarati Muslims' is usually used to signify an Indian Muslim, from the state of Gujarat in West India, who speaks Gujrati as a first language and follows certain customs different from the rest of Indian Muslims.

The district is home mainly to the Chakee, and other Gujarati Muslims such as the Ghanchi, Chhipa and Memon. There are also small groups of Muhajirs, Pakhtuns and Balochis, over 99% of this population is Muslim. The population of Lyari Town is estimated to be nearly one million.

Historically Lyari is known as the mother of Karachi. It has provided a base for the prosperous growth and development of the mega-polis Karachi is today.

Lyari derives its name from the river, which used to flow into the Arabian Sea. Its riverbed extended from Lalukhet (present Liaquatabad) to the Port Trust yard. Rainwater drained from the mountains to the sea via two larger watercourses. Between the two courses there existed 20–25 fisher folk's huts. The spot was then called Dirbo. It later came to be known as 'Kalachi-jo-Goth', that is, 'the village of Kalachi', the fisherwoman. Thus the first settlement of common people here bore the name of Lyari and historically became the fast developing city, internationally known as Karachi, the first capital of Pakistan.

Over the course of time, as shipping and trade rapidly developed, the existing port facilities became inadequate. It became necessary to reclaim land for housing purposes from the Lyari bed. On the other side of the Lyari River, 'Khadda' (present UC No. 04 Lyari Town) had already been built up to accommodate fisherman, who were removed from Machi Meanee in 1870.

## Liaquatabad

Liaqatabad Town, named after Liaquat Ali Khan, is located in a central part of Karachi. It has North Nazimabad to the north, Gulberg and Gulshan Town to the east, Jamshed Town to the south across the Lyari River, and SITE Town to the west across the Orangi Nala. The population of Liaquatabad Town is estimated to be 650,000, of which 99% are Muslim.

This is one of the most populated and busy areas of Karachi, housing a variety of income groups and their settlements. The low and middle-income settlements like Firdous Colony, Mujahid Colony and Gharib Abad have double and triple-storey houses, commercial areas and adequate amenities. Middle to high-income settlements like Rizvia Society, Nazimabad No. 1 and Sharif Abad have single and doublestorey bungalowtype houses, open spaces and commercial areas. The commercial areas of Liaquatabad Town, such as the Super market area, UC 10 area, Qasimabad, Bandhani Colony and Sharifabad have specialized markets, dealing in furniture, spare parts, marble workshops, sanitary ware, metal workshops and many other smaller markets for retail items and household goods.

Within and around these markets are found thousands of hawkers, who like in Saddar, cater to both commuters and shoppers alike. Only 3% of the hawkers of Liaquatabad Town come in from its adjoining areas, 90% of them live in the same vicinity: this reduces the daily cost of commuting. They had moved to the area after Partition and have been settled here ever since. Contrary to popular belief, hawking is a family business. According to the old hawkers the work situation has deteriorated over the past 20 years due to the political nature of the areas. Nowadays, owing to the deteriorated condition of law and order in the city, businesses remain closed for three—four days of the week, which affects their daily income.

Most hawkers here use cabins or pushcarts to sell various items. The police, and sometimes the government, is paid Rs 30 on a daily basis as *bhatta*. There is a regular *kunda* (illegal electrical connection) system here, and those who are honest have obtained legal connections at Rs 500. A guard is employed for those who leave their wares at their place of work. Garments and other goods that are easy to carry or more valuable hence more liable to theft, are carried back home.

Due to the large middle and upper income, residential population in the area, the hawkers are ensured profitable business. Their average daily net income is approximately Rs 300–500 (they were unwilling to quote the correct amount as they think that they might have to pay income tax on it). They are located along the entire length of the main road, which plies thousands of bus trips every day; this area is under police and municipal jurisdiction. The buyers are usually residents, passers-by or the general public.

The hawkers of Liaquatabad are under political patronage of the MQM, as a majority belongs to this political party.

## Dehli Colony

Dehli Colony is a low-income settlement situated within the Clifton area and surrounded by high-income areas. It is a well-serviced area with several amenities, transport links within reach and a satisfactory level of services. The small businesses and hawkers from this area further provide a variety of goods and services.

The communities residing here mostly belong to the Jamiat-e-Punjabi-Saudargaran-e-Dehli (The association for Delhi-Punjabi merchants & businessmen). However, there are other communities like Punjabis, Muhajirs, and Pathans in the area as well. They belong to lower middle and middle-income groups Originating from a business community, people here have invested in diversified trades and the area is known for certain specialties, such as traditional Delhiwala food, hand embroidered clothes (especially the ones worn at weddings) and services like hired chefs for marriage parties, drivers, household maids and other craftsmen and technicians. People have also invested in their properties and constructed multi storeyed houses on 80—240-square yard plots that are common in the area. The different communities enjoy cordial relations with each other and are willing to take on work on self-help basis. Owing to saturation, however, there are a lot of traffic and sewerage problems in the colony.

Areas like Dehli Colony, which are centrally located and provide ample employment opportunities, are attractive for tenants. Due to the proximity of work opportunities and amenities, the real estate value of the land is also high.

Informal businesses and hawkers in the area do well as they acquire a sufficient clientele from the adjoining upper income areas. They are organized and situated mostly on the service roads, in the form of encroachments. Hawkers have their own pushcarts, on which they sell fruit, vegetables, clothes, toys, fish and other food and household items. Being mobile, these hawkers also go into the adjoining areas and provide home delivery of their goods.

The hawkers of Dehli Colony live in the same area, before which they worked at the city centre. Most of them have been hawking since 1984 and have now involved their sons in their businesses. Compared to what it was earlier, their income has also increased. Most of them take their wares home when they close for the day, but there is a watchman system for those who leave their pushcarts/goods on site. They pay Rs 20 to the watchman for the security of their pushcart. They hire labour to transport the goods they purchase from the main market. Most of them have their own motorbikes and some use public buses.

### Kashmir Mujahid Colony

Kashmir Mujahid Colony is located behind the PIDC building in Civil Lines, Sadder Town. It stretches over 4 acres of land and is dominated by Kashmiri migrants who arrived in the area in 1950. Today this area comprises of 223 housing units that house approximately 2000 people. Sindhis, Pukhtuns, and Punjabis live here along with the Kashmiris. A majority of the population resides in single and double-storey, 100 sq. yards houses with loadbearing walls and tiled roof systems. Regardless of not having achieved legal status as yet, the colony has been fully serviced with utilities and paved streets over the last decade.

The livelihood of the majority of the people is related to services sector, catering to the adjacent upper income areas, the port and government offices. The location is ideal for easily commuting to the city's activity centres. Owing to its situation in the city, the area is in high demand with real estate values ranging between Rs 2,500,000–3,000,000. The females of the area are limited to their household chores, representing the better financial status of the people. There is a predominance of Muslims in the colony.

80% of the people living here are owners of their houses, while the remaining 20% are tenants. Residents have tried several times to gain legal status through the SKAA, but because of the longstanding conflict over unclear boundaries of jurisdiction between the Pakistan Railways and SKAA, all efforts have ended in vain and the settlement is currently under threat of eviction, due to the revival and extension of the Karachi Circular Railway.

### Umer Colony

Umer Colony is the combined name given to the settlements located on either side of the railway line, near the Baloch Colony flyover, from where they stretch for one kilometre towards the Cantonment Station. Although they have almost the same character and history, the settlements have been given different names. They do, however, fall under different wards of the provincial assembly: PA-114 and PA-115. The settlement towards Shahrah-e-Faisal is called Umer Colony No. 1, whilst the settlement on the opposite side is known as Umer colony No. 2. In this study we are focusing on Umer Colony No. 1.

The settlement consists of 1100 houses built over 12.75 acres of land. It started in 1956 originally as an area that would provide domestic and other manpower services to the adjoining P.E.C.H.S., K.A.C.H.S. and M.A. Society. However, it was soon occupied by higher income groups as well. Residents mostly live in 60-square yard plots that are single storey and have G.I. or cemented sheet roofing over loadbearing walls. 20% live in multiple storeyed buildings supported by an RCC structure with either RCC or tile-girder roofing. As per market values, these plots cost between Rs 0.7—1.0 million today. The area is not completely leased.

The majority of people are migrants from Punjab and Khyber Pakhtunkhwa. Hindu and Christian minorities co-exist with the colony's Muslim majority. These people are mostly labourers with skilled, unskilled, permanent, and temporary job categorizations. The adjacent middle to higher income areas are the main job market not only for the men, but also women who mostly find work as maids there.

People manage the provision of utilities and services on a self-help basis. Ground water and government supply are both used; a floodwater drain has been converted to a sewage drain, while the KESC has supplied electrical connections to the entire area. There is no proper system of solid waste management and waste picking.

### Neelum Colony

Neelum Colony is a formally developed settlement for low-income people established by the Cantonment Board Clifton (CBC). The reason behind creating a low-income settlement in a posh locality was to provide a services' sector to the area. It was assumed that the low income families would provide domestic and other manpower services to the posh families living in the adjacent areas. The demand in the job market increased so rapidly that Neelum Colony was short on space and manpower; eventually, Shah Rasool colony was created as an extension of Neelum Colony, albeit with a relatively different socio-economic profile and dynamics.

Since the area was formally planned, all plots uniformly measure 60 sq. yards and are serviced by formalized utilities. There is a majority of self-owned homes here, in comparison to the adjacent Shah Rasool Colony, where tenants are in majority. The colony is also home to tenants, but in a lower proportion. Building structures are mostly built in RCC and plastered, having ground plus one or more floors. Another important aspect is the widespread presence of extended families here, which again is higher than those at Shah Rasool Colony.

There is a preponderance of migrants from the country's rural areas, especially those of Khyber Pakhtunkhwa. People are better off here as compared to the residents of adjacent Shah Rasool Colony; however, jobs and the businesses are dependent on the surrounding posh areas, resultantly, the location is of great importance.

# Glossary

| | |
|---|---|
| ACHS | Al-Riaz Cooperative Housing Society |
| AKPBS,P | Aga Khan Programme for Basic Services, Pakistan |
| AWT | Army Welfare Trust |
| BoR | Board of Revenue |
| CBO | Community based Organization |
| CDGK | City District Government Karachi |
| DC | Deputy Commissioner |
| DHA | Defence Housing Authority (formerly the Pakistan Defence Officers' Cooperative Housing Society) |
| FAR | Floor area ratio |
| HBFC | House Building Finance Company |
| KBCA | Karachi Building Control Authority |
| KCHSU | Karachi Cooperative Housing Society Union |
| KCR | Karachi Circular Railways |
| KDA | Karachi Development Authority (formerly the Karachi Improvement Trust) |
| KESC | Karachi Electricity Supply Company |
| KIT | Karachi Improvement Trust |
| KMC | Karachi Metropolitan Corporation |
| KPT | Karachi Port Trust |
| KSDP | Karachi Strategic Development Plan |
| KWSB | Karachi Water and Sewerage Board |
| LDA | Lyari Development Authority |
| LERP | Lyari Expressway Rehabilitation Project |
| MDA | Malir Development Authority |
| ML&C | Military Lands & Cantonments Group |
| MPGO | Master Plan Group of Offices |
| OCHS | Overseas Cooperative Housing Society |
| OPP-RTI | Orangi Pilot Project Research and Training Institute |
| PDOCHS | Pakistan Defence Officers' Cooperative Housing Society (now the Defence Housing Authority) |
| PECHS | Pakistan Employees Cooperative Housing Society |
| PQA | Port Qasim Authority |
| SBCA | Sindh Building Control Authority |
| SDULO | Sindh Disposal of Urban Land Ordinance |
| SITE | Sindh Industrial and Trading Estate |
| SKAA | Sindh Katchi Abadi Authority |
| SLGO | Sindh Local Government Ordinance |
| SMCHS | Sindhi Muslim Cooperative Housing Society |

**Local Terms:**

| | |
|---|---|
| *Bhatta* | Bribe extracted through coercion |
| *Bisi* | Community savings scheme |
| *Goth* | Village |
| *Katchi abadi* | Informal housing |
| *Nazim* | Mayor |
| *Thallawala* | Builders' merchant |

# References

Akhtar, S., & Dahnani, M. R. (2011). *Industrial land use and land value pattern in Karachi City.*

An, G., & Becker, C. M. (2013). Uncertainty, insecurity, and emigration from uncertainty, insecurity, and emigration from Kazakhstan to Russia. *World Development, 42,* 44-66.

Anderson, B. A., & Silver, B. D. (1986). Infant mortality in the Soviet Union: Regional differences and measurement issues. *Population and Development Review, 12*(4), 705–738.

ARCOP/CK-NBBJ. (2011). Sindh Education City Master Plan.

Asian Development Bank. (2005). *Karachi Megacities Preparation Project Volume 1.*

Baloch, Y. (2011). Forced evictions in Karachi: Socio-economic and political consequences: [Presentation for Urban Resource Centre, NED University, on 14 October 2011, online on URC website] www.urckarachi.org

Cox, W. (2012). World urban areas population and density: a 2012 update. *New Geography,* 5 March.

Das, S. (2001). *Kashmir and Sindh: Non-convergence in the Third World: Nation-Building, Ethnicity and Regional Politics in South Asia.* Anthem Press.

World Bank Group. (2014). Dealing with construction permits in Karachi—Pakistan. http://www.doingbusiness.org/data/exploreeconomies/pakistan/sub/karachi/topic/ dealing-with-construction-permits

Desai, V., & Loftus, A. (2012). Speculating on Slums: Infrastructural Fixes in Informal Housing in the Global South. *Antipode.*

Farani, M. (2011) *Manual of Land Revenue Laws—A Compilation.* National Law Book House, Lahore.

Gazdar, H., & Mallah, H. B. (2011). *Housing, Marginalization and Mobility in Pakistan: Residential Security as Social Protection.* Centre for Social Protection Research Report 04. New Dehli: Institute for Social Studies Trust (ISST) Indian Habitat Centre. http:// www.socialprotectionasia.org/Conf-prgram-pdf/4-SPA-FinalPaper-No-04.pdf

Gilbert, A. (2003). *Rental housing: An Essential Option for the Urban Poor in Developing Countries.* Nairobi: United Nations Human Settlements Programme (UN-HABITAT)

Government of Karachi. (1971). *Karachi Development Authority (KDA) Disposal of Land Rules.*

Government of Pakistan. (1998). Census Reports.

Government of Sindh. (1980). *Sindh Disposal of Plots Ordinance.*

Hasan, A. (2011). *The Re-planning of Saiban City, Lahore.* International Institute for Environment and Development. [Unpublished paper]

Hasan, A. (2009). *Subsidizing Interest Rates.* [Unpublished note]

Hasan, A. (2008). *Housing Security and Related Issues: the case of Karachi.* UN-HABITAT. [Unpublished paper]

Hasan, A. (2000). *Housing for the Poor.* Karachi: City Press.

Hasan, A. (1999). *Understanding Karachi—Planning and Reforms for the Future.* Karachi: City Press.

Hasan, A., Sadiq, A., & Ahmed, S. (2010). *Planning for High Density in Low-income Areas: A Case Study from Karachi.* London: International Institute for Environment and Development (IIED).

Hasan, A., & Mohib, M. (2009). *Urban slums reports: The case of Karachi, Pakistan.* University College of London, Development Planning Unit. Accessed Oct. 2013. http://www.ucl.ac.uk/dpuprojects/Global_Report/pdfs/Karachi.pdf

Hasan, A., Polak, C., & Sadiq, A. (2008). *The hawkers of Saddar Bazaar.* Karachi: Ushba Publishing International.

Henry L. Stimson Centre. (2010). *Case study Lagos: Growth without infrastructure.* www.stimson.org/images/uploads/Lagos_Case_Study.pdf

Hossain, S. (2006). *Social characteristics of a megacity: Case of Dhaka City, Bangladesh.* TASA Conference. University of Western Australia and Murdoch University.

Housing Building and Finance Company (HBFC). HBFC official website. www.hbfcl.com/

Humayun, A., & Jafri, A. (2010). Karachi's Ethnic Tinderbox. *Small Wars Journal,* 2 Dec. www.smallwarsjournal.com/blog/journal/.../611humayunjafri.pdf

Hussain, F. (2012). General observations of surveyors. [Unpublished note].

Ismail, A. (2009). *The saving of Zubo Goth.* [Unpublished paper.]

Karachi Port Trust (KPT). KPT official website. http://www.kpt.gov.pk

Kazakhstan to Russia. (2013). *World Development,* 42, 44-66.

Khan, A. (2002). Pakistan's Sindhi Ethnic Nationalism: Migration, Marginalization, and the Threat of 'Indianization'. *Asian Survey,* 42 (2), 213-229.

Kool, M., Verboom, D., & Van der Linden, J. (1988). *Squatter settlements in Pakistan; The impacts of upgrading.* Lahore: Vanguard.

Lyari Expressway Resettlement Project and Karachi Circular Railway Rehabilitation Project. Lyari Expressway Resettlement Project official website. http://www.lerpkarachi.com.pk/

Mahmood, Zaigham. (2010). *Pakistan: Low-income housing initiatives.* World Bank. http://siteresources.worldbank.org/EXTFINANCIALSECTOR/Resources/2828841239831335682/6028531 1239831365859/Rizvi_LowIncomeHousing Pakistan_overviewpaper.pdf

Malir Development Authority. MDA official website. http://mda.com.pk/

Master Plan Group of Offices (MPGO). (2007). *Karachi Strategic Development Plan-2020.* City Government Karachi.

Moreno, L. (2008). *The architecture and urban culture of financial crisis.* The Bartlett workshop transcripts. Figaropravda c/o UCL Urban Lab.

Mujtaba, H. (2012). *Lyari: Land of Magic.* Wichaar. 30 April. [originally published in 1997].

Ngwane, T. (2010). *Xenophobia in Bottlebrush: An Investigation into The Reasons Behind The Attacks on African Immigrants in An Informal Settlement in Durban,* Research Paper, University of KwaZulu Natal Centre for Civil Society. [Commissioned by Atlantic Philanthropies.]

Orangi Pilot Project (OPP). OPP Official website. www.oppinstitutions.org/

Orangi Pilot Project. (2011). *127th Quarterly Report (July-September 2011).*

Pakistan Railways. Pakistan Railways official website. http://www.pakrail.com/

Payne, G., Durand-Lasserve, A., & Rakodi, C. (2007). *Social and Economic Impacts of Land Titling Programmes in Urban and Peri-urban Areas:* A review of the literature.

http://www.gpa.org.uk/ [Presented at the World Bank Urban Research Symposium, Washington DC, 14-16 May]

Planning Commission of Pakistan. (2011). *Task Force Report on Urban Development*. Government of Pakistan.

Port Qasim Authority (PQA). PQA official website. www.portqasim.org.pk/

Qureishi, S. (2010). The Fast Growing Megacity Karachi as A Frontier of Environmental Challenges: Urbanization and Contemporary Urbanism Issues. *Journal of Geography and Regional Planning*, 3(11), 306-321.

Rasheed, A. (2001). *Taliban*. Karachi: Oxford University Press.

Sassen, S. (2001). *The Global City: New York, London, Tokyo*. Princeton, NJ: Princeton University Press.

Sehgal, I. (1990). Model for Metropolitan Government. Ikram Sehgal blog. Posted on Oct. 9. http://www.sehgalfamily.com/?p=1974

Shah, S. (2010). *Karachi, Pakistan's Biggest City, On Edge of Gang-led Civil War*. McClatchy.

The Asia Foundation. (2008). *Consumer Financing in Pakistan: Issues, Challenges and Way Forward*. Islamabad: Consumer Rights Association of Pakistan.

Transparency International. (2010). National Corruption Perception Survey 2010. Transparency International official website. http://www.transparency.org/cpi2010/results

Regional differences and measurement issues. *Population and Development Review*, 12(4), 705–738.

Van der Linden, J. & Selier, F. (1991). *Karachi: Migrants, Housing, and Housing Policy*. Lahore: Vanguard.

Water and Sanitation Project Report. (2010), *Benchmarking for Performance Improvement in Urban Utilities—A Review in Bangladesh, India, and Pakistan*. Water and Sanitation Program. The World Bank.

Weinstein, L. (2008). Mumbai's Development Mafias: Globalization, Organized Crime and Land Development. *International Journal of Urban and Regional Research*, 32, 1 March.

## NEWSPAPER ARTICLES

Aligi, I. (2009). Balloting of plots for CDGK employees held. *The Daily Times*, 10 Dec.

Ayub, I. (2009). Land mafia's hand found in estate-agent killings. *Dawn*, 28 Dec.

Baloch, S. (2011). Mosques on Amenity Plots: Do Not Go to Jail, Pass Go, Collect 200. *The Express Tribune*, 19 Apr.

Chishti, A. K. (2011). The Political Economy of NATO Trucks. *Friday Times*, 15 Sept.

Correspondent. (2009). Only CM has right to allot land. *Dawn*, 30 July.

Correspondent. (2004). Low cost housing: a low priority. *Dawn*, 25 Jan.

Correspondent. (2005). 14 builders blacklisted, projects sealed. *Dawn*, 31 July.

Correspondent. (2003). Balloting for Malir scheme plots. *Dawn*, 24 Aug.

Correspondent. (2011). 55 Housing Schemes across the Country under Probe. *Financial Post*, 3 Mar.

Correspondent. (2011). Karachi's Population Explosion Far Greater Than Experts' Calculations. *Pakistan Today*, 6 Dec.

Correspondent. (2012). Sindh Government Unhappy Over Railways Selling State Land. *The Express Tribune*, 8 Nov.

Correspondent. (2011). Construction growth to outpace GDP this decade. *The Indian Express*, 5 Mar.

Correspondent. (2004). Balloting of Plots in Low—Price Housing Schemes in Taiser Town Still Pending. *The Pak Tribune*, 14 Aug.

Cowasjee, A. (2007). Shoot the messenger. *Dawn*, 22 July.

Cowasjee, A. (2002). For the endangered species. *Dawn*, 16 June.

Ghori, H. K. (2010). Anti-encroachment Drive Put on Hold in Karachi. *Dawn*, 22 July.

Hasan, A. (2012a). The Impending Migration. *Dawn*, 2 December. http://dawn.com/2012/12/04/the-impending-migration/

Hasan, A. (2012b). Sindh local government: The Real Issues. *The Express Tribune*, 10 Jan.

Hashim, A. (2008). Parking businesses thrive on I. I. Chundrigar Road. *Dawn*, 8 Dec.

Jawad, A. (2011). Wali Khan Babar Murder: One by One, 4 Men Linked to Investigations Bumped Off. *The Express Tribune* 16 Apr.

Khan, T. (2010). Ethnic Violence Rules Karachi Politics. *The National*, 29 Dec.

Newspaper item. (2001). *Dawn*, 16 Oct.

Newspaper item. (2006). *Dawn*, 1 June.

Newspaper item. (2004). *Dawn*, 25 Jan.

Newspaper item. (2004). *Dawn*, 25 Jan.

Newspaper item. (2004). *Dawn*, 27 July.

Newspaper item. (2012). *The Express Tribune*, 16 Feb.

Newspaper item. (2002). *The News*, 10 Oct.

Newspaper item. (2009). *The News*, 11 Nov.

Newspaper item. (2009). *The News*, 18 Apr.

Newspaper item. (2008). *The News*, 24 Sept.

Newspaper item. (2001). *The News*, 25 Jan.

Newspaper item. (2004). *The News*, 31 Mar.

Newspaper item. (2004). *The News*, 5 May.

Newspaper item. (2008). *The News*, 6 Feb.

Newspaper item. (2001). *The News*, 7 May.

Rana, P. I. (2009). Ship-breakers yearn for basic amenities. *Dawn*, 11 June.

Rind, H. M. (2012). REITs to Help Draw Investment. *The News International*. 4 Dec.

Sahoutara, N. (2012). Karachi's Entire Land Record to go under Microscope. *The Express Tribune*, 5 Dec.

Siddiqui, T. (2012). SC Freezes Allotment, Mutation of Government Land in Sindh. *Dawn*, 29 Nov.

## PERSONAL COMMUNICATIONS

Ahmed, N. (2013). Email to authors, 14 Feb.

Ahmed, N. (2013). Chairman—Tameer Bank. Interview with Moizza B. Sarwar, 2 Jan., Karachi.

Arsalan, R. (2011). Managing Director—SKAA.

Badiuzzaman, S. (2012). Interview with Moizza B. Sarwar, 31 Dec., Karachi.

Bilqees. (2011). Domestic helper. Interview with authors, 22 Oct., Karachi.

Farid, Sadiq, R. (2011). Interview with authors, 8 Sept., Karachi.

Hussain, M. (2011). Estate Agent—Pak Estate Agency North Nazimabad. Interview with authors, 22 June, Karachi.

Jaffery, A. R. Abbas. (2011). Purchaser of flat in Al-Ghafoor Agency. Interview with authors, 26 July, Karachi.

Janti. (2011). Office boy in a foreign mission. Interview with authors, 21 Oct., Karachi.

Javed, H. (2011). Estate Development Officer—Land Dept CDGK. Interview with Asiya Sadiq, 30 Sept., Karachi.

Khan, J. (2011). Developer—Momal Pride, Al-Adil Builders. Interview with authors, 21 July, Karachi.

Khan, Naser et al. (2011). Interview with authors, 8 Oct., Karachi.

Khan, Y., & Iqbal, A. (2012) Interview with Arif Hasan, 30 May, Karachi.

Mazahar, R. M. (2011). Developer—Rao Mega City. Interview with authors, 6 Oct., Karachi.

Moinuddin, S. (2011). Developer and Lawyer. Interview with authors, 22 Nov., Karachi.

Nuruddin. (2011). Former developer; and Advisor—Chairman Pakistan Institute of Engineers Karachi. Interview with authors, 15 Aug., Karachi.

Riaz ul Haque. (2011). Representative—HBFC. Interview with authors, Karachi.

Riaz un Nabi, S. (2011–12). Assistant Manager—HBFC. Interviews with Moizza B Sarwar, Karachi.

Sadiq, F., & Sadiq, R. (2011). Estate Agents—Omer Colony No. 1 PECHS. 8 Sept., Karachi.

Shahid. (2011). Manager—Khuda Ki Basti 3 site. Interview with authors, 21 July, Karachi.

Siddiqui, I. (2013). Interview with Moizza B. Sarwar, 2 Jan., Karachi.

Siddiqui, K. (2011). Chief Physical Planning and Housing, Government of Sindh. Interview with Asiya Sadiq, 14 Oct.

Sohail. (2011). Estate Agent Bismillah Estate—Taiser Town, Scheme-45. Interview with authors, 21 July, Karachi.

Zaheerul Islam. (2012). Former Head of Mass Transit Unit Karachi. Interview with Moizza B Sarwar, 27 Dec., Karachi.

Zaidi, F. (2011). Property Salesman—Federal B Area Block 10. Interview with authors, 6 July., Karachi.

## VIDEOS

Aaj TV. Program 'Benaqab' on builder's mafia in Karachi. Aaj TV. 'Do Bigha Zameen'. [Film clips on YouTube] http://www.youtube.com/watch?v=6CXb7afR8yQ> 27 Oct 2009 http://www.youtube.com/watch?v=YFGnYFlK2Rs&feature=related http://www.youtube.com/watch?v=JDuut4ODcmI&feature=related

Amer Ahmed Khan (Samaa TV) and Mohammed Salahuddin (Geo News). Report on the operation against park encroachments initiated by an order of the Supreme Court. Samaa TV and Geo News. [Film clip on YouTube]: http://www.youtube.com/watch?v=eREsRxd8MY4

Amir Bhatti. Geo FIR. Geo TV. [Film clip on YouTube] https://www.youtube.com/watch?v=bR-1sYSz8tg

ARY News. Report on land grabs in Karachi. ARY News. [Film clip on YouTube] http://www.youtube.com/watch?v=-ho9hocHeYY

Correspondent. Interviews estate agents and victims of scam in Gulistan-e-Jauhar, Karachi. Geo TV. [Film clip on YouTube] http://www.youtube.com/watch?v=FhfF5STy1fo#

Express News. Forced encroachment on the rooftops of residential flats in Gulistan-e-Jauhar (Rabia City Block 11 & 13). Express News. [Film clip on YouTube] http://www.youtube.com/watch?v=hubBd2LOWrY&feature=related

Express News. Report on police operation against the land 'mafia' on National Highway. Express News. [Film clip on YouTube] http://www.youtube.com/watch?v=QdIgWT Q58hA&feature=related

Hassam Khan. The story of Kidney Hill/ Ahmed Ali Park/ Faluknuma. Samaa TV. [Film clip on YouTube] http://www.youtube.com/watch?v=TWcJpSoJY7E&feature=related

Hassam Khan & Asif Jameel. Samaa TV. [Film clip on YouTube] http://www.youtube. com/watch?v=KJLY9rJxfPE

Mahera Omar. Getz Pharma and NGO Shehri-CBE. [Film clip on YouTube] https://www. youtube.com/watch?v=kzI80WqAzB0

Mahera Omar. Film on Gutter Baghicha. NGO Shehri-CB [2 part film clips on YouTube] http://www.youtube.com/watch?v=PJXSg7WkhFY; http://www.youtube.com/ watch?v=OokvKHrVRos

Mohammed Salahuddin. Report on land grabbing. ARY News. [Film clip on YouTube] http://www.youtube.com/watch?v=LMiKWwZsEtM&feature=related

NGO Shehri-CBE. The takeover of Karachi city parks by the land mafia. NGO Shehri-CBE. [Film clip on YouTube] http://www.youtube.com/watch?v=NHVll_QXaxg

NGO Shehri-CBE. The takeover of Karachi city parks by the land mafia. NGO Shehri-CBE. [Film clip on YouTube] http://www.youtube.com/watch?v=NHVll_QXaxg

Qazi Hasan. Report on Karachi's land scams. Geo TV. [Film clip on YouTube] http://www. youtube.com/watch?v=U3rIHlZDY-g#

Quaid Ali Shah. Report on the Collapse of a 4-storey building in Orangi Town during the flood season. Samaa TV. [Film clip on YouTube] http://www.youtube.com/watch?v=v UvsPEjC4Rw&feature=related

Salman Lodhi. Special report. ARY News. [Film clip on YouTube] http://www.youtube. com/watch?v=x_FEjocw9I8

Samaa TV. Clips. Samaa TV: [Film clip on YouTube] http://www.youtube.com/ watch?v=_hCVWgoAtUE&feature=related; http://www.youtube.com/watch?v=_ iXbV5pP9JE&feature=related

Samaa TV. MNA Sufyan Yusuf on program 'Aap Ki Baat.' Samaa TV. [Film clips on YouTube] http://www.youtube.com/watch?v=HFn-lykk3VA#; CNBC. Qudsia Kadri (Chief Editor of the Daily Financial Post and President, MWPJO) on program Agenda 360.' CNBC. http://www.youtube.com/watch?v=_kSI44_YRjk

Wali Khan Baber. Report on Pehlvaan Goth. Geo News [Film clip on YouTube] http:// www.youtube.com/watch?v=sML_DYGUac8

Zille Haider. Report on a land ownership dispute. Geo News [Film clip on YouTube] http:// www.youtube.com/watch?v=3If_Ixc9opU&feature=related

# Index